Beyond Dialogue

To Michael O'Brien, for all your help

Beyond Dialogue

Building Bonds Between Christians and Muslims

Craig Considine

polity

First published in 2025 by Polity Press

Polity Press
65 Bridge Street
Cambridge CB2 1UR, UK

Polity Press
111 River Street
Hoboken, NJ 07030, USA

ISBN-13: 978-1-5095-5526-0
ISBN-13: 978-1-5095-5527-7(pb)

A catalogue record for this book is available from the British Library.

Library of Congress Control Number: 2024936851

Typeset in 11.5 on 14pt Adobe Garamond
by Cheshire Typesetting Ltd, Cuddington, Cheshire
Printed and bound in Great Britain by CPI Group (UK) Ltd, Croydon

The publisher has used its best endeavours to ensure that the URLs for external websites referred to in this book are correct and active at the time of going to press. However, the publisher has no responsibility for the websites and can make no guarantee that a site will remain live or that the content is or will remain appropriate.

Every effort has been made to trace all copyright holders, but if any have been overlooked the publisher will be pleased to include any necessary credits in any subsequent reprint or edition.

For further information on Polity, visit our website:
politybooks.com

Contents

Introduction

DEUCE and the Synthesis of Civilizations

Working in the field of Christian and Muslim relations is not for the faint-hearted. Since time immemorial, Christians and Muslims have engaged in a litany of cruel and inhumane actions towards one another. Engrained in the collective consciousnesses of both populations is a memory of the other as an invading force that seeks converts, power, and resources. Issues pertaining to civilizational expansion and empire building have marked these relations since the Arab-Byzantine wars of the seventh century.

The unresolved geopolitical entanglements between the West and the Ummah (the global community of Muslim believers) have created cultural, religious, and social dynamics that are complex and difficult to resolve. The relationship between these civilizations is contentious, highly politicized, and represents many threats to peaceful coexistence on the world stage. Those like me who advocate for peace and pluralism face resistance from those who consider any kind of synthesis between Christians and Muslims as antithetical to their respective traditions. Extremists on both sides consider themselves to be the formal custodians of not only civilization, but God, and they see their civilizations and religions as commanding the subjugation of anyone who is deemed to be an outsider or threat.

Given the state of Christian and Muslim relations today, the naysayers point to the saying "get real, there will never be peace." This book challenges that claim by showing how "getting real" also means working toward coexistence and human flourishing. Positive examples do exist and have existed throughout history. In finding the common routes to peace, we see Christians and Muslims abiding by the best elements of their respective civilizational values and faith traditions.

For Christians and Muslims to settle their differences and live in harmony, there is an urgent need for attitudinal changes, paradigm shifts, and creative solutions. Put another way, as Pope Francis once said, they need to bequeath to their children a culture that is capable of "devising strategies of life, not death, and of inclusion, not exclusion." Solutions are contained within the Christian and Islamic traditions themselves and the histories of the civilizations born of them. I do not see these solutions as hopelessly idealistic or utopian. In fact, I have witnessed them in action, as this book will show. I hope that readers take the models and examples to heart and learn from them.

DEUCE

This book presents the acronym DEUCE as a mechanism to build more bonds between Christians and Muslims, and subsequently between the West and the Ummah. DEUCE stands for Dialogue, Education, Understanding, Commitment, and Engagement (Considine 2017a: 177). It can be used as a general concept to explain effective interfaith work, or it can be used as an actual step-by-step process to deploy in local communities.

Dialogue, the first element of DEUCE, is about initiating contact and starting conversations with other human beings. In my lectures around the world, I often tell audiences that this initial stage of dialogue should focus on "being human" rather than simply "being Christian" or "being Muslim." Focusing on shared identities and our common humanity – on issues like being a son, father, dad, husband, friend, or citizen – helps to foster connections across both real and perceived divides. I also tell audiences that "effective listening" is a lost art, but one that is essential for effective communication, and eventually understanding. Ceremonial exchanges – like enjoying a meal, organizing a book club, or co-hosting an interfaith event – are useful tools in engaging in meaningful dialogue.

Human beings are able to efficiently engage in **Education**, the second element of DEUCE, once dialogue establishes rapport and trust. Education involves a more serious and structured dialogue to generate "sympathetic intelligence" on topics like cultural practices, national identities, religious beliefs, sacred texts, and theological doctrine. The purpose of education is not to "convert" other participants to their religion or political ideology. Participating in educational endeavors also does not ask Christians or Muslims to compromise their religious beliefs or agree on the lowest common denominators about the respective traditions of the other. Rather, it is to enhance knowledge of each other's identities, lived experiences, realities, and views. Education is about gaining a more nuanced and thorough understanding of the various issues that typically divide two or more populations.

The third element of DEUCE – **Understanding** – refers to a state of being which is achieved by deliberate efforts to form friendships with other human beings. Understanding is synonymous with the idea of "finding consensus" in complex and fluid environments. It is also akin to "seeing eye to eye" or agreeing to move toward common goals even if there might be differences or disagreements. Understanding also should be differentiated from "knowing." While the two are related, knowing is static while understanding is active. If Christians and Muslims are able to understand one another, they are more likely to make sense of each other's decisions in a given situation. They would also be more likely to predict how people might respond to certain situations, which is a form of conflict resolution.

Commitment is the fourth element of DEUCE. It points to being dedicated or loyal to a particular cause, movement, or relationship. By committing to common goals and agreeing to a similar vision for society, Christians and Muslims are able to demonstrate camaraderie, care, and trust, all of which are critical to building bonds in a given society. Commitment to civil projects is particularly critical to a community's overall health and well-being. Unless Christians and Muslims commit themselves to a common set of principles, then both populations will continue suffering from human maladies like discrimination, racism, and xenophobia.

The fifth and decisive step of DEUCE is **Engagement**, which refers to Christians and Muslims being physically and socially active and committed to working together on projects bigger than themselves or immediate communities. Engagement might entail building multi-faith complexes, establishing a network of centers, leaders, and organizations, and jointly facilitating events for the common good. Instead of waiting for changes, there are Christians and Muslims that have taken – and are taking – responsibility in making the societal changes that they desire. This book brings their stories and teachings to life.

The Clash, Dialogue, and Synthesis of Civilizations

I will be addressing DEUCE through a theoretical framework that includes three concepts – the Clash of Civilizations, the Dialogue of Civilizations, and – my unique contribution – the Synthesis of Civilizations.[1] The latter term refers to Christians and Muslims working together by using the best of their cultural resources and religious traditions to create a new kind of community, and a new way of understanding the relationship between Christianity and Islam.

It is important to note that "synthesis" does not refer to a religious synthesis, or what some scholars refer to as "religious syncretism." I am not advocating for a new religion that combines principles of Christianity and Islam. To be clear, I am advocating for a "civic synthesis," whereby diverse groups of people work together in the public realm to build a new kind of multi-ethnic and multi-religious community.

The Synthesis of Civilizations is tied to the title of this book – "beyond dialogue." My theory is that there is indeed something beyond the framework of the Dialogue of Civilizations, and that DEUCE is a useful tool to use in furthering deeper bonds between Christians and Muslims.

The Dialogue of Civilizations is currently the world's major trend in interfaith dialogue, sponsored by the efforts and teachings of Pope Francis, whose papacy outlined the need for a Culture of Encounter between Christians and Muslims, and the United Arab Emirates (UAE) government, with whom he has worked closely. While the Dialogue of Civilizations welcomes Christians and Muslims to engage the other, there is no guarantee that their encounters will lead to fruitful developments between the populations. My point here relates to a popular criticism of interfaith dialogue – that it fosters tolerance, which is a good thing, but that it does not foster pluralism. The latter is the process whereby human beings of diverse backgrounds embark upon the "energetic engagement" with religious diversity. On this point, it differs from tolerance, which passively accepts diversity without actually engaging it. Pluralism, on the other hand, embraces diversity and stresses the importance of meaningful relationships for the betterment of the public good.

Both the Synthesis of Civilizations and the Dialogue of Civilizations are antithetical to the Clash of Civilizations. This concept argues that the primary source of conflict in the world is rooted in culture and religion. Its proponents claim that the West and the Ummah are mutually incompatible because of their different belief systems, civilizational values, and historical experiences. The Clash of Civilizations gained credibility following the attacks of 9/11, which – for many Westerners and Muslims worldwide – was another event in a long war between Christians and Muslims. It manifested in recent development like the United States' "Muslim travel ban," terrorist attacks by Muslim extremists on the European continent, and the tumultuous end of US engagement in Afghanistan.

But this pessimism about positive interfaith relations does not depict the full extent of Christian and Muslim relations. Positive encounters between Christians and Muslims have a history that long predates the "War on Terror." While the chapters of this book do not shy away from addressing the very real conflicts between those acting in the name of Christianity and Islam, we would be foolish to think that they capture the truth.

Structure of the Book

Beyond Dialogue will provide a historical and contemporary overview of Christian and Muslim relations in seven key geographical areas of the world, in the following order – the Arabian Peninsula, Europe, Asia Minor, South Asia, Africa, the United States of America (USA), and the Holy Land. Each of the seven chapters begin with the letter "H," and every chapter serves as a sociological concept that guides my analysis. These seven "H's" are Humanity, Hybridity, Heterogeneity, Honor, Harmony, Healing, and Holiness. Throughout the book, readers will see examples of DEUCE woven into real-life examples from across the globe and through the centuries. My hope is that readers will see the value of DEUCE and gain a better understanding of the potential for better relations between Christianity and Islam, the two biggest religions in the world.

In each chapter, I focus on specific "borderlands," a term that was inspired by the work of Gloria Anzaldúa (d. 2004), an American scholar of cultural theory. These locations represent the physical, spiritual, and symbolic boundaries that separate the West and the Ummah. By focusing on borderlands, readers are given a glimpse into the tense relations between Christians and Muslims, but also cultural hybridity, as these sites are susceptible to collaboration and mixing. To analyze the borderlands, I turn to the concept of the Grey Zone, which is a metaphor for the physical spaces of coexistence. These spaces are threatened by extremists in the West and the Ummah, who both view the world as divided into two camps – Christians or Muslims – and share the goal of destroying spaces of harmony and humanity.

My own lived experiences and personal observations will be recurring themes in the following pages. In some ways, I am similar to Louis Massignon (d. 1962) – the French Catholic priest and scholar – who once described himself as "standing at the crossroads, on the terrain of spiritual contact between Christianity and Islam" (Moncelon 1990: 537). I am not French like Massignon, but I am Catholic, and I have also stood at diverse sites of contact between Christians and Muslims.

This is my latest contribution to the body of knowledge as I continue my interfaith work. I am confident that DEUCE can be a utilitarian approach to bridging real or perceived differences that is able to greatly enhance harmony between Christians and Muslims.

CHAPTER 1

Humanity
The Arabian Peninsula

There are few places in the world more difficult to be a Christian than Saudi Arabia. Consider the story of Fatima, a Saudi woman who converted to Christianity from Islam in her mid-twenties. After her conversion, she started blogging under the pseudonym Rania, the Arabic woman's name meaning "eye-catching" or "noticeable" (Open Doors Australia 2013). Fatima was certainly both.

Her first blog post had a comment posted to it, which read – "You worship a foolish, crucified, cursed Lord. We are not honored by Saudi Arabian Christians. If I had you in my hands, I would slaughter you twice."

Gracefully, Fatima responded by referencing the eighth beatitude of Jesus, who declared, "Blessed are those who are persecuted for righteousness' sake, for theirs is the kingdom of heaven."

Things spiraled downwards for Fatima after her first post. Her brother went into a fit of rage when he found out that she had converted to Christianity. One day, in fear for her life, Fatima locked herself in her bedroom and started blogging. The title of that particular post was "I am in big trouble."

Fatima was right. Her brother, disgusted by her conversion to Christianity, eventually mangled her face by throwing acid on it. He then cut out her tongue. She later died from her injuries.

Fatima's story raises concerning questions on the presence of DEUCE and the well-being of humanity in Saudi Arabia, the birthplace of Islam. I define humanity as the quality of being benevolent, hospitable, inclusive, kind, and sympathetic towards one's fellow human beings, who constitute one human race. The opposite of humanity – inhumanity – is the state or quality of being cruel, exclusive, extreme, monstrous, and even violent towards one's fellow human beings, let alone one's sibling.

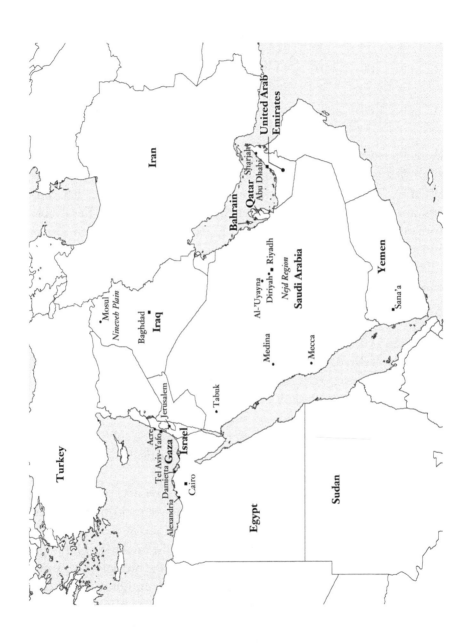

Today, Saudi Arabia ranks as the thirteenth most difficult country in the world to live in as a Christian (Open Doors USA n.d.a.). There is not a single official church in the country. Handing out Bibles is illegal. Converts to Christianity, foreign-born Christians, and native-born Christians all face systematic discrimination, intolerance, and prejudice, all of which fester in societies steeped in extremism and supremacy.

How, exactly, did Christianity become virtually intolerable in Saudi Arabia?

PART ONE – THE CLASH OF CIVILIZATIONS

Wahhabism and the House of Saud

The eyes of the world turned to Saudi Arabia in the days following 9/11. Fifteen of the hijackers, who launched their terrorist attacks by crashing commercial flights into the Twin Towers in New York City and the Pentagon in Washington D.C., were Saudi nationals. The attacks killed 2,977 people (9/11 Memorial and Museum n.d.). It was the single largest loss of life resulting from a foreign attack on American soil in the history of the USA.

My previous book *The Humanity of Muhammad – A Christian View* (Considine 2020) started with my personal experience on that fateful day. As a fifteen-year-old junior at Needham High School in Massachusetts, I had little context – and a lack of education or understanding – to make sense of the terror-driven media narratives about Islam and Muslims. I had no Muslim friends, I had never visited a mosque, and I never learned about Islamic history in Catholic school or public school. I had a lot of questions as to what happened on that day.

Naturally, the American government had questions, too. It started pointing the blame at Al-Qaeda – a transnational terrorist network – and the Taliban – an Islamist government – in Afghanistan. Most Americans had never heard of either group at the time. Questions also swirled on whether Muslim-majority countries around the world may have assisted the terrorists in their attacks.

Clarity on the perpetrators' identities was provided in December 2002, when a joint House of Representatives and Senate intelligence committee provided evidence of possible links between the government of Saudi

Arabia and some of the fifteen Saudi citizens involved in the attacks (Ottaway 2016).

Osama Bin Laden (d. 2011), the Saudi-born founder of the pan-Islamic terrorist organization known as Al-Qaeda, emerged as the ringleader of the attacks of 9/11. In May 1998, when interviewed in Afghanistan by ABC, he outlined his vision for the Clash of Civilizations, stating:

> *It is far better for anyone to kill a single American soldier than to squander his efforts on other activities . . . We believe that the worst thieves in the world today and the worst terrorists are the Americans. Nothing could stop [Muslims] except perhaps retaliation in kind. We do not have to differentiate between military or civilian. As far as we are concerned, they are all targets (Public Broadcasting Service n.d.).*

The Clash of Civilizations is a term that captures the perceived antagonistic relationship between Christians and Muslims. It was popularized by Samuel P. Huntington (d. 2008), the former political scientist from Harvard University, following the collapse of the Berlin Wall and the fall of the Soviet Union in the early 1990s. He argued that the primary source of future conflicts will be rooted in "cultural values" rather than "economic values" (like capitalism versus communism) (Huntington 1993: 22). To drive home his thesis, Huntington's book publisher – Simon and Schuster – created a book cover that juxtaposed two flags – the American flag (representing the West) and the white crescent placed against a green backdrop (representing the Ummah).

Bin Laden was famous for spreading discontent and resentment in the West by calling the American-led "War on Terror" a greedy and immoral war designed to bolster Western oil interests. He referred to Saudi Arabia as a "colony" of the USA and Saudi leaders as the "puppets" of Western leaders for allowing American military bases inside the birthplace of Islam.

Many media commentators suggested that 9/11 was the result of Wahhabism, which is recognized as a primary driver of "Islamic terrorism" and the "catchall term to describe all forms of Islamic militancy" (Pew Research Center 2005). In the West, Wahhabism is synonymous with extremism. In the Ummah, it is synonymous with the conservative Hanbali school of jurisprudence and the strictest interpretation of the

Sharia. It has been identified as the only form of religion that can be openly taught or practiced in Saudi Arabia (Rohmaniyah and Woodward 2012: 3).

Wahhabism is named after Muhammad Ibn Abd Al-Wahhab (d. 1792), a jurist and theologian of the eighteenth century. He saw himself as a *mujaddid*, or a "restorer of the faith," and encouraged a literal interpretation of the Qur'an and *ahadith*. Al-Wahhab was a strict proponent of *tawhid*, the Arabic term meaning the "oneness of God" or the "unity of God." For those who may not be familiar with the term, *tawhid* celebrates Allah as indivisible, monolithic, and singular (Phillips 2018). For Al-Wahhab, it was incompatible with the Trinity – the Christian doctrine claiming that the Father (God), the Son (Jesus), and the Holy Spirit represent the true essence of God. From a Wahhabi perspective, the Trinity is the "ultimate evil" (Abdul-Rahman 2023). It positions Christians as "unsaveable," or victims of what Pope Francis called the "throw-away culture," in which human beings are discarded and excluded as outcasts and potential villains because they do not align with hegemonic worldviews.

Christians, it should be noted, do not worship three gods. Worshipping three gods amounts to polytheism. Rather, Christians typically worship one God who they believe exists as three distinct, co-equal, co-eternal persons, sharing all the attributes of deity, agreeing completely in will and purpose, and existing eternally in divine, loving relationships with one another (Phillips 2018). There also are Unitarian Christians who adhere to a strict monotheism in the unitary nature of God. An understanding of these distinctions and views is important for furthering constructive dialogue and beneficial engagement between Christians and Muslims.

Al-Wahhab was particularly harsh in maintaining a puritanical view of religious sites. He eschewed *bid'ah* – the Arabic term meaning "innovation" – including practices like decorating graves, mysticism, and worshipping saints. He considered all these practices to be *shirk*, or the sin of polytheism.

Al-Wahhab encountered problems while living in Iran in 1736 and then again in his birthplace of Al-'Uyayna in 1744. He ended up finding refuge in Diriyah, an agricultural settlement that was then emerging as a commercial center.[1] There, he was granted protection by Saud Bin Muhammad Al-Muqrin (d. 1725), an *emir* of the Nejd region of the

Arabian Peninsula. Ibn Saud has been described as an ambitious and competent warrior. He is the progenitor of the current line of the Saudi royal family. His ally Al-Wahhab provided the House of Saud with military support and guidance on matters of religion and statecraft. Their connection was deepened when Al-Wahhab's daughter married Abdul-Aziz, a son of Ibn Saud.

Few would contest that Al-Wahhab shaped the present-day country of Saudi Arabia. It is commonly believed that he turned the House of Saud from limited rulers of a middle-sized settlement with a talent for business and diplomacy, into the guardians of Islam's Holy Places. His legacy, however, is a mixed bag (Crawford 2014). He is either remembered as a "pious religious activist" who fought to establish a regime of Islamic godliness, or a "hateful figure" who condemned Christianity, Sufism, and Shiaism.

Wahhabism has been the dominant force in Saudi Arabia since the days of Al-Wahhab and Al-Muqrin. Abdulaziz Bin Abdul Rahman Al-Saud (d. 1953), who founded Saudi Arabia, revived his dynasty's support for Wahhabism in the years before World War II by founding a militant tribal organization known as the Ikhwan (Britannica n.d.c.). Wahhabis also seized control of the Grand Mosque of Mecca in 1979, rose up in rebellion in the mid-1990s, kept women from driving cars until 2018, and preached incessantly against the opening of the kingdom to secular Western culture (Ottaway 2021).

The Saudi government, nonetheless, has been undertaking a radical and rapid restructuring of its country, the most far-reaching changes since the creation of Saudi Arabia in 1932. There are initial signs that Saudi Arabia is embracing the core principles of DEUCE.

De-Wahhabization and Mohammad bin Salman

Leading Saudi Arabia's transformation is Mohammad bin Salman, colloquially known as MBS, who is the Saudi Crown Prince, the prime minister, and de facto ruler of Saudi Arabia. He has won plaudits from Western leaders for his reforms that push for a "moderate Islam" to modernize Saudi Arabia.[2]

MBS lambasted his kingdom's Wahhabi establishment in a speech during Ramadan in 2021. In language never used by a Saudi monarch, he called into question the "enslavement" of Saudi religious leaders due to the prevalence of Wahhabi indoctrination:

> *If [Al-Wahhab] were with us today and he found us committed blindly to his texts and closing our minds to interpretation and jurisprudence while deifying and sanctifying him, he would be the first to object to this. There are no fixed schools of thought and there is no infallible person. We should engage in continuous interpretation of Qur'anic texts, and the same goes for the traditions of the Prophet (see Hassan 2022).*

MBS added that a *fatwa* – or an authorized Islamic legal ruling – "should be based on the time, place, and mindset in which they are issued." With these words, he declared that the prevailing Wahhabi tradition is faulty and out of date. "We cannot grow, we cannot attract capital . . . we cannot progress with [their] extremist thinking in Saudi Arabia," he said at the end of his speech.

Part of MBS's de-Wahhabization efforts includes welcoming a stream of Western male and female artists, bands, dancers, and singers to enhance understanding of the West in Saudi Arabia. He has engaged with Jewish Americans and Christian Americans on tours of historical sites relating to the Abrahamic tradition in Saudi Arabia. One of the Christians, the evangelical Pastor Joel Richardson, became the first person in the history of Saudi Arabia to give a "Christian tour" of the Arabian Peninsula (Bostock 2021).

While MBS's efforts are revolutionary, one could say that the first signs of DEUCE and de-Wahhabization in Saudi Arabia occurred under the rule of His Majesty King Abdullah Bin Abdul Aziz (d. 2015). In 2006, he issued the Confirmation of Policies with the USA, which stated that Saudi Arabia would commit itself to "[guaranteeing] and [protecting] the right to private worship for all, including non-Muslims who gather in homes for religious practice" (Human Rights Watch 2012). Six years later, in partnership with the governments of Austria and Spain, he founded the King Abdullah Abdul-Aziz International Centre for Interreligious and Intercultural Dialogue (KAICIID), otherwise known as the International Dialogue Center, in Austria. This unique intergovernmental organization, which includes Austria, the Holy See (Vatican), Saudi Arabia, and Spain, was founded to promote the concepts of DEUCE (King Abdullah

Abdul-Aziz International Centre for Interreligious and Intercultural Dialogue n.d.). The KAICIID envisions a world where there is cooperation, justice, understanding, reconciliation, and respect between the civilizations of the world. The organization also works to end the abuse of religion to justify oppression, violence, and conflict.

Despite these humane developments, there remains an elephant in the room – Saudi Arabia is a theocracy, a form of government that demands conformity to a state-sponsored religion. Its constitution says that the country is "a sovereign Arab Islamic State. Its religion is Islam. Its constitution is Almighty God's Book, The Holy Qur'an, and the Sunna (Traditions) of the Prophet (PBUH)" (Kingdom of Saudi Arabia n.d.).

Several articles in the Saudi Arabian Constitution might be seen as problematic for Christians advocating for more religious freedom. Article Seven of the Constitution states that the Saudi state derives its authority from the "Book of God" – the *Qur'an* – and the *ahadith*, the collection of sayings by Prophet Muhammad. The article adds that these are the "ultimate sources" of references for the laws of Saudi Arabia. Article Nine of the Constitution states that the Saudi people shall be raised in the "Islamic creed." Article Ten states that the Saudi state will aspire to promote "family bonds and Arab-Islamic values." While this is not overtly discriminatory toward Christians, it leaves little – if any – space for the freedom of religion for Christians and other religious populations in the country.

Nevertheless, there are civilizational changes emerging around the Arabian Peninsula. Saudi Arabia is reckoning with its history of Wahhabism. That bodes well for today's Christians in Saudi Arabia, a country that holds promise and potential in terms of practicing DEUCE in the years ahead. Their greater acceptance of DEUCE represents a potential pathway for the country's evolution, which will also benefit other countries around the Arabian Peninsula as their transformation develops.

PART TWO – THE DIALOGUE OF CIVILIZATIONS

After decades of isolation and rigidity, the Saudis appear to be in favor of DEUCE-friendly concepts like interfaith dialogue, educational reforms, cross-cultural understanding, and interethnic engagement. The latter is best illustrated by their interest in joining the Abraham Accords, an American-sponsored peace agreement that normalized relations between Israel and several Arab countries, one of which – the UAE – has emerged as a global center for the Dialogue of Civilizations.

The Abraham Accords

Hope for a regional peace around the Arabian Peninsula was on the horizon before 7 October 2023, the day that Hamas – a Palestinian Islamist political group and terrorist organization according to many Western countries – crossed the border from their stronghold in the Gaza Strip and killed 1,200 people in southern Israel. In the months before that day, there were movements towards a potential normalization agreement between Israel and Saudi Arabia, as MBS noted in an interview with Fox News. "Every day, we get closer [to normalizing with Israel]," he said (Al-Jazeera 2023). The inclusion of Saudi Arabia in the Abraham Accords was envisioned as a "tectonic shift in Middle East geopolitics," the likes of which have not been seen since the fall of the Berlin Wall and the end of the Cold War in 1989 (Kurtzer-Ellenbogen et al. 2023).

Caroline Glick, a Jewish American and Israeli author and journalist, attended the official signing of the Abraham Accords at the White House in 2020.[3] For her, the ceremony was a "moving and jarring" experience (Glick 2020). It occurred at the same location where the Oslo Accords were signed in 1993.[4] To Glick, the Oslo Accords were nothing more than "political theatre" and constituted a "fake peace" with the Palestinians. For her, the Abraham Accords signaled a "genuine peace," because Arab countries recognized Israel's right to exist. "You cannot make peace with people who justify your murder and seek your destruction," Glick rightly noted, "You can only make peace with those who accept you as you are for what you are."

Others praised the Abraham Accords for ushering in a "culture of peace" and a "new dawn in interfaith relations and security alliances in the Middle East" (Alketbi 2022). This new dawn, as the signees of the Abraham Accords committed themselves to, would be ushered in by offsprings of DEUCE, including academic initiatives, cultural exchanges, interfaith dialogue, people-to-people programs, and scientific progress between the nations of the accords. The signees also committed themselves to countering extremism, which they agreed promotes division, hatred, and terrorism in the region and around the world.

I had the opportunity to witness first-hand the significance of the Abraham Accords during my tour of Qasr Al-Watan, the presidential palace of the UAE. As I was marveling at the palace's majestic Great Hall, particularly its 37-meter diameter dome, a male tourist asked me to take a picture of him and his wife. He handed me his phone and I quickly noticed the Hebrew language on his screen. I proceeded to ask him about his experiences in the UAE and he told me that he loved the country for its hospitality and openness. He also mentioned that it was "unthinkable" just years before that Israelis would be welcomed as visitors to an Arab nation. These transformations were made possible by the UAE's promotion of DEUCE principles.

It is fair to say that the Abraham Accords drastically altered relations between the UAE and Israel, whose relations have never been stronger. For the first four months of 2023, bilateral trade between the UAE and Israel was valued at $990.6 million, with an expectation that it would reach $3 billion for the year and $3.45 billion for 2024 (Feierstein and Guzansky 2023). Between 2020 and 2023, bilateral trade between the two countries exceeded $6 billion.[5] The partnerships formed by Emiratis and Israelis point to the vital role that economic integration plays in promoting peace and security. They also point to the idea that long-standing divisions can be resolved through collaboration (commitment and engagement) and diplomacy (dialogue, education, and understanding).

The Abraham Accords also cemented ties between the UAE and Israel in the defense industry. The Israelis supplied the Emiratis with air defense systems after missile and drone attacks in Abu Dhabi, the Emirati capital, were conducted by the Houthis, a Yemeni party identified as a terrorist organization by Western countries, in 2022. The UAE's air defenses against the Houthis are backed by the American military forces, who – alongside the Saudis and Emiratis – are concerned with the rise of Islamist groups like the Muslim Brotherhood[6] in Yemen specifically, and other parts of the world.

The Abraham Accords are not without their fair share of critics. One criticism is that they did almost nothing to advance a resolution between the Israelis and the Palestinians. One journalist said that the agreements left the Palestinians "more alienated than ever" and that they represented "bitter lemons for [them]" because it "ripped up any residual solidarity that Arab nations once sought to convey for [their] plight" (Scheindlin 2022b). Palestinian leaders themselves spoke of the betrayal of their Arab allies for reaching an agreement with Israel without first making progress toward creating the State of Palestine (Pamuk and Lewis 2021). They added that Arab Muslim countries had set back the cause of a just peace by abandoning the demand that Israel return land to the Palestinians (Holland 2020).

A second criticism is that the Abraham Accords were not designed to further Abrahamic relations, but rather to counter Iran, a common enemy of both the UAE and Israel. The Houthi-dominated government in Sana'a, the capital of Yemen, is backed by the Iranian government. The UAE, on the other hand, supported the former Yemeni government by deploying its own troops to Yemen alongside Saudi Arabian forces. The joint Emirati-Saudi mission was to restore the Sunni-led government driven out by the Houthis. These political entanglements point to a wider proxy war in the region between Saudi Arabia, Israel, the UAE, and their allies on one side, and the Houthis, the Iranians, and their allies on the other. The dynamic represents a Clash *within* Civilization as much as it points to the need for the Dialogue of Civilizations.[7]

In addition to being recognized as an opponent of Iran and the Muslim Brotherhood, the UAE is known for opposing Islamist political movements that are backed by Turkey and Qatar (Fiore 2020). Over the last few decades, the UAE adopted opposite stances to Turkey and Qatar toward the Muslim Brotherhood. The Emirati approach to the Muslim Brotherhood and its allies is driven largely by the country's response to the Arab Spring, suspecting that the movement might embolden those dissidents seeking political reform (Baskan 2019). To prevent these reforms from taking shape, the UAE started cracking down on the Muslim Brotherhood in 2011 and later launched a punitive campaign that culminated in its 2014 declaration of the Muslim Brotherhood as a "terrorist organization."

A third criticism is that the Abraham Accord signees are undemocratic countries that undermine democratic values both at home and in international relations (Scheindlin 2022a). This is a fair criticism. Tools for measuring democratic quality show that Bahrain, Morocco, the UAE, and Sudan all score low on "democracy" (Democracy Matrix

2023). Israel performs well alongside other Western democracies, but international organizations like Amnesty International and Human Rights Watch also accuse it of orchestrating an "apartheid" against the Palestinians.

While opposition to the Abraham Accords stems from the Clash of Civilizations, it also stems from the fear of "religious syncretism," a potential byproduct of engaging in the Dialogue of Civilizations. The idea that Christians and Muslims (and Jews) are forming a "single community" has prompted critics to raise their concern about the possible emergence of a new religion – dubbed "Abrahamism" – which has been described as "straight out of a dystopian movie" and a composite of Judaism, Christianity, and Islam. One journalist argued that although the term Abrahamic sounds bright and merciful, its actual content is dark and misleading, because it uses religion in the service of American foreign policy and Israel in the Middle East (Sharqawi 2022).

Even Christians advocating for the Dialogue of Civilizations have stressed their opposition to "Abrahamism." His Holiness Pope Tawadros II, the leader of the Coptic Orthodox Church of Alexandria, described it as "categorically unacceptable" because it is a political idea rather than a religious one (Egypt Today Staff 2022). He added that the Abrahamic religion is "set out to destroy the constants" of Judaism, Christianity, and Islam. Similarly, in a Russia Today Arabic interview, Egyptian General Khairat Shukri claimed that "Abrahamism" is "no less dangerous than Zionism" (Mirza 2021). Even Sheikh Ahmed El-Tayyeb, who co-authored "A Document on Human Fraternity" with Pope Francis, agreed with Pope Tawadros II and General Shukri's claim that merging Judaism, Christianity, and Islam is not advisable. He stated:

> . . . it is impossible for humankind to concur in one religion, given differences among people in colors, creeds, minds, languages and even fingerprints. All this is a historical and scientific fact, and before this it is a fact confirmed by the Holy Qur'an (Al-Sherbini 2021).

Sheikh El-Tayyeb, nonetheless, kept the door open for DEUCE by stating that dialogue and education are important in promoting human fraternity, which is crucial in preserving peace, security, and stability (Egypt Today Staff 2022).

Pope Francis has himself been accused of promoting "Abrahamism." His advocacy for the Dialogue of Civilizations has been described as "equalizing religions" and directly contradicting the historical Catholic Church position that Catholicism is the only "true religion" (Sammons 2023). By conflating Catholicism and Islam, the critics claim, Pope Francis and Sheikh El-Tayyeb endorse religious indifference and a potentially tyrannical "one world religion."

In defense of Pope Francis's promotion of the Dialogue of Civilizations, Bishop Miguel Ayoso Guixot, the President of the Pontifical Council for Interreligious Dialogue, stated, "It is not about creating a 'melting pot' in which all religions are considered equal," he noted, "but [recognizing] that all believers, those who seek God, and all people of good will without religious affiliation are equal in dignity." Bishop Guixot added that engaging in Abrahamic initiatives "invites us to reflect upon and value our own identities, without which authentic interreligious dialogue is impossible" (Watkins 2019). His comments are critically important to understanding a key takeaway of this book – that the Synthesis of Civilizations is not intended to fuse religions together in the hope of creating a new religion, but rather to foster a stronger "civic-community" that allows the five principles of DEUCE to flourish.

Few countries have committed themselves more to Abrahamic initiatives than the UAE. The Hamas–Israel conflict has only temporarily hampered the impact of the Abraham Accords. It is likely that they will survive the conflict and flourish in the years ahead. Adopting an understanding of DEUCE will help to build improved bridges on the pathway to peace.

Sheikh Zayed's Vision and the Year of Tolerance

Understanding the UAE's embrace of the Abraham Accords is impossible without understanding the life and vision of Sheikh Zayed Bin Sultan Al-Nahyan (d. 2004), the founding father of the UAE. Sheikh Zayed was the youngest son of Sheikh Sultan Bin Khalifa Al-Nahyan, the ruler of Abu Dhabi from 1922 to 1926. At that time, Abu Dhabi was a poor and underdeveloped city. Its economy was primarily based on fishing and pearl diving, and simple agricultural settlements were scattered across the oases.

While serving as the ruler of Abu Dhabi in the late 1960s, Sheikh Zayed welcomed the UK's decision to withdraw from the Arabian Gulf in 1971. In the subsequent years – with the assistance of Sheikh Rashid Bin Saeed Al-Maktoum (d. 1990) – Sheikh Zayed called for a federation of seven emirates, all of which united to form the UAE on 2 December 1971. Before his death, he renamed the Sheikh Mohammad Bin Zayed Mosque in Al-Mushrif, a district in the capital Abu Dhabi, as *Mariam, Umm Eisa*, which translates from Arabic to "Mary, the mother of Jesus."

Sheikh Zayed's vision – grounded in benevolence, compassion, and unity – has been illuminated over the years in the UAE's pursuit of peace. His vision reached a climax in 2019, the year that his son – Sheikh Khalifa Bin Zayed Al-Nahyan (d. 2022) – designated the Year of Tolerance. This initiative was designed to confirm and solidify the UAE as a global capital of tolerance and a bridge of communication between people of diverse cultures (United Arab Emirates Government Portal 2022). It had five primary goals – to deepen values of coexistence and tolerance; to host a series of dialogues and projects between various cultures and civilizations; to launch cross-cultural programs; to focus on policy-oriented issues regarding dialogue, cross-cultural communication, and tolerance; and to promote tolerance in the media. All of these initiatives are clear manifestations of DEUCE in action.

The Year of Tolerance witnessed a landmark visit by Pope Francis, the first pope to ever arrange a papal visit to the Arabian Peninsula. In Abu Dhabi, he led a public mass for an estimated 180,000 people at the Zayed Sports City stadium. According to the Vatican, people in attendance hailed from 100 countries. They included asylum seekers and migrants, many of whom previously hailed from the Philippines and South America.

Pope Francis's visit to the UAE also included another important milestone – the signing of "A Document on Human Fraternity for World Peace and Living Together," which I mentioned previously. He signed it in tandem with Sheikh El-Tayyeb. The document was praised around the world for its commitment to humanism. Miguel Moratinos, the High Representative for the United Nations Alliance of Civilizations (UNAOC), called it a "blueprint for humanity," namely in that it reaffirms "the dignity and worth of every human being regardless of this person's religion, belief, ethnicity, gender, or culture" (Moratinos 2021). A part of the "Document on Human Fraternity" reads:

In the name of God and of everything . . . Al-Azhar al-Sharif and the Muslims of the East and West, together with the Catholic Church and the Catholics of the East and West, declare the adoption of a culture of dialogue as the path; mutual cooperation as the code of conduct; [and] reciprocal understanding as the method and standard (A Document on Human Fraternity for World Peace and Living Together 2019).

These words captured what Pope Francis referred to as the Culture of Encounter, which encourages people to engage with one another in the vast spaces of humanity, society, and spirituality, in the hope that more emphasis on DEUCE concepts could lead to a potential lasting mutual peace between conflicting communities. These spaces are sites for potential collaboration and knowledge building, as well as hope for a more peaceful future.

In addition to these humanitarian offerings, "A Document on Human Fraternity" made it clear that freedom of religion is a prerequisite to any healthy and thriving community or nation. The agreement guarantees the protection of places of worship for all religious populations. It added that any violent or terrorist attack on a place of worship is a "deviation" from the teachings of Christianity and Islam, as well as a clear violation of human rights and freedom of religion, which are unattainable without a recognition of the importance of DEUCE.

The years preceding the Year of Tolerance also revealed elements of the Dialogue of Civilizations in the UAE. In 2016 His Highness Sheikh Mohammed Bin Rashid Al-Maktoum, the current prime minister and vice president of the UAE and the Ruler of Dubai, made structural changes to his cabinet by creating the post of Minister of State for Tolerance and Coexistence. His Highness Al-Maktoum ushered in this change in the spirit of the UAE's commitment to eradicate cultural, ideological, and religious bigotry in society (United Arab Emirates Government Portal 2022). Furthermore, on the International Day of Tolerance in November 2017, Al-Maktoum named the pedestrian bridge over the Dubai Canal as the "Tolerance Bridge," a move that symbolized tolerance as "a fundamental value in the UAE community where people from over 200 nationalities live in harmony without racism, discrimination, or intolerance" (United Arab Emirates Government Portal 2022).

Critics, nevertheless, have claimed that the Emirates – along with other Gulf states – engage in superficial interfaith outreach as part of its broader alignment of political interests between them and Israel, which share a common foe in Iran (Associated Press 2020). Critics also question the UAE's commitment to freedom of religion because Emirati Christians themselves are unable to express their Christian faith publicly. There are strict laws against proselytization by non-Muslims in the country. Those who engage in proselytization or conversion can face harsh punishments. The UAE also does not allow Christians to pray in public, although churches across the country are able to display crosses. Emirati Muslims who convert to Christianity risk losing inheritance and parental rights, being forced to marry, being fired, or placed under pressure to work for "free" (Open Doors USA n.d.c.). There is also widespread media censorship in the UAE and dozens of activists are in jail for speaking out against the Emirati government. Political parties also are banned.

Despite these issues, the UAE has long welcomed Christianity and Christians to their country. Christian news outlets such as Christian Broadcasting Network and Trinity Broadcasting Network operate in the country. Christian literature and media are available in bookstores in leading Emirati cities like Abu Dhabi, Dubai, and Sharjah. Contemporary Christian bands and musicians have also performed in the country. At the institutional level, the Emirati government recognizes various Christian denominations, including Catholics, Orthodox, and Protestants. Other smaller denominations include several Evangelical and Pentecostal churches and the Church of Jesus Christ of Latter-day Saints, whose followers are known as Mormons.

As of 2023, there are a total of ten Catholic churches in the Emirates. Of all the Christian denominations in the UAE, the Catholics have the largest and most historically significant presence in the country. I have visited two of their churches – the Saint Francis Church (which I return to later in the chapter) and Saint Joseph's Cathedral. In my visit to the latter, I was struck by the faithfulness and energy of Abu Dhabi's small but growing Catholic population, which has had a presence in the UAE for decades.

Saint Mary's of Dubai and DEUCE in Emirati History

In 1966 – the year oil was discovered in Dubai – His Highness Sheikh Rashid Bin Saeed Al-Maktoum donated a small portion of land to a Roman Catholic mission led by Father Eusebio Daveri, who eventually established – with the permission of Emirati leaders – a church named Church of the Assumption. The Catholic community in Dubai dedicated the church to Mary, the mother of Jesus, during an inauguration in which His Highness Al-Maktoum hosted His Eminency Monseigneur Magliacani. The Comboni Missionary Sisters,[8] who are known for their cultural diversity and intercultural lifestyles, expanded Saint Mary's by creating a Catholic school in 1976 to accommodate the growing Christian community in the city.

Although the original church was demolished in 1989, the community built a new church that they named Saint Mary's Roman Catholic Church.[9] Choosing the mother of Jesus as the name bearer of the church is an affirmation of the shared views on Mary in the Christian and Islamic traditions. The Qur'an, like the Bible, recognizes her purity, virginity, and wisdom. Many stages of Mary's life are verified in the Islamic holy book, including the Annunciation, her pregnancy, Jesus's miraculous birth, and her death. Mary, in short, is a bridge between Christianity and Islam.

Saint Mary's accommodates 2,000 persons and hosts dozens of services in languages including Arabic, English, Malayalam, and Urdu. It is located near a busy four-lane road in central Dubai. As of 2023, it has over 2,000 students and is considered one of the best English-medium schools on the Arabian Peninsula (Saint Mary's Catholic Church Dubai n.d.). It is the school through which many Emirati youth graduate. It provides a comprehensive education that incorporates interreligious principles and moral sciences within its curriculum. That kind of curriculum encourages the benefits of DEUCE concepts between students of diverse backgrounds and teaches young people how to achieve coexistence and justice in an increasingly globalized and multicultural world.

The Christian members of the Saint Mary's community contribute to the broader culture of peace in the UAE. The school's intercultural curriculum improves cultural awareness, empathy, and well-being for not only its members, but for the wider Emirati society. It also encourages conversations that can create deeper human connections, which is key to actualizing the Synthesis of Civilizations.

PART THREE – THE SYNTHESIS OF CIVILIZATIONS

The Synthesis of Civilizations, as I noted in the Introduction, is not pointing to the fusion of Christianity and Islam or any promotion of religious syncretism. It is, however, pointing to a "civic synthesis" in which people of all walks of life engage with one another in the five principles of DEUCE – dialogue, education, understanding, commitment, and engagement. At first glance, readers might think that the Synthesis of Civilizations only occurs in times of coexistence, harmony, and peace. Curiously, it also appears amidst inhumanity and war zones.

Restoring Humanity and the Spirit of Mosul

In an increasingly interlinked world, human connectedness matters more than ever. It strengthens a country's immune system against extremism and violence. But no city or country, regardless of its commitment to pluralism, is immune from extremism and violence.

Take, for instance, the city of Mosul, which means "the linking point" or "the bridge" in Arabic. Located in northern Iraq, it is one of the oldest cities in the world. For millennia it has served as a strategic location due to its crossroads and bridge between north and south, east and west.

Being at the crossroads of civilizations, Mosul inevitably emerged as a melting pot of diverse cultures and groups. The city has been described as the crucible of pluralism in Iraq and the embodiment of coexistence among the countries' various ethnic, linguistic, and religious groups (United Nations Educational, Scientific, and Cultural Organization 2022: 8).

Because Mosul is so multicultural, it was targeted by ISIS, which swept into the city and proclaimed it its capital in 2014 (United Nations Educational, Scientific, and Cultural Organization 2022: 8). When it seized control, ISIS presented the Christians of Mosul and the wider Nineveh Plain with three choices – convert to Islam, pay a tribute (or the *jizya*), or flee the city. Hundreds of thousands of Christians ended up

24

fleeing. By the summer of 2014, the entire Nineveh Plain was practically empty of Christians for the first time since the seventh century. ISIS controlled the city until 2017.

ISIS's treatment of the Christians of Mosul became the subject of international headlines. During the occupation, it turned churches into torture and execution chambers, bomb factories, shooting ranges, and jihadi training schools for children. Included among the many humiliations for Christians was the exhumation of the graves of priests and clergy, whose bodies were searched for gold and valuable items (Martany and Al-Khatib 2022).

One Christian leader of Mosul – Sister Diana Momeka of the Dominican Sisters of Saint Catherine of Siena – shared her firsthand experiences with ISIS. She told members of the US House of Representatives' Committee on Foreign Affairs in 2015 that:

> the current persecution that our community is facing is the most brutal in our history. Not only have we been robbed of our homes, property, and land, but our heritage is being destroyed as well. [ISIS] has and continues to demolish and bomb our churches, cultural artefacts and sacred places like Mar Benham and his sister, a fourth century monastery, and Saint George's Monastery in Mosul. Uprooted and forcefully displaced, we have realized that ISIS plans to evacuate the land of Christians and wipe the earth clean of any evidence that we ever existed. This is cultural and human genocide (Momeka 2015).

In the aftermath of ISIS's pillaging, UNESCO concluded that the city's heritage sites were "reduced to rubble" and that its religious monuments and cultural antiquities were severely damaged (United Nations Educational, Scientific, and Cultural Organization n.d.b.). Eighty per cent of the "Old City" of Mosul was destroyed (United Nations Educational, Scientific, and Cultural Organization 2022: 8). Not only did the war destroy the city's vital infrastructure, but it also diminished the Christian population, increased fear, created pessimism for the future of Christianity in Iraq, and all but ended any opportunities to engage in DEUCE.

One of the churches attacked by ISIS – the Mar Tuma Syriac Catholic Church – dates back to the nineteenth century. ISIS used its church grounds as a prison and courthouse (The National 2022). It also destroyed Saint George's Monastery, which it also used as a prison for the Yazidis, the Kurdish religious group that combines elements of Judaism, Christianity, Islam, and ancient Persian religions. ISIS even melted the main statue of Saint George to use as ammunition (Neurink 2022). The church graveyard was also destroyed.

Yet, amidst the killing and destruction, there were signs of the Synthesis of Civilizations in Mosul. Christians and Muslims – both of whom were targeted by ISIS militants – started rebuilding the city *together*. Engagement in the public sphere, as demonstrated here, is critically important to extending the concepts of DEUCE throughout Iraq. It could be the harbinger of changes to come.

In the first Mass celebrated in the rebuilt church of Saint George's Monastery, Father Najeeb Michaeel – the Chaldean[10] archbishop of Mosul – welcomed Iraqi military officers and officials who played a role in its rebuilding (Neurink 2022). Bishop Michael noted during the Mass that the reopening of Saint George's would have been impossible if it were not for the commitment and engagement of local Muslims who cleaned up the churches after ISIS left.

The rebuilding of the Convent of Our Lady of the Hour – also known as the Al-Saa'a Church or the Latin Church – is another example of DEUCE in Mosul. The site, founded by the Dominicans in 1870,[11] included a church, a seminary, a school for children, a school for women teachers, and a hospital. Al-Saa'a has historically served as a "sanctuary" for Christians and Muslims alike.

Humanity, in short, is the "spirit of Mosul." While upholding humanity is paramount, it is also essential that we understand the dangers of destroying cultural heritage and religious sites. World leaders must recognize that these are not just matters of architectural or historical significance, but also matters of promoting peace, tolerance, and understanding in the face of inhumanity.

Reviving the Spirit of Mosul

Humanity often reveals itself in the most inhumane moments. It often begins on the periphery of society by people who have been excluded from mainstream societies. People on the periphery experience inhumanity, but they also know humanity when they see it.

The people of Mosul amplified humanity by creating the "Revive the Spirit of Mosul" initiative, a 2018 collaboration between the UAE, the European Union (EU), and UNESCO. These three entities engaged with the people of Mosul to encourage reconciliation, restore interfaith harmony, and foster social cohesion between Christians and Muslims. The UAE revived the spirit of Mosul by donating $50.4 million to the restoration of Al-Saa'a and Al-Tahera churches. The restoration of the Al-Saa'a Church was the subject of several bilateral consultations with both experts and local stakeholders, a process that helped to generate a sense of local ownership of Mosul itself (United Nations Educational, Scientific, and Cultural Organization 2022: 15). Furthering a sense of local ownership helps to ensure that DEUCE is responsive to the needs and the priorities of communities that are devastated by extremism and war.

The Revive the Spirit of Mosul initiative also restored interfaith spaces and educational environments by restoring the "House of Prayer," a building bordering the Dominican convent that serves as a multipurpose educational and cultural center for the local community (United Nations Educational, Scientific, and Cultural Organization 2022: 15). On the educational front, the UAE rehabilitated schools so that they could serve "as places where [people] learn to live together," with the ultimate goal being the transmission of "openness and respect," or what UNESCO called the "foundations for a peaceful future" (United Nations Educational, Scientific, and Cultural Organization 2022: 5).

Leaders involved in Revive the Spirit of Mosul also committed themselves to education through the arts and cross-cultural collaborations. A creative space called The Station was completed in June 2021 to serve as a "hub for young people working on cultural and creative industries to meet, learn, and exchange ideas" (United Nations Educational, Scientific, and Cultural Organization 2022: 20). UNESCO partnered with Action for Hope, a non-governmental organization, in "Listening to Iraq," a program that provided training to 24 musicians from Mosul.[12] It also backed a project called "Prevention of Violent Extremism Through Education," which was designed to further interfaith dialogue, non-violence, and peacebuilding in the face of extremism.

Another element of Revive the Spirit of Mosul was the recovery and restoration projects on the city's library, which originally housed a collection of manuscripts dating back to the ninth century (United Nations

Educational, Scientific, and Cultural Organization 2022: 16). The multi-faith collection contained ancient Aramaic and Syriac texts, but also Muslim, Jewish, and Yazidi papers on history, literature, and mathematics.

Preserving ancient books and manuscripts is critically important in furthering the heritage of Mosul and promoting education – the second component of DEUCE – in Iraq. Alongside his allies, Father Michaeel worked to remove 800 manuscripts from sites under imminent attack from ISIS. His heroic efforts forced him to flee to Irbil, where he was given refuge, and later received support from UNESCO, who collaborated with him by digitizing and restoring the ancient manuscripts. According to Father Michaeel, the preservation effort embodied "a spirit of trust, confidence, and peaceful coexistence between Iraq's numerous communities" (United Nations Educational, Scientific, and Cultural Organization 2022: 16). These kinds of efforts remind us that preserving knowledge can play a useful role in DEUCE promotion, and thus building bonds between Christians and Muslims.

Efforts to revive the Spirit of Mosul not only serve as messages of hope, healing, and humanity, but they also remind us that DEUCE is alive and well even in areas that have been decimated by conflict and warfare. Engaging in DEUCE can help to ensure that the city of Mosul lives up to its name – "the bridge" – in the years ahead.

The Abrahamic Family House in Abu Dhabi

The Spirit of Mosul was reinvigorated by a 2021 visit to Iraq by His Holiness Pope Francis, who held a symbolic Mass in Irbil in front of the ruins of the Al-Tahera church and prayed for all the victims who were killed during the war. The Pope also held an interreligious gathering in Ur, believed to be the birthplace of the prophet Abraham, who is revered in Judaism, Christianity, and Islam.

His visit was staged in a stark, but poignant way. A simple, tent-like structure – with white drapes to protect participants from the sun – was set up next to Abraham's house (Bordoni 2021). Collectively, a group of interfaith leaders humbly offered the following prayer:

As children of Abraham, Jews, Christians, and Muslims, together with other believers and all persons of good will, we thank you for having given us Abraham, a distinguished son of this noble and beloved country, to be our common father in faith. We thank you . . . for the example of courage, resilience, strength of spirit, generosity, and hospitality set for us by our common father in faith . . . Open our hearts to mutual forgiveness and in this way make us instruments of reconciliation, builders of a more just and fraternal society.

This kind of unity between Jews, Christians, and Muslims is often referred to as the Abrahamic tradition. The term "Abrahamic" was introduced by Louis Massignon, the French Catholic scholar of Islam and pioneer of Christian and Muslim relations. Massignon believed that Christians and Muslims worshiped the God of Abraham, that Muhammad was a sincere spokesperson of God, that the Qur'an is divinely inspired, that Islam had a positive mission in the history of salvation; and that Arabic is a language of divine revelation (Griffith 1997: 193). All these positions broke with conventional and traditional Christian doctrine and teachings. All promote the spirit of Mosul as well as DEUCE.

Massignon's unconventional views contributed to *Nostra Aetate* (1965), the Catholic Church's landmark document concerning the history and state of Christian and Muslim relations. Thanks in part to Massignon's vision, it is regarded as the most important agreement between Christians and Muslims. It stated:

In her task of promoting unity and love among men, indeed among nations, [the Catholic Church] considers above all in this declaration what men have in common and what draws them to fellowship . . . The Catholic Church rejects nothing which is true and holy in these religions . . . [but rather looks] with sincere respect upon those ways of conduct and of life, those rules, and teachings, which, though differing in many particulars from what she holds and sets forth, nevertheless often reflect a ray of that Truth which enlightens all men.

With *Nostra Aetate*, the Catholic Church ended its old missionizing way of perceiving Muslims by speaking about Islam in terms of deep respect. In doing so, it set itself up to engage in DEUCE.

Massignon, however, never lived to see the fruits of *Nostra Aetate*, one of which is the Abrahamic Family House on Saadiyat Island in Abu Dhabi, the capital of the UAE. It is one of the region's examples of a wider acceptance of DEUCE concepts, especially in terms of the fifth concept – engagement.

The Abrahamic Family House is a multi-religious space consisting of a synagogue, a church, and a mosque. While it is not literally "one house" (as in one building), the interfaith space evokes coexistence and unity between Jews, Christians, and Muslims. None of the three places of worship are more dominant than their counterpart (For Human Fraternity n.d.). Each of the distinct places of worship sits on a podium, unified by their cube-like design, height, and scale. All three structures are colored in an off-white hue and built in a mixture of concrete, marble, and oak. The equal volumes of the three houses are meant to reflect a clear visual and metaphorical harmony among the three spaces and the three religions (Proctor 2023). As an artform, the Abrahamic Family House represents the Synthesis of Civilization in materialized form, which is the ultimate goal of DEUCE.

Yet, there are clear differences in each building's design, symbolic of the faith represented in each place of worship. Each house is designed to meet the seating needs of the congregation and the direction of prayer of each respective religious tradition. The church faces toward the east and the rising sun, the synagogue looks toward Jerusalem, and the mosque faces Mecca. Within each of these places of worship, visitors can read about distinct religious services, listen to holy scripture, and experience the sacred rituals of Judaism, Christianity, and Islam.

I had the opportunity to attend the inauguration of the Abrahamic Family House in February 2023. It was a memorable experience, particularly the final ceremony. A Jewish boy, Christian girl, and Muslim boy each brought a cube representing each house of worship to the center platform of the forum, which is shared by Jews, Christians, Muslims, and visitors to the site. There, the three young Emiratis interacted with one another in a civil, friendly, and joyful manner. They were surrounded by a large circle of people which constituted the few hundred attendees of the inauguration. Collectively, we formed a protective ring around the youth. Priests, imams, rabbis, intellectuals, politicians, judges, academics, activists, and an array of other groups from around the world watched as the Emirati youth showed us what the future could look like – humane, tolerant, and peaceful. This symbolism, replete with DEUCE concepts, was emotional for many and powerful to witness firsthand.

The Abrahamic Family House is historic for other reasons. The Ben Maimon Synagogue at the location is the country's first ever purpose-built synagogue. Its multi-layered façade represents the Sukkot, the Jewish festival where Jews harvest palm trees and build tents in their gardens as designated areas for gathering and eating with family members and guests. It is said to champion the Jewish virtues of community and tradition. It is named after Moses Ben Maimon (d. 1204) – or simply Maimonides – the Jewish jurist, philosopher, and physician of medieval Judaism.

Born into a scholarly family in Córdoba in 1135, Maimonides spent his boyhood and teenage years growing up in Spain, which was then ruled by Muslims. His education, however, stalled in 1148, the year he was captured by the Almohads, a group of Muslims who forced the Jewish population of Córdoba to either convert to Islam or flee the country. After the Almohad takeover of Córdoba in 1148, the Maimons practiced Judaism in secrecy and in the privacy of their homes. They disguised their Jewish identity as much as possible and even dressed to appear like Muslims in public.

The Maimons permanently left Córdoba in 1159 and fled to Fez, then to Palestine, and finally to Al-Fustat, a city near Cairo. In Egypt, Maimonides studied medicine and became a practicing physician. His reputation spread rapidly, and he soon became the primary physician of Sultan Salah Al-Din Yusuf Ibn Ayyub (d. 1193), better known as Saladin, the twelfth-century military leader, who I examine in the next chapter.

Next to the Ben Maimon synagogue is the Church of Saint Francis of Assisi, named after Saint Francis (d. 1226), the founder of the Franciscan orders. The Saint Francis Church, as it is commonly known, is designed to celebrate communal ceremony and togetherness. The entrance of the church is equipped with a water element manifesting as a ritual of "crossing over" (For Human Fraternity n.d.). The church's interior is designed to be "constantly in luminous flux, reminding visitors of their proximity with that which is transcendent and divine" (For Human Fraternity n.d.).

Saint Francis is best known for his journey in 1219 from Acre to Damietta, Egypt. He visited the Holy Land just before the decisive battle of the fifth Crusade, which ended in a defeat for the Crusaders, which I also examine in the next chapter. After the battle, Francis and Brother Illuminato, his traveling companion, traveled into Egyptian territory occupied by Sultan Malik Al-Kamil (d. 1238). The sultan hosted Saint

Francis and Brother Illuminato and engaged with them in a constructive dialogue on faith and God. Early retellings of the meeting describe Al-Kamil as willingly listening to Saint Francis as he tried to convert the sultan to Christianity (Sadowski 2019). For Al-Kamil, an educated man who appreciated cultural exchanges, the meeting was another opportunity to show Islamic hospitality and learn more about Christianity.

Sultan Al-Kamil must have been shocked at Saint Francis's courteous and peaceful approach in the middle of a war zone. It was radically different from Al-Kamil's violent encounters with the Crusaders. The sultan was so impressed with Saint Francis that he granted him and Brother Illuminato free and secure passage throughout his territories, a rare privilege for Christians in Muslim territories during the Crusades. His decision reflects an understanding that not all Christians were enemies of Muslims.

Saint Francis' subsequent writings reveal that the meeting had a profound impact on his views of Muslims. When he eventually returned to Italy, Saint Francis urged his fellow Christians and public officials to have bells rung during the day to call Christians to prayer, a practice he had witnessed with the Islamic call to prayer. His meeting with the Sultan serves as a "strong impetus and example for dialogue among peoples and religions today" (Damietta Cross-Cultural Center n.d.).

Rounding out the Abrahamic Family House is the Sheikh Ahmed El-Tayyeb Mosque. The El-Tayyeb Mosque promotes sequence, layering, and a rhythmic journey that begins with observing, which is followed by a spiritual ablution that culminates in prayer. The lofty, vertical faults of the mosque uplift its visitors, allowing them to feel enveloped in a space of veneration and historic belief (For Human Fraternity n.d.). It is named after Sheikh El-Tayyeb, the current head of Al-Azhar University in Cairo, and the co-author of "A Document of Human Fraternity" with Pope Francis.

The Abrahamic Family House also includes a fourth space – an educational space – which is crucial in fostering DEUCE. This fourth space, which is not affiliated with any religion, is meant to "exemplify human fraternity and solidarity . . . while [preserving] the unique character of each faith" (Gomes 2021). It serves as a center of learning, "where all people can come together as a single community devoted to mutual understanding and peace" (For Human Fraternity n.d.). A variety of daily activities and programs at the Abrahamic Family House is supplemented by regular international conferences and world summits that focus on harmonious coexistence across – and within – communities. In order for DEUCE to be enacted, such educational opportunities must be encouraged and supported by all people from all denominations.

Islamic Civilization and Spaces of Light

As noted throughout this chapter, I have visited the UAE on several occasions to engage in the Dialogue of Civilizations alongside Christian, Jews, Muslims, and people from all walks of life. The final experience I would like to share is my tour of the Sheikh Zayed Grand Mosque and Library in Abu Dhabi. My tour guide – His Excellency Yousef Al-Obaidli, the Director-General of the mosque and library – told me that the entire structure was designed to show the architectural marvels and styles of different Islamic civilizations. He added that the center's primary message is that of coexistence, openness to other cultures, and tolerance. At the end of my tour, His Excellency Al-Obaidli presented me with one of the Grand Mosque's distinctive publications, fittingly titled "Spaces of Light."

If my experiences in Abu Dhabi gave me a predilection, it is that the UAE is likely to continue growing in its role as a regional leader of the Dialogue of Civilizations and perhaps even the Synthesis of Civilizations. Moreover, the emerging tolerance of Saudi Arabia augments a future in which the birthplace of Islam is known more for its humanity than its inhumanity. The "true Islam" has been misinterpreted and selfishly manipulated by numerous countries and groups over many centuries, while the hope of an interfaith revival by humanity is represented in the "Spaces of Light."

Like Saudi Arabia and the UAE, Western countries are dealing with their unique culture and their own respective concerns about their national identities, particularly in the relationship between Christendom, the Ummah, and the EU, to which we now turn in the next chapter.

CHAPTER 2

Hybridity
Europe

When I was growing up, my dad – Christopher – told me stories about Ardeamush, our ancestral townland in Lisdoonvarna, Ireland. Ardeamush – meaning "James' height" in Irish – is located a few miles from the famous Cliffs of Moher in County Clare. Some scholars say that our surname – Considine – is the Anglicized version of the Irish surname MacConsaidín, meaning "Son of Constantine." The surname derives from Constantine the Great (d. 337), the Emperor of Rome who Christianized the Roman Empire in 323. Others claim that the first Considine – Consaidín O'Briain (d. 1194) – was the Bishop of Killaloe and a fifth-generation descendant of Brian Bóruma, or Brian Boru, the first high king of Ireland. Believe it or not, this sets the ground for the concept of hybridity, the "H" for this chapter.

Given our family's historical ties to Ireland, my dad was thrilled when I was accepted into Trinity College Dublin to start a PhD program in 2010. My dissertation explored the meaning of Irishness through the lens of young men living in Ireland. Being Irish held deep historical and religious meanings for my interviewees. One participant talked about Saint Patrick, the patron saint of Ireland, as someone who "cleansed" the country of paganism and brought the "holy culture" of Catholicism to the Irish people (Considine 2017a: 111). Another participant described himself as "fully Irish" because his family spoke Irish, played Gaelic sports, and knew Irish dancing (Considine 2017a: 167). Most importantly, my interviewees did not look like me, nor were they Catholics like me. They were actually second-generation Pakistani Irish Muslims. In Ireland, I learned that hybridity had many faces.

I described some of my participants in my earlier book – *Islam, Race, and Pluralism in the Pakistani Diaspora* – as "cross-cultural navigators" – or people that are neither culturally "Irish" nor "Pakistani," but rather

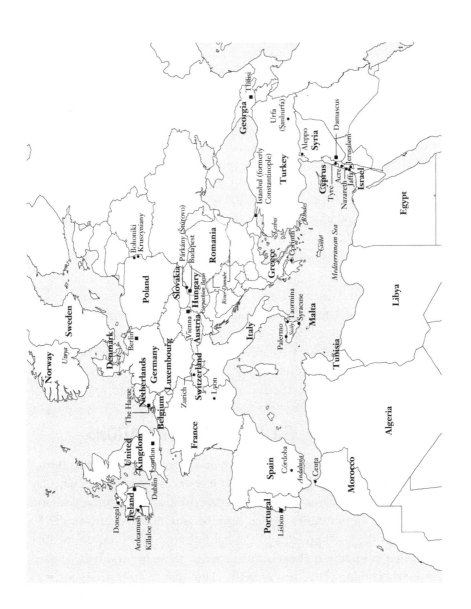

coterminous Irish and Pakistani. While they may not have been ethnically Gaelic or practicing Catholics, they were still culturally Gaelic and believers in monotheism like most Christians. As ethnically South Asian and practicing Muslims themselves, they also disrupted traditional notions of being Muslim, Pakistani, and South Asian. Their identities remind readers that cultural identities are never pure or static, but rather always dynamic and organic.

Hybridity is the term that I like to use in describing the civilizational interplay between the West and Islam on the European continent. The term has multiple metaphors – amalgamation, fusion, and creolization (Burke 2018). It has been associated with the work of Homi K. Bhabha, a British-Indian scholar, who theorized that cultures are created in a Third Space – the space "in-between" two cultures (Bhabha 1994: 37). This in-between space is marked by cross-cultural exchanges and the Synthesis of Civilizations. I also refer to this as the Grey Zone.

But the idea that European culture and Islam are compatible is interpreted by some Europeans as a threat, which inevitably contributes to Islamophobia and Islamophobic hate crimes in Europe today. In my own PhD study, I found that young Pakistani men living in Dublin were repeatedly called "Paki" – a term with racialized and Islamophobic underpinnings. One interviewee even told me that his "brown skin color" made it impossible for him to ever be connected to the perception of one's individual Irishness, which is a far cry from the intents of DEUCE.

PART ONE – THE CLASH OF CIVILIZATIONS

While the idea of synthesizing Western and Islamic values sounds promising, it has also been the subject of controversies across the present-day EU. Hybridity has not always been perceived as a welcome addition in European communities, which have been dominated historically by white Christians. Opponents of the hybridization of European identity claim that culturally homogeneous societies are stable and better suited for social cohesion. They also typically claim that homogeneous societies are safer than heterogeneous ones. There are also historical reminders that homogeneous societies are not safe from the Clash of Civilizations.

Closing the Drawbridge to Fortress Europe

From the early Muslim communities' struggle against the Byzantine Empire, to the Crusaders of Western Europe who invaded the Holy Land, to European colonization of the Ummah, to terrorism carried out in the name of Islam by Muslims in the twentieth and twenty-first centuries, there is certainly not a shortage of conflict to cover in examining relations between Europeans and Muslims worldwide.

Today, the civilizational interplay between Christians and Muslims is particularly tense on the borderlands of Europe and non-Europe. The outposts of Europe – or the defenses that "protect" Europeans from non-Europeans – have become destinations for migrants and flashpoints for the Clash of Civilizations. These "hotspots" are oftentimes symbolic of Fortress Europe, the term popularly used to describe the European response to migration from Muslim-majority countries. Fortress Europe is characterized by anti-immigrant sentiments, border fortifications, detention centers, exclusion, and rampant Islamophobia. It does not even welcome the possibility of engaging in DEUCE.

Ceuta, the former Spanish colonial enclave on the coast of northwest Africa, is a manifestation of Fortress Europe. With Spain's incorporation into the EU in 1985, the city emerged as an outpost of Europe along the border with North Africa. It has been described as "Europe's Rio Grande," the river which creates the border between the southern USA and northern Mexico, and which is known for its apprehensions and expulsions of migrants (Gramlich and Scheller 2021). In recent years, the Ceutan government has been criticized for its treatment of migrants, many of whom are Muslims (Escarcena 2022: 64). It defends the city with a network of fences that were built in the early 1990s. The fences help to restrict access to incoming migrants, but it does not always stop them.

Some desperate migrants never even make it to Ceuta. Under the cover of a night-time sky in February 2014, a group of 200 sub-Saharan Africans attempted to enter Ceuta through El-Tarajal, a city on the border of Morocco. Many of the migrants were arrested by Moroccan authorities. Those who were not arrested swam to the stretch of coast that was supported by the Ceutan fences. Once they arrived there, the migrants encountered the Civil Guard – one of the two national police forces in

Spain. The Civil Guard used rubber bullets, tear gas, and anti-riot equipment against them. Other migrants were left by the Civil Guard to drown in the Mediterranean Sea.

Ceuta is not the only outpost of Europe. Lesbos, the Greek island near the Turkish coastline, is another hotspot in the defense of Fortress Europe. It became the center of Europe's migration crisis in 2016. Initially, the local Lesbos population supported migrants with food, shelter, and solidarity, but the situation quickly turned into an unmanageable humanitarian disaster. Two European journalists described what they saw when visiting the Greek island in 2017:

> *Those wishing to visit ground zero of European ignominy must simply drive up an olive tree-covered hill on [Lesbos] until the high cement walls of Camp Moria come into view. "Welcome to prison," someone has spray-painted on the walls. The dreadful stench of urine and garbage greets visitors and the ground is covered with hundreds of plastic bags. It is raining, and filthy water has collected ankle-deep on the road. The migrants who come out of the camp are covered with thin plastic vapes and many of them are wearing only flipflops on their feet as they walk through the soup. Children are crying as men jostle their way through the crowd. Welcome to one of the most shameful sites in all of Europe (Christides and Kuntz 2017).*

Dismayed at the inhumane images and deplorable conditions coming out of Lesbos, Pope Francis arranged a visit to Mavrovouni, one of the migrant camps on the island, at the beginning of his papacy. There, he explicitly criticized Fortress Europe for closing its "drawbridge" to non-Europeans. In closing the bridge between Europe (the West) and non-Europe (the Ummah), he said that the Mediterranean Sea had become "a grim cemetery without tombstones" and "a mirror of death" (Stamouli 2021). He compared these conditions to previous generations when the Mediterranean Sea served as the cradle of human civilization, a nod to the success of hybridity.

Pope Francis's speech at Lesbos was described by a Greek journalist as "not a mere act of commemoration," but a reminder of "our duties as sincere Christians at the gates of Europe" (Tzoitis 2021). For me – a Catholic – it is a call to DEUCE, as the Pope suggested in his own words: "Problems are not resolved, and coexistence improved by building walls higher, but by joining forces to care for others according to the concrete possibilities of each and in respect for the law."

Pope Francis and his allies, nevertheless, face opposition from Europeans who believe that Muslims jeopardize the culture and security of the EU. To critics of their philosophy, DEUCE between Christians and Muslims should be discouraged, because any potential "fusion" between Western principles and Islamic values is impossible. These kinds of beliefs and dynamics, which promote exclusion and xenophobia, have deep roots in European history. Hybridity is the exception and not the norm. It is also an overt challenge to DEUCE acceptance among Europeans.

The Crusaders in the Holy Land

The question of whether the West and the Ummah are still living in the shadows of the Crusades is worth considering. Osama Bin Laden drew parallels to the Crusades by accusing Americans of being "new crusaders" engaged in a colonial war to subjugate the Ummah. The American President George W. Bush, following the 9/11 attacks, announced that the West was embarking upon a new "crusade" to rid the world of Islamic terrorism. In England, the English Defence League (EDL) – a notable political organization – uses the Cross of Saint George, the Crusaders' principal symbol, as its logo (Godwin n.d.). In like manner, in January 2019, three members of a militia group in the USA were jailed for plotting the mass murder of Muslim Americans (Jones 2019). The group's ethos was outlined in a four-page manifesto that lambasted the American government for allowing Muslims into the country. In case any doubt remained about their feelings toward Muslims, they called themselves "The Crusaders."

Most scholars start the Crusades in March 1095.[1] On this date, Pope Urban II (d. 1099) received an ambassador from the court of Alexios I Komnenos (d. 1118), the emperor of the Byzantine Empire. Emperor Komnenos asked Pope Urban II for financial and military assistance in the Byzantines' war against the Seljuk Turks, who had seized Anatolia, the easterly-most region of the Byzantine Empire. Pope Urban II accepted Alexios I's invitation in 1095 at the Council of Clermont, where he called upon English, French, and German knights to embark on a Holy War – which became the First Crusade – to wrestle the Holy Land from the Ummah.

Pope Urban's infamous speech at Clermont,[2] a town west of the city of Lyon in south-central France, described the recent atrocities conducted by Muslims on Eastern Christians.[3] He shared stories about Muslims slicing open the abdomens of Christians and tying their organs to stakes. The Pope also recalled the destruction of churches and how they were replaced by mosques. At Clermont, he identified Muslims as an "accursed and foreign race" and the "enemies of God."

Thousands of English, French, and German knights accepted Pope Urban's call to war in the Holy Land. The Crusaders marched across the European continent, swore an oath of allegiance to Emperor Komnenos in Constantinople, and carried southwards to their final destination of Jerusalem. By 1098, Baldwin II of Bourcq (d. 1131) – a Norman knight – seized Edessa, now the city of Urfa in Turkey, and turned it into the first Latin-speaking settlement in the Greek-speaking Byzantine Empire. In the following year, on 15 July, the Crusaders conquered Jerusalem after about a month-long siege.

Jerusalem in 1099 and Ceuta in 2014 have similar, yet diverse dynamics regarding the civilizational interplay between the West and Islam. In 1099 in Jerusalem, the Fatimid Empire was defeated by the Crusaders, who were driven by religious supremacy and a thirst for land and power. In 2014 in Ceuta, Muslim migrants were denied their humanity and some forbidden from crossing the outpost of Fortress Europe. The roles were flipped. In one case, the Christians are "defending" and in the other case they are "invading."

The Crusaders were viewed by Muslims in the Holy Land as the terrorists of their time. Once victorious in Jerusalem, the Crusaders systematically ransacked the city, looted it for its historical artifacts, and massacred thousands of Jews and Muslims. According to the *Gesta Francorum*,[4] the Crusaders were "killing and slaying even to the Temple of Solomon, where the slaughter was so great that our men waded in blood up to their ankles." They also turned Al-Aqsa and the Dome of the Rock into Christian places of worship on the Temple Mount. To prevent the spread of disease in Jerusalem, the mounds of dead bodies were burned in huge pyres by Muslims before they were massacred in cold blood (Cartwright 2018). By 1100, the Crusaders created the State of Jerusalem under the rule of Baldwin, who – as leader of the State of Jerusalem – received the title of "Defender of the Holy Sepulcher."

The grotesque and shocking images of war would never be entirely forgotten by the Ummah. Witnessing the invasion of the Crusaders must have been shocking to the Muslims of the Holy Land. Islamic sources typically view the First Crusade as a wave of Christian aggression, cruelty, and plunder of the more civilized Ummah, which had some of the most urbanized and culturally rich cities in the world. Even Pope Urban II recognized that the Crusaders were "inferior" to the Muslims of the Holy Land. In Clermont, he stated:

> Your land is shut in on all sides by the sea and mountains and is too thickly populated. There is not much wealth here, and the soil scarcely yields enough to support you. On this account you will kill and devour each other, and carry on war and mutually destroy each other . . . [So set] out on the road to the Holy Sepulcher, take the land from that wicked people, and make it your own.

The impression that Europe was "backward" in comparison to the Ummah contributed to the sense of Muslim trauma after their defeat in the First Crusade. Their view was that the barbaric, inferior, and regressive people from the edges of the known world conquered the culturally sophisticated, militarily superior, and divinely protected centers of the civilized world. There was, to put it lightly, a lot of soul-searching on the part of the Muslims during and after the First Crusade.

For the Crusaders, holding onto the lands seized from Muslims was not an easy task. They eventually met stiff resistance in Imad Al-Ding Zengi (d. 1146), who ruled over much of the Levant and Mesopotamia in the 1140s. He seized Edessa, the first Crusader state, in 1144. Its seizure – and the Spanish Crusaders' seizure of Lisbon, Portugal from Muslims – are seen as the first two decisive battles of the Second Crusade, with its epicenter in Syria.

Nur Al-Din, the son of Zengi and the ruler of Aleppo – a principal city in northern Syria – defended Damascus against a besiegement by Conrad of Germany (d. 1152) and Louis VII of France (d. 1180) in 1148. By 1154, Zengi had secured Damascus and, in doing so, unified the various Muslim groups of Syria. His general, Asad Al-Din Shirkuh (d. 1169), proceeded to seize Egypt in a six-year struggle from 1163 to 1169. His victory set the stage for the Third Crusade.

It was Shirkuh's nephew – Salad Al-Din Yusuf Ibn Ayyub (d. 1193), better known in the West as Saladin, who became the Muslim hero of the

Third Crusade.[5] He is best known as the counter-crusader of the Ummah who defeated the Crusaders at the Battle of Hattin on 4 July 1187. Four months later, on 2 October 1187, the Crusaders surrendered Jerusalem to him. Saladin's victory in Jerusalem was followed by a string of other victories in the Crusader cities of Acre, Caesarea, Jaffa, Nazareth, and Tiberias.

In response to his victories, Pope Gregory VIII (d. 1187) issued a pontifical decree – *Audita tremendi* – calling for the Third Crusade. Out of the total number of six crusades, the Third Crusade is regarded by historians as the most complex.[6] While it is true that it led to death and destruction, it also witnessed numerous cases of interethnic cooperation (understanding), political and military alliances (commitment), exchange of goods and science (education), and limited religious tolerance (dialogue).

For the Crusaders, the Third Crusade was led by three Christian kings – Frederick I (or "Barbarossa" – d. 1190), the Holy Roman Emperor, Philip II (d. 1223), the king of France, and Richard I ("The Lionheart" – d. 1199), the king of England. At the Battle of Acre in 1191, King Philip II and Richard I reconquered the city, but Saladin's army remained intact. The Christians and Muslims met shortly after in the Battle of Arsuf. While the Crusaders were once again victorious, their armies were dealt a severe blow. Their ultimate goal of recapturing Jerusalem now seemed unlikely. At a stalemate, the Crusaders and Muslims signed the Treaty of Jaffa on 2 September 1192, thus ending the Third Crusade. Richard returned to England in 1192. Saladin died the next year.

Scholars have described Richard the Lionheart and Saladin as "frenemies," a hybrid term that merges "friends" and "enemies." The latter was celebrated by Western Christians in later generations for his chivalry and generosity. He entered into several treaties with Richard which allowed the Crusaders to maintain a presence in a small coastal strip of land the stretched from Jaffa to Tyre. Under his rule, Christian merchants and pilgrims were allowed to freely enter Jerusalem and the native Christian populations were allowed to remain in the city. He even showed leniency in dealing with the Crusaders who had fought against the Muslims by sparing their lives following their defeat. The Christians had a presence in the Holy Land until the Crusaders lost Jerusalem for the final time during the Sixth Crusade in 1244.

European Christians once again became "conquerors" of the Holy Land in the twentieth century. When Henri Gouraud (d. 1946), the

French general during World War I, captured Damascus from the Ottoman Empire in 1920, he stood in front of the grave of Saladin and said, "Awake, Saladin – we have returned!"

With all this history in mind, it is easier to understand why the Crusades are seen by many Muslims as a medieval and contemporary threat, which undermines the Ummah, whether it be subtle through cultural transformations (the Dialogue of Civilizations) or overt through colonization, conflict, and war (the Clash of Civilizations). For me, they are an attack on the Ummah, and they are antithetical to hybridity and DEUCE concepts.

Christian–Muslim Alliances at the Battle of Vienna

The invasion dichotomy or pendulum once again swung back to the European continent in the fifteenth century, when Fortress Europe experienced its worst attack since the sack of Rome in 410. In 1453, the Ottoman Empire sacked Constantinople, the crown jewel of Christendom and the capital of the Byzantine Empire. After its sacking, the Ottomans expanded into the Balkan region of Eastern Europe. By 1683, their territory in Europe stretched as far west as modern-day Budapest (Hungary), and nearly stretched as far west as Vienna (Austria), which the Ottomans invaded on two separate occasions.

The Battle of Vienna – the second of the two Ottoman invasions – was a titanic Clash of Civilizations that forever changed the course of history between the West and the Ummah (Herbjørnsrud 2018). It pitted Mehmed IV (d. 1693), the Ottoman Emperor, against Leopold I (d. 1705), the Hapsburg monarch and the emperor of the Holy Roman Empire. To protect Vienna, Leopold I joined forces with Jan (John) Sobieski III (d. 1696), the king of Poland. Together, they put an end to the Ottomans' westward expansion into Eastern Europe.

But the details of the Battle of Vienna are much more complex than the simplistic binary of "Christian victory" and "Muslim defeat" (Herbjørnsrud 2018). The conflict has many twists, one being the critical Christian–Muslim alliance that enabled the defeat of the Ottoman Empire.

King Sobieski, the primary general working on behalf of Leopold I, did not depend solely on Christian support in defending Vienna against the Ottomans. Part of his Polish army included cavalrymen from the Lipka Tatars, a Muslim ethnic group of Polish ancestry.[7] During the Battle of Vienna, these Tatar Muslims wore straw springs in their helmets to avoid being mistaken for Crimean Tatars, who were fighting for Mehmed IV (Herbjørnsrud 2018). King Sobieski showed his affinity for his Muslim friends in a letter to his wife Marysieńka. He wrote that the Lipka Tatars were "guarding the [Muslim] prisoners and are proving to be loyal and trustworthy" (Herbjørnsrud 2018), a clear sign toward the emergence of hybridity and the prevalence of commitment, the third concept of DEUCE.

The Lipka Tatar Muslims were so committed to the defense of Vienna that they even saved King Sobieski's life after he was cut off from his army by the Danube River at the Battle of Párkány, which commenced shortly after the Battle of Vienna. According to tradition, King Sobieski appointed Lieutenant Krzeczowski, the Muslim who had saved his life, to colonel. He also granted him an estate in Kruszyniany, in present-day eastern Poland. Kruszyniany is one of the last of the villages that remain the home of Polish Tatars to this day, the other village being Bohoniki (Karlińska 2020). The village's famous wooden mosque is over 300 years old and is the oldest Lipka Tatar mosque in Poland. Unfortunately, in 2014, vandals defaced the building with xenophobic drawings. Local Christians responded by restoring the mosque, which was a positive step toward social cohesion, a key element of hybridity.

It is worth noting that the bonds between the Polish Catholics and the Lipka Tatar Muslims predated the Battle of Vienna. In 1674, after becoming the king of the Commonwealth of Poland, King Sobieski freed the Lipka Tatars from all taxation. He also allowed the building of mosques, which were forbidden during the Counter-Reformation, the period of Catholic resurgence following the Protestant Reformation (Herbjørnsrud 2018). These DEUCE-like reforms were set in motion when King Sobieski became more familiar with Turkic culture in the 1650s, when he served on a diplomatic mission in Constantinople – the capital of the Ottoman Empire. There, he educated himself on the Tatar and Turkish languages and studied military traditions and tactics by generals of the Ottoman Empire. Without engaging in education, the king would have likely never committed himself to a hybrid alliance with Muslims.

The Polish–Lipka Tatar alliance is a reminder that the Battle of Vienna was not simply driven by the Clash of Civilizations, but by the Clash *within* Civilizations. The interethnic and interreligious loyalties crossed many borders of ethnicity and religion. Mehmed IV, for example, was allied with Louis XIV (d. 1715), the Roman Catholic "Sun King" of France, who the Hapsburgs famously nicknamed "The Most Christian Turk," a phrase which points to an opposition of hybridity. Mehmed IV also allied himself with Emeric Thököly (d. 1705), a Lutheran Protestant aristocrat who fought against the Hapsburgs at the Battle of Vienna.[8] In 1682, Thököly was named king of Upper Hungary – today, mostly Slovakia. Upper Hungary later became a vassal state under the Ottomans. By paying tribute to Mehmed IV, the Protestant Hungarians received religious freedom, something that the Catholic Papal States would not grant them.

A reoccurring theme throughout this book is that Christian and Muslim relations are sometimes impacted as much by a Clash *within* Civilizations as a Clash between Civilizations. This is evident in the Battle of Vienna, which halted Islamic expansion into the European continent and secured a lasting alliance among European Christian countries. Its legacy is still remembered by Austrians and other Europeans, though not always in favor of the promotion of DEUCE.

The Gates of Vienna and the Great Replacement Theory

Advocates of hybridity in Europe face stiff opposition from Europeans who promote a Clash of Civilizations worldview. They cast a competition between "us" – the white European Christians – against the "them" – the brown Muslims of the world.

The Hapsburg victory at the Battle of Vienna is the motivation of "Gates of Vienna," a well-known website within the anti-Islam movement in the West (Bridge Initiative 2020). The ethos of the website is captured by the banner on its homepage, which states, "At the siege of Vienna in 1683, Islam seemed poised to overrun Christian Europe. We are in a new phase of a very old war." The articles on the website focus on the present-day "Muslim invasion"[9] of Europe.

The Gates of Vienna website became the subject of controversy in 2011, the year that Anders Behring Breivik – a Christian Norwegian – killed

77 Norwegians at a Labor Party youth summer camp on Utøya island.[10] It was the worst terrorist attack in Norway's history. He defended his act of terrorism by claiming that Norwegians were under attack from within by Muslims and their elitist, left-wing, and Marxist sponsors. Breivik's worldview was outlined in a 1,500-page manifesto titled "2083 – A European Declaration of Independence." He chose the year 2083 to foreshadow what Europe might look like at the 400-year anniversary of the Battle of Vienna. His vision of Europe in 2083 included the continent being fully Islamized and morphing into "Eurabia," a metaphor for the Arab-Islamic demographic takeover of the European continent.

In 2083, Breivik cited the Gates of Vienna website over 86 times (Bridge Initiative 2020). In one article published in July 2011, he left a comment that read – "Only the forced deportation of the Muslims will suffice." A total of 700 pages of his manifesto are considered to be "Islamophobic" (Richards 2014: 43). He also stoked fears in the manifesto by promoting the Great Replacement Theory, which posits that the white majority in Europe is being "replaced" by non-whites (Wilson and Flanagan 2022). Advocates of this message claim that European civilization is being destroyed by global capitalists – or to some proponents of the theory, by the Jewish people and Israel – who are implementing policies that push Muslim migrants out of Africa and the Middle East and to the EU.

The Great Replacement Theory has been the subject of public opinion polls in France. One poll found that almost two-thirds of French citizens believe that white European Christians are being "threatened with extinction" by Muslim migration (Arab News 2021). The same poll revealed that the fear of "Eurabia" was prevalent across the French political spectrum, but most pronounced among supporters of Marine Le Pen, the leader of the National Rally party. Ninety percent of the National Rally supporters, according to the poll, believed that the "replacement" of whites by non-whites is a likely scenario. The poll also revealed that 52 percent of supporters of Emmanuel Macron, the leader of the En March party and the president of France as of 2024, believed in the Great Replacement Theory.

One of the EU's loudest advocates of the Great Replacement Theory is Viktor Orbán, the current prime minister of Hungary. In a 2022 speech in Romania, Orbán argued that countries where Europeans and non-European people mix are "no longer nations – they are nothing more than a conglomeration of peoples" (Gijs and Fota 2022), a quote which shows his opposition to hybridity. He also suggested that the Carpathian Basin – a region shared by Hungary and Romania – should be populated by a "pure race." "We are willing to mix with another," he said, "but we do not want to become mixed race." Such ethnocentric comments are clearly a barrier to hybridity in Hungary and other parts of Europe. Ethnocentrism limits DEUCE and opposes the idea that Christians and Muslims can live in cooperation and harmony with one another.

PART TWO – THE DIALOGUE OF CIVILIZATIONS

The idea that Europe's success lies in ethnic or racial homogeneity leaves little, if any, room for DEUCE or the integration of Muslims into European societies. Thankfully, there are other contemporary models being initiated across multiple European countries to engage in the Dialogue of Civilizations and build a peaceful relationship between Christians and Muslims.

The New Europe and the Schengen Zone

If any event raised the question of what it means to be European, it was World War II. By 1945 – the last year of the war – Europe was in a devastated state. Millions of Europeans were dead, countless numbers either injured or displaced, and six million Jews were murdered in the Holocaust. In the immediate post-World War II environment, European leaders started reimagining Europe as a continent where DEUCE, with its ability to create cross-cultural engagements, mutual dependency, and peace – could flourish.

One leader of the time – Sir Winston Churchill (d. 1965), the former prime minister of the UK – captured the New Europe in a 1946 speech in Zurich, Switzerland. He said that the whole of Europe needed a remedy which, as if by a miracle, would transform the continent and "make all Europe as free and happy as Switzerland today" (Council of Europe n.d.). Churchill added, "We must build a kind of United States of Europe."

The New Europe – anchored in core democratic values including civil liberties, human dignity, and a transnational European culture – manifested on 7 May 1948 at the Hague Congress, where delegates across Europe created a new European political assembly. They called it the Council of Europe. On 5 May 1949, at St. James' Palace in London, ten European countries – Belgium, Denmark, France, Ireland, Italy, Luxembourg, the Netherlands, Norway, Sweden, and the UK – signed the initial Council of Europe treaty. Between 1949 and 1970, eight other countries – Austria, Cyprus, Greece, Iceland, Malta, Switzerland, Turkey, and West Germany – joined the council.

A second institution arose out of the New Europe – the Schengen Zone. In Schengen, Luxembourg in 1985, the countries of Belgium, France, Germany, Luxembourg, and the Netherlands agreed to gradually allow the free movement of their own citizens across the national borders of the signees without needing a passport or visa checks. In 1990, these countries signed the Schengen Agreement, the treaty which led to the creation of the Schengen Zone, in which internal border checks were largely abolished. Quickly, the zone expanded to include Italy, Portugal, Spain, and Greece in 1990, 1991, 1991, and 1992, respectively.[11] Today, it remains one of the largest areas of open borders between member countries in the world (Schengen Visa Info n.d.).

Turkey – an Islamic nation, and the focus of the next chapter – is noticeably missing from the EU and the Schengen Zone, a fact that points to European opposition to mixing with Turkish Muslims.

There are several reasons why Turkey is not part of the "New Europe." For starters, the leader of the ruling Justice and Development Party (AKP) – Recep Tayyip Erdoğan – has authoritarian tendencies. He has cracked down on freedom of the press and human rights, both of which are core EU principles. A second reason is international relations. The EU and Turkey are locked into a longstanding dispute over Cyprus. Turkey has occupied the northern part of the island since 1974, which it invaded that year. It also refuses to recognize the Republic of Cyprus, a member state of the EU. A third reason is religious freedom. Turkey is constitutionally a secular state, but it is increasingly Islamist. While churches dot its landscape, Turkey does not officially recognize Christian groups like the Armenians or Catholics. A fourth reason is the sheer size of Turkey. If allowed entry to the EU, Turkey would be the bloc's largest population and territory by far. Europeans fear that admitting the Turkish population would upset the balance of power on the continent. For these reasons, the EU suspended Turkish accession talks in 2019.

For the foreseeable future, it seems logical to expect that Turkey will continue being a boiling cauldron of change. If it proceeds with its attempt to join the EU or even actually joins the EU at some point, that will have a great bearing on building bonds between Christians and Muslims and the acceptance of DEUCE on the European continent.

Turkey, however, is not absent from another part of the New Europe – the North Atlantic Treaty Organization (NATO), the post-World War II military alliance between Western countries, which effectively became the European army. On 4 April 1949, ten European countries – Belgium, Denmark, France, Iceland, Italy, Luxembourg, the Netherlands, Norway, Portugal, and the UK – joined Canada and the USA as its initial members. Three years later, in 1952, Turkey joined NATO and sided with Western powers in the Cold War. Since then, Turkey has emerged as a controversial member of NATO for its role in working with the enemies of NATO, a topic that I turn to in the next chapter.

The identity conflicts and migration crises faced by Europeans today raise questions on whether the promises of the New Europe, which is anchored by DEUCE values, will come to fruition in the twenty-first century. The European civic identity that emerged out of the rubble of World War II has proven to be fragile, particularly on the borderlands between Europe and non-Europe. It is slowly being replaced by European identities rooted in narrow cultures, ethnicities, and historical ties to the "homeland." If Europeans increasingly see themselves in these terms, then more cross-cultural communication between Christians and Muslims will be needed in the years ahead, which represents a significant challenge to DEUCE in Europe.

Coexistence and Conflict at the Cathedral-Mosque in Córdoba

I knew hardly anything about Islam or Islamic history when I enrolled in Dr. Akbar Ahmed's "World of Islam" class as a sophomore at American University in 2004. To say I was surprised to learn about the history of Islamic Spain would be an understatement. I was even more surprised to learn that Islamic Spain created an unprecedented society that enabled a rich cultural synthesis between the Arabs, Berbers, Christians, and Jews (Ahmed 2003: 50).

The city of Córdoba was the crown jewel of Islamic Spain. In 756, Abd Al-Rahman I (d. 788) – the Umayyad ruler – declared it an independent emirate, and himself the *emir* of Al-Andalus. Al-Rahman's grandson – Abd Al-Rahman II (d. 852) – transformed it into a majestic city of international renown for its art and humanity (Mezquita-Catedral De Córdoba n.d.b.). The next two rulers of the city – Abd Al-Rahman III (d. 961) and Al-Hakam II (d. 976) – brought it to the pinnacle of its influence. Al-Rahman III reconciled the various conflicts between Arabs, Berbers, Christians, and Jews on the Iberian Peninsula. He granted Jews and Christians the right to practice their religion without harassment or persecution from the government. Al-Hakam II, on the other hand, created the Library of Córdoba, which housed more than 400,000 volumes – more than all the other libraries of Europe put together. He also formed a joint committee of Arab Muslims and Iberian Mozarab Christians to translate Latin and Greek books into Arabic. This emphasis on education and understanding is a positive step for the betterment of Christian and Muslim relations.

La Convivencia, meaning "the coexistence," or – more literally – "living together," is the name given to this time in Spanish history.[12] La Convivencia has been used as a convenient shorthand for the religious pluralism that characterized the Iberian Peninsula – and by extension the Mediterranean region as a whole – from the early eighth century to the fifteenth century (Wolf 2017). It is a reminder of the times in European history when the West and the Ummah were walking side-by-side, as Charles III, the future king of the UK said in a 1993 speech at Oxford University:

Not only did Muslim Spain gather and preserve the intellectual content of ancient Greek and Roman civilizations, it also interpreted and expanded upon that civilization and made a vital contribution of its own in so many fields of human endeavor – in science, astronomy, mathematics, algebra (itself an Arabic word), law, history, medicine, pharmacology, optics, agriculture, architecture, theology, [and] music. Averroes [d. 1198] and Avenzoor [d. 1162], like their counterparts Avicenna [d. 1037] and Rhazes [d. 935] in the East, contributed to the study and practice of medicine in ways from which Europe benefited for centuries afterwards (Prince of Wales 1993).

The Andalusian scholars mentioned by King Charles III are known for synthesizing Aristotelian philosophy and Islamic philosophy. They also successfully persuaded the Andalusian rulers to develop a government based on the *Republic* by Plato. Medieval Europe was a pupil – and in a sense a dependent – of Andalusia and the wider Ummah. Together, the West and the Ummah moved human civilization forward in pursuing knowledge and working together to preserve the world's heritage (Carnevale 2020).

The twenty-first century presents much different circumstances. Spain represents a battleground in the civilizational interplay between the West and the Ummah. This is no more evidence than at the "Cathedral-Mosque of Córdoba."

When the Muslims conquered Spain in 711, the main church of Córdoba – the Basilica of Saint Vincent of Lérins[13] – was shared by Christians and Muslims and divided into Christian and Islamic halves. The arrangement of sharing the structure ended in 756, when Abd Al-Rahman I – the *emir* of Córdoba – crowned the city by building the new Grand Mosque of Córdoba on the site of the Visigothic church.[14] Although he ended Christian worship on the site, Abd Al-Rahman maintained the Christian architectural influence by including Greek, Roman, and Visigothic towering arches and art in its interior and exterior design (Mezquita-Catedral De Córdoba n.d.a.). By 1236, when Córdoba returned to Christian rule, the building was reconverted into a church. At the time, it was the second biggest surface area mosque in the world, after the Holy Mosque of Mecca.

During the Renaissance, between the years 1523 and 1599, the Cathedral-Mosque had significant reconstruction which resulted in its present structure (United Nations Educational, Scientific, and Cultural Organization n.d.a.). In the sixteenth century, the Bishop of Córdoba proposed demolishing the mosque and building a new cathedral, but he faced opposition. Emperor Charles V (d. 1558), a powerful sixteenth-century ruler of the Hapsburg dynasty, decided to insert a new gothic cathedral right in the middle of the mosque. This period of "de-Islamicization" on the site was reversed in 1816, the year that Patricio Furriel restored the *mihrab*, or prayer niche, hidden until that year under the altarpiece of the old San Pedro chapel. The Cathedral-Mosque's *mihrab* also is located in a small octagonal recess roofed with a single block of white marble. The walls of the octagon are lined with Byzantine-style mosaics laced with gold. Later in the nineteenth century, Velázquez Bosco (d. 1923) also restored the Islamic legacy of the building.

Today, the Cathedral-Mosque is distinguished by its neo-Moorish revival architecture, a blend of European and Moorish styles that marks Spanish identity. It serves as an architectural hybrid that synthesizes the artistry of the West and the Ummah and is a testimony to cultural synthesis (United Nations Educational, Scientific, and Cultural Organization n.d.a.; Giese and Acosta 2021: 536). In 1984, UNESCO declared it a "World Heritage Site" and described it as a "masterpiece of human creative genius," as well as a "manifestation of a considerable exchange of human values" (Mezquita-Catedral De Córdoba n.d.b.). Its current status would have never been possible if previous generations of Christians and Muslims did not engage in the principles of DEUCE.

But DEUCE, unfortunately, is often limited by political leaders. In 1998, the Roman Catholic leaders of the Cathedral-Mosque worked to turn the status of the site into a "Cathedral," as it was previously known as the "Cathedral-Mosque." Several years later, a group of Spanish Muslims appealed to the Church to permit them to conduct their Islamic prayers in the cathedral (Cimmino 2017). The Church rejected their petition in 2006. In response to the rejection, Mansur Escudero – the former president of the Córdoba-based Islamic Council – protested the decision by performing prayers outside of the Cathedral-Mosque (Cimmino 2017). In the same year, the Diocese of Córdoba tried to register ownership over the site, but the city council of Córdoba denied them. Valeriano Lavela, the secretary general of the Córdoba council, argued that the landmark does not belong to the Church, but rather "each and every citizen of the world from whatever civilization and regardless of people, nation, culture, or race" (see Burgen 2016). The city council added that the Mosque-Cathedral is not a public domain asset that can be owned by any power, public administration, or religious group.

Matters were complicated further in 2014, when Muslim activists formed a grassroots association – La Plataforma Mezquita-Catedral, or the Platform for the Mosque-Cathedral of Córdoba – to campaign for changes to the name of the site (Burgen 2016; Hedgecoe 2015). La Plataforma Mezquita-Catedral claimed that the Catholic Church had taken the Cathedral-Mosque out of public hands by "taking advantage of a loophole in property legislation and registering itself as the sole owner of the building" (Hedgecoe 2015). A Plataforma online petition, designed to wrestle the site from the Catholic Church's control in order to put it into the hands of public management, gathered more than 350,000 signatures (Kassam 2014). Left-wing politicians, like Rafael Rodríguez, the former Andalusian minister for tourism and member of the United Left party, said the diocese had a "fundamentalist" attitude and appeared to be "prioritizing religious beliefs over common sense and the natural history of the monument." Rodríguez added, "[Erasing the term 'mosque'] does not seem either reasonable or acceptable to me" (Kassam 2014). For me, it represents a rejection of the Dialogue of Civilizations, and thus of hybridity itself.

It is important to consider the term "erasure" in understanding the political dynamics in play around the site. Some Spaniards claimed that the practice of collective indifference renders certain groups invisible.

In the fall of 2014, a number of Spaniards reported that the term "Mosque of Córdoba" had disappeared from searches on Google Maps. Activists claimed that if a tourist in Córdoba had Googled directions to the mosque in mid-November 2014, that tourist would have only found a reference to the "Cathedral of Córdoba," denoting the space solely as a Catholic house of worship (Calderwood 2015). Its disappearance sparked a national and international controversy. Fifty-two member states of the Islamic Educational, Scientific, and Cultural Organization (ISESCO) described the name change from a "mosque" to a "cathedral" as "an attempt to obliterate the landmarks of Islamic history in Andalusia," adding that it was "a provocation for Muslims around the world, especially for the Muslims of Spain" (see Hedgecoe 2015). An online petition of Muslims and their allies opposing the removal of the term "mosque" claimed that the Bishop of Córdoba was guilty of "symbolic appropriation," which is not compatible with values emanating from DEUCE or the promotion of hybridity.

Right-wing political groups in Spain, on the other hand, claimed that the future of the site will be ceded to Muslims for their exclusive religious use. Enrique Rubio of Vox, a national conservative party, claimed that the plan to "re-convert" the site into a mosque was orchestrated by Islamic states like Iran and Saudi Arabia (Hedgecoe 2015). The canon of the Cathedral of Córdoba, José Juan Jiménez, counterargued the political left by describing it as "hostile to everything the Church represents" (Hedgecoe 2015).

The Cathedral's position was dealt a blow in 2016, when the city council of Córdoba declared that "religious consecration is not the way to acquire property" (see Burgen 2016). Seven years later, in March 2023, the Spanish government formally recognized the Cathedral of Our Lady of the Assumption as the property of the Roman Catholic Church (Arab News 2023). Demetrio Fernandez, the Bishop of Córdoba, applauded the recognition because it did justice to the fact that the Great Mosque of Córdoba was built on the seventh-century Visigothic Church. He claimed that it pushed back against the idea that the city's history was more Muslim than Christian. Opponents of the Spanish government's ruling claimed that it "diluted" Islamic history at the site. The Plataforma Mezquita called it "an offensive against the indisputable and evidential Islamic influence of the entire monumental ensemble" (Arab News 2023).

While the Córdoba controversy is far from resolved, at least there is ongoing dialogue, which is a positive circumstance representing a minimal understanding of the importance of DEUCE. There also seems to be relative acceptance of the term Cathedral-Mosque in Spanish society (Hedgecoe 2015). The hyphen conjoins the West and Islam and represents the historical and religious links between Christians and Muslims. It stands for a hypothetical Third Space of cultural synthesis. De-hyphenating the name and space means that the building no longer represented common values and shared history between the West and Islam. It could stand as an example of Fortress Europe in that it excludes Islam or Muslims, or it could stand for the New Europe, a vision supported by inclusion and tolerance.

PART THREE – THE SYNTHESIS OF CIVILIZATIONS

Out of all the examples of the Synthesis of Civilizations shared in this book, the European context has the richest examples in terms of artistic and cultural fusions between the West, Christians, Islam, Muslims, and other groups. Interestingly, the hybridity was acquired after Christians and Muslims engaged in the Clash of Civilizations, especially in Sicily, an Italian island off the coast of Italy. Today, a hybrid culture is forming in buildings like the House of One in Berlin, Germany and the Peace Cathedral in Tbilisi, Georgia.

Sicilian Synthesis in Medieval Times

Sicily, an Italian island, is joined with Tunisia and other Muslim-majority countries in North Africa by the Strait of Sicily. Historically, it has been a key island in the civilizational interplay between the West and the Ummah. The island was first settled in 750 BC by the Phoenicians, who created the island's first colony at Motya. Subsequent generations witnessed the arrival of Greek groups like the Corinthians in 733 BC and the Rhodians and the Cretans in 689 BC. These Greek forces united against the Carthaginians and fought them for control of the island over a long period of time (580–376 BC). From 264 to 241 BC, the Carthaginians and the Romans fought the First Punic War. In 254 BC, the Romans captured Palermo, one of Sicily's most important cities. Fifty-three years later, in 201 BC, Syracuse – another major Sicilian city – joined the Republic of Rome, which named Sicily its new province.

The culture and demographic makeup of Sicily was drastically altered in the mid-seventh century when the Aghlabid Muslims, the dynasty that ruled over a significant portion of modern North Africa, started raiding Byzantine lands. The Aghlabids' territory – which made up the present-day countries of Eastern Algeria, Tunisia, and Western Libya – was called Ifriqiya, a medieval state created by the Umayyads in 703 after their victory over the Byzantines.[15] In 827, the Aghlabids were invited to Sicily by Euphemius, a Byzantine general trying to overthrow Michael II (d. 829), the Emperor of Byzantium.[16] Upon their arrival, the Aghlabids quickly deposed Euphemius and started a series of raids against Byzantine castles on the island. They seized Syracuse in 878 and then Enna, a fortress in the middle of the island, in 878. The raids would last until 902, the year that Taormina – the main Byzantine city on the island – fell to the Aghlabids. It took seventy-five years for the Aghlabid Muslims to conquer Byzantine Sicily. It is seen as a major victory for the Ummah in their civilizational struggle against the West and Christendom at large.

Palermo – the capital of present-day Sicily – emerged as the Aghlabid capital on the island. In 846, Sicilian Muslims used it as a base to invade and eventually sack Rome. In the ninth and tenth centuries, the island's Muslim population grew, and an Islamic-Arab culture formed in the city. Many Sicilians between the ninth and thirteenth centuries understood Siculo-Arabic or Sicilian Arabic, particularly in Val di Mazara in western Sicily, and Val di Noto in southern Sicily (Metcalfe 2002: 290). It emerged through the mixing of Arabs, Berbers, Normans, Lombards, and others. Linguistically, Siculo-Arabic fused Romance and Arabic elements. Scholars use the term to refer to the archaeological, architectural, historical, linguistic, and philosophic material of the period of Islamic rule (827–1091) and the Norman rule (1091–1282) of Sicily (Agius 2007: 25–6).

Sicilian Muslims saw their power wane under the reign of Ibn Al-Thumna (d. 1062), the *emir* of Sicily. In 1061, he hired two Norman brothers – Robert Guiscard (d. 1085) and Roger of Hauteville (d. 1101) – to assist him in a civil war.[17] Within two years, the Muslim Arabs of Sicily and the Norman Christian newcomers were no longer allies. In 1060, the Sicilian *emir* of Syracuse – Ibn Al-Timnah – asked the Normans for help against his rival Ibn Al-Hawas, the leader of the Kalbid ruling class of the city of Palermo. At the Battle of Cerami in 1063, De Hauteville defeated Al-Hawas. The Battle of Cerami started the gradual "Normanization" of Sicily.

In 1071, under the command of Guiscard, the Normans won a decisive victory at the Battle of Palermo. They converted the city's principal mosque into a new cathedral and built a new church – the San Giovanni dei Lebbrosi – on the remains of the Islamic castle of *Yahya*, the Arabic term for John (Metcalfe 2002: 294). In addition to destroying mosques, the Normans imposed a tax on Muslims that was slightly higher than that of Christians. The tax is similar to the *jizya*, a tax which previous Sicilian Muslim leaders imposed on Christians as *dhimmi*, or "protected people."

By 1091, the Norman Christians had seized all of Sicily and parts of southern Italy from the Muslim Arabs. While their dominance might point to a Clash of Civilizations, it is worth remembering that the Normans committed themselves to freedom of religion by allowing the remaining Muslims of Palermo to maintain the Sharia – or "Islamic law" – which was preserved and safeguarded so that Muslims could settle their own civil disputes according to Islamic teachings (Metcalfe 2002: 295–6). Around this period, Muslims also played important roles in the cultural life of Sicily, particularly in the western part of the island, where they served as craftsmen, farmers, and merchants.

After their takeover of Sicily, the Norman kings governed in a manner fitting of the Synthesis of Civilizations. Under the reigns of Roger II (d. 1154), William I (d. 1166), and William II (d. 1189), the island flourished as a multi-ethnic, multinational, and multi-religious society. It was unlike any other civilization to date. Roger II's rule, in particular, is why some scholars avoid attaching terms like "the Normans" or "Norman kingdom" to this period of Sicilian history. Applying these terms runs the risk of "transmitting a rash of preconceived ideas about the character, dynamics, and development of authority on the island" (Metcalfe 2002: 299).

Roger II developed a nation that was not particularly "Norman" in character. His administration consisted of both Christians and Muslims advisors and key government officials. After his coronation, he issued a *tari* – the gold quarter dinar first issued in Islamic Sicily – bearing a cross with a Greek inscription on one side and his name in Arabic on the other side.[18] The side with Roger in Arabic also had the date and mint of the *hijra*.[19] On the mantle of his coronation, he included an Arabic inscription marking the year – 1133–4 – of its manufacture. The mantle was designed in an Islamic style with paintings that paired Christian and Islamic scenes. Historians believe that it was created by Arab Muslim craftsmen in Palermo.

The cultural and religious proximity between Christians and Muslims in Sicily was described by Ibn Jubayr (d. 1217), an Arab Muslim geographer and poet. During its period of Norman Christian rule, he walked past Saint Mary of the Admiral, a Greek Byzantine church in Palermo. He described the hybridity that he saw in the city:

> *[T]he Christian women's dress in [Palermo] is the dress of Muslims; they are eloquent speakers of Arabic and cover themselves with veils. They go out at this aforesaid festival [Christmas] clothed in golden silk, covering in shining wraps, colorful veils and with light gilded sandals. They appear at their churches bearing all the finery of Muslim women in their attire, henna, and perfume (translated by Broadhurst 1952: 307).*

This depiction – along with the emerging Siculo-Arabic language – points to a cultural synthesis between Christians and Muslims. Evidence also is found among the Christians of Corleone in 1178, over one third of whom had names with non-Arabic or mixed elements (Metcalfe 2002: 312). Among these names are al-Rahib ("the Monk"), al-Qissis ("the Priest"), Abu l-Salib ("of the Cross"), and al-Nastasi ("The Resurrection" in Greek) (Metcalfe 2002: 313). These names show that Sicilians made a conscious and considered decision to promote DEUCE concepts in their communities.

Sicily's hybridity is still evident on the island today. Patrizia Spallino, an Arabic language professor at the Officini di Studi Medievali in Palermo, noted that the Tunisian Arabic that used to be spoken on the island over 1,000 years ago is still spoken in everyday words and places. The port neighborhood of Marsala in Palermo, for example, derives its name from the Arabic word *marsa Allah*, meaning "port of God."

There is more evidence of cultural synthesis in Sicily. It is also evident in Norman architecture. Several buildings dating from 1130 to 1194 in Palermo evoke a synthesis of Byzantine, Islamic, and Romanesque styles (Fein n.d.). The central Fountain Hall of the La Zisa Towers, which were built in 1164 and 1175, are decorated with Arabic inscriptions that describe the space as "paradise on earth made manifest" (Fein n.d.). Islamic-style star-shaped panels surmount the nave of the Capella Palatina, which was built between 1131 and 1240. The Capella Palatina also includes Islamic paintings on its wood ceilings, which have been preserved unchanged (Youth Committee of the Italian National Commission for UNESCO n.d.). The Church of San Giovanni degli Eremiti, a site dating to the tenth century, has been described as a unique adaptation of Arab construction to a Christian custom (Youth Committee of the Italian National Commission for UNESCO n.d.).

The hybridity evident in Sicilian history – and in its historical buildings today – provide Christians and Muslims with evidence of cross-cultural collaboration, which oftentimes leads to the Synthesis of Civilizations and new kinds of cultures. The Synthesis of Civilizations in medieval Sicily shows that Christian-Muslim conflict is not "inevitable," and that DEUCE enriches societies.

Berlin's House of One and Tbilisi's Peace Cathedral

The acceptance of DEUCE is unfolding today with the planning of two buildings, one in Germany and the other in Georgia.

The House of One in Berlin, Germany is similar to – but slightly different from – the Abrahamic Family House in Abu Dhabi, which you read about in the last chapter. While the Abrahamic Family House consists of a synagogue, church, and mosque side-by-side, but separated, the House of One will have three Houses of Prayer – a synagogue, church, and mosque – under the roof of a single building. Put another way, the House of One represents hybridity taken to a higher degree. It is a further blending, where the divisions between communities are minimized even further, but communities are able to maintain their religious distinctiveness.

The House of One emerged after years of dialogue between Rabbi Andreas Nachama, Father Gregor Hohberg, and Imam Kadir Sanci. They are motivated by the idea that Jews, Christians, and Muslims are capable of coexisting and thriving in Berlin and beyond. Their project is backed by the German government, which granted the House of One €47 million. Another €10 million were provided by the Berlin state government, and an additional €9 million have come from individual donations (Connolly 2021).

Like the Abrahamic Family House's common educational space, the House of One has a central shared space – the House of Learning – which all visitors will pass through to access the synagogue, church, and mosque. As a passageway, the House of Learning naturally promotes engagement between Jews, Christians, Muslims – and also visitors or tourists, who may be of non-Abrahamic faiths or no faith at all. One local Jewish leader said that he welcomed the House of One because it encourages dialogue, education, and understanding, and that it offers a space where religious people can talk "with each other" instead of "about each other" (Connolly 2021).

Commitment – the fourth stage of DEUCE – also manifests in the founding treatise of the House of One (House of One 2011). The project is rooted in a constitution that identifies four key commitments – a culture of non-violence, a culture of solidarity, a culture of respect, and a culture of equal rights. These four commitments run counter to the Old Europe before World War II.

The House of One has also worked closely with the Peace Cathedral in Tbilisi, the capital of the Republic of Georgia, a borderland country between the West and the Ummah.[20] The Peace Cathedral includes a synagogue for Jews, a church for Christians, a mosque for Muslims, and a "fellowship hall." This space allows Jews, Christians, and Muslims to engage in dialogue, education, and understanding with each other. It also has adult and children's libraries and an interfaith dialogue center (Brumley 2022).

The detractors of the Peace Cathedral – as well as the House of One and the Abrahamic Family House – claim that these kinds of hybrid religious spaces only water down or merge Judaism, Christianity, and Islam into "Abrahamism," the "new religion" that I addressed in chapter 1. To be clear, religious syncretism is not the aim or goal of the Peace Cathedral. The project's director – Bishop Malkhaz Songulashvili – said that it respects the liturgical integrity of each community, each in their own space, and has little interest in religious syncretism (Brumley 2022).

Turning back to the House of One, it is located at Leipziger Strasse on the foundations of a thirteenth-century church – the Petrikirche. This historic church was badly damaged during World War II and destroyed during the Cold War.[21] With the creation of the House of One, the area will experience a restoration of its symbolic importance as a locus of interplay between religion and civic life, while taking into account the fluid circumstances of our time (House of One 2011).

Given the historical European events associated with World War II, the evolution of the House of One and the Tbilisi Peace Cathedral represent a currently extant initiative to educate people that DEUCE represents significant positives steps in European societies at large.

European Identity in the Twenty-First Century

In summary, the history between the West and Islam on the European continent is a long and complicated one. On one hand, it is a history of ethnocentrism, invasions, population transfers, religious supremacy, and war. On the other hand, it is a relationship marked by cross-cultural exchanges, community building, cultural fusion, collaboration, interfaith understanding, and – in the best of times – peace.

Wherever one stands on the political spectrum, it is hard to dismiss the evidence of hybridity as an essential part of European identity. In the years ahead, it will be interesting to observe whether European identity will be rooted in a "Christian cosmopolitanism" based on integration, universality, and synthesis, or a European identity rooted in a "Christian crudeness" based on exclusion, ethnocentrism, and religious supremacy? Bridge-builders and DEUCE devotees gravitate toward the former as it aligns more with our common humanity. Unfortunately, the latter is on display in present-day Turkey, which I turn to next.

CHAPTER 3

Heterogeneity
Turkey and Its Neighbors

The last chapter started with a historical backdrop of the origins of my surname, Considine. As I noted, it is believed by some scholars to be the Irish language spelling of Constantine, the former Roman emperor and founder of the Byzantine Empire. In 330, Emperor Constantine moved the capital of the Roman Empire – Rome – 850 miles to the east, to the ancient Greek colony of Byzantium. "New Rome," which was later renamed Constantinople ("the City of Constantine") by Constantine's successors, served as the Byzantine capital for over 1,000 years. When I visited Constantinople – now named Istanbul – in 2011, I was struck by the deep Christian roots of the city.

While one does not typically associate Christianity with Turkey, few countries in the world have such a unique and varied Christian history. Most of the New Testament is believed to have been written on present-day Turkish soil by Christians. Paul the Apostle (d. 64), who was born in Tarsus, is believed to have walked from Assos to Troy to share the message of Christianity with the gentiles. The Turkish city of Antioch, once an important province in the Roman Empire, was one of the ancient cradles of Christianity.

Turkey has always been a crossroads of the civilizational interplay between human civilizations. The Byzantines, Greeks, Hittites, Ottomans, and Persians – along with lesser-known civilizations – all invaded, conquered, flourished, and left the ruins of their mighty empires on present-day Turkish soil. Istanbul – like Turkey's history – is a borderland between the West and the Ummah and represents heterogeneity in terms of its cultural diversity and cross-cultural landmarks. I approach heterogeneity as the important recognition that diversity – be it cultural, ethnic, or religious – is a healthy addition to a given society. Heterogeneity differs from hybridity – the theme of the last chapter – in

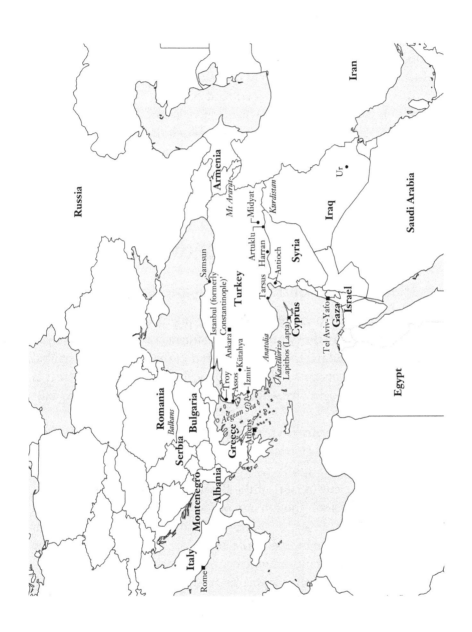

that recognizing diversity is a first step towards embracing hybridity. In many ways, Turkey – with its multiple ethnic and religious groups in an area where, geographically, East meets West – is dichotomous, swinging back and forth, oscillating like a pendulum between conflict and harmony.

Today, Turkey is home to mainly Turkish Muslims, but also Armenians, Assyrians, Caucasians, Greeks, Jews, and Kurds. Its diversity, however, does not mean that Christians are included, or even welcomed, in Turkish society. While diversity can exist in-and-of itself, inclusion is a different concept. It requires an energetic engagement with diversity. At this point in time, DEUCE in Turkey is hardly the norm with such a complex cultural and historical dynamic, nor is DEUCE viewed as necessarily important in the social and political realms of Turkish society.

PART ONE – THE CLASH OF CIVILIZATIONS

Triumph and Transformation at the Hagia Sophia

No Turkish city captures the civilizational interplay between the West and Islam better than the city of Istanbul. Situated on the Bosporus Strait – the waterway marking the border between Europe and Asia – Istanbul is a city of stark contrasts. When I visited, I noticed quickly that it is an ancient, yet modern city where multiple civilizations appear to exist side-by-side.

No symbol represents Istanbul's complex identity more than *Hagia Sophia*, the Greek term which translates to "Holy Wisdom."[1] Built as a Christian basilica nearly 1,500 years ago, it was first dedicated by Emperor Constantius (d. 361) of the Byzantine Empire in the year 360. Constantine II (d. 340), the son of Constantine the Great, referred to it as the *Megale Ekklesia*, or the "Great Church." As the primary church in Constantinople, the capital of the empire, it served as the site where twelve centuries of Byzantine emperors were crowned.

The structure of Hagia Sophia as it stands today was completed by Justinian I (d. 565), the Byzantine emperor, who built it to honor Constantine the Great, the founder of Constantinople. To build the Great Church, Justinian used the best possible architectural material from the various provinces around the Byzantine Empire. The marble used for the building's ceiling and floor were produced in Anatolia and Syria, while the bricks for the walls came from as far away as North Africa. The Hagia Sophia's 104 columns were imported from the Temple of Artemis in Ephesus, a city in western Turkey known today as Izmir, as well as from Egypt. These materials, and the diverse lands from which those materials originated, provide evidence of DEUCE in previous civilizations and generations before the present day.

While the Hagia Sophia has long endured as an epicenter of Christendom, it is also known for its role in the Clash of Civilizations.[2] On 29 May 1453, the Ottomans conquered Constantinople, a victory that sent shockwaves throughout Christendom. Sultan Mehmed II (d. 1481) – known as Mehmed the Conqueror of the Ottoman Empire – quickly converted the Hagia Sophia into a mosque. For the Ottomans, its conversion represented an Islamic triumph over both Europe and Christendom. They proceeded to replace the original Christian-themed mosaics of the Greek Orthodox tradition with Islamic calligraphy. Panels were hung on the columns of the nave featuring the names of the first four caliphs – Allah (God), Prophet Muhammad, and the two grandsons of Muhammad. The mosaics on the main dome showing images of Jesus were covered by gold Islamic calligraphy. Heterogeneity, in a nutshell, was rejected.

The Ottoman sultans who followed Mehmed II were crowned "emperor" in the former basilica. They all claimed the title of *Qayser-I Rum*, or "Roman Emperor." The Ottomans believed that they were the rightful heirs of the Roman Empire because they now possessed its most prized gem – Constantinople. The Hagia Sophia itself remained a mosque until the Ottoman Empire collapsed following its defeat against Western powers in World War I. The modern-day country of Turkey emerged in 1923 out of the ashes of the empire's collapse.

In 1934, under the leadership of Mustafa Kemal (d. 1938), the first Turkish president, the new nation of Turkey restored the original Byzantine mosaics[3] and secularized the building by turning it into an interfaith museum, a decision that recognized the diversity of the Hagia Sophia's heritage. The building became an international symbol for cross-cultural communication and interfaith dialogue. It also served as a sign that Turkish authorities made accommodations in dealing with its own religious heterogeneity.

The Conversion of the Hagia Sophia

Recent political events in Turkey, on the other hand, have introduced the question of whether the Turkish government is committed to recognizing Turkey's Christian heritage. Recep Tayyip Erdoğan, the President of Turkey as of 2024, sparked an international controversy when his government converted the Hagia Sophia into a mosque in July 2020. He did so after a Turkish court annulled the site's "museum" status, stating that its use as anything other than a mosque was "not possible legally" (British Broadcasting Corporation 2020b). Shortly after the court released its decision, Erdoğan issued a presidential decree that transferred the management of the site from the Ministry of Culture to the Presidency of Religious Affairs (Sariyuce and Reynolds 2020). The Hagia Sophia's first Islamic call to prayer – the *azhan* in Arabic – was broadcast on all of Turkey's main news channels soon after the court's decree (British Broadcasting Corporation 2020b). A spokesperson for the Turkish government defended the conversion – and hinted at a DEUCE-embodied culture – by claiming that the building's Christian artifacts would be preserved and that foreign tourists would not be restricted from visiting the site, but few Turkish Christians had faith in the government.

According to critics of the conversion, the Hagia Sophia's new status was a clear sign that the Turkish government was not committed to building a civic or secular-oriented society. Nor was it a sign that the Turkish government was interested in engaging in DEUCE anytime soon. Some of the harshest criticism came from neighboring Greece, whose Minister of Culture called it "an open provocation to the entire civilized world" (Sariyuce and Reynolds 2020). Ecumenical Patriarch Bartholomew, the leader of the world's Orthodox Christian community, warned that the conversion would "turn millions of Christians from around the world against Islam" (see Ioannou 2020). Mike Pompeo, the Secretary of State of the USA at the time, viewed the change in the Hagia Sophia's status as "diminishing the legacy of this remarkable building and its unsurpassed ability – so rare in the modern world – to serve humanity as a much-needed bridge between those of differing faith traditions and cultures" (Sariyuce and Reynolds 2020). Pope Francis added that he was "pained" by the erasure of Christianity at the site, a quote which reminds us that the erasure of Christianity occurs in the Ummah, just as the erasure of Islam occurs in the West (Córdoba, Spain, for example).

In defense of the Dialogue of Civilizations, several critics of the Turkish government emerged within Turkey and around the Ummah. One Turkish academic claimed that Erdoğan's primary motive was to spark a battle between secularists and Islamists. The academic wrote that:

> a fight over mosque versus museum slots easily into a religion/modernity binary. It can also be used to create an Islam/Christianity binary as Hagia Sophia was originally built as a church and functioned as such for nine centuries until the Ottoman Conquest of Istanbul . . . [The reconversion] awakens historical allusions and underlines the real or perceived dichotomy between the Ottoman Empire and the Republic [of Turkey] . . . Erdoğan will focus on international condemnation to fan the flames of identity conflicts, presenting these reactions as interference in Turkey's internal affairs – if not outright Islamophobia. Given that certain European countries have their own problems with accommodating Muslim places of worship, European criticisms can easily be framed as hypocritical and anti-Islamic (Çevik 2020).

According to a poll conducted in 2020 (see Çevik 2020), a majority of the Turkish population regarded the conversion as an attempt by the government to divert attention from economic problems and reverse the declining support of the Justice and Development Party – the AKP – the ruling political party at the time.

The increasing erasure of Turkish Christianity is due largely to the rise of Islamism, a form of religious nationalism that merges Islam with governance (Open Doors USA n.d.a.).[4] Akyan Erdemir, a former Turkish parliamentarian, claimed that the conversion relegated Turkey's Christian communities to "an inferior rank of conquered minorities," a status which represented the "glorification of the Ottoman 'spirit of conquest'" (Gilbert 2021). Another Turkish activist opposed the conversion saying that it was not only "bad news" for Christians, but "bad news for the world" (see Ioannou 2020). Additionally, journalist Saud Al-Sarhan claimed that Erdoğan was spreading a "Turkish-led religious-national pan-Islamist global movement that racializes 'Muslims' as a group hostile and antithetical to the West." Al-Sarhan added that he was "abandoning the project of the modern Turkish Republic (and the ideas of its founder Mustafa Kemal Atatürk)" (Al-Sarhan 2020). Erdoğan, he stated, was "further widening the gap between East and West."

Given the current political and religious issues extant in Turkey today, it is anticipated that Turkey occupies a key juncture in the world relative to the Dialogue of Civilizations and the acceptance thereof. However, given the current political climate in Turkey, the movement toward DEUCE may take years to evolve, if it ever does. Pressures emanating from the region – and from Turkey's relationship with the West, as well as the Ummah – mean that Turkey's physical location as a borderland will continue in the future.

Discrimination Against Christians in Modern-Day Turkey

For many Christians living in Turkey today, the conversion of the Hagia Sophia into a mosque was another blow to their already marginalized status. The country only accepts three non-Muslim groups as official religious minorities – Armenians, Orthodox Christians (Greeks), and Jews (Minority Rights Group International n.d.). This means that Christian groups, like the Assyrians,[5] are not officially recognized by the Turkish state. The historic Greek Orthodox Halki Seminary remains closed as of 2024. According to the US State Department, Turkey has restricted efforts of Christians to train their clergy domestically (United States Department of State 2022). In January 2022, an Armenian Christian parliamentarian condemned the demolition of a seventeenth-century Armenian church in Kutahya that had previously been protected under local law. These developments have led to an exodus of Christians in one of the most important locations in Christendom.

Protestants living in Turkey have also reported widespread discrimination, including an increase in hate speech (particularly on social media), no legal recognition as a church, and a lack of missionaries to train Turkish pastors (Casper 2022). The lack of legal recognition by the Turkish state means that Christians are denied free utilities and tax exemption (Casper 2022). In 2020, Protestants in Istanbul tried registering a Christian school first as an association, then as a business, and then simply as a regular private school, but their request was denied by the government (Casper 2022).

Notwithstanding these forms of discrimination, Turkey offers Christians a relative degree of freedom of religion, certainly more so than countries like Saudi Arabia, as discussed in chapter 1. Catholic Armenians, for example, have an archbishop in Istanbul, while the Greek Orthodox community has its own Patriarchate. In Yesilko, on the European side of Istanbul, the Saint Ephrem Syriac Orthodox Church, the first-ever church built during the era of the Turkish republic, opened in 2023 (Al-Bawaba 2023). Greek Patriarch Bartholomew led Mass at the Hagia Yorgi Church for Christmas in 2022 and Greeks living in the northwestern province of Erdine celebrated the same holiday with prayers and rituals at the Sveti Georgi Church in the Barutluk neighborhood (TRT World 2022a). Their ability to engage in these practices suggests that there is a chance, albeit a small one, of embracing heterogeneity in Turkey today.

Erdoğan appears to offer only platitudes in reaching out to Christians. He extended his Christmas greetings to Turkish Christians and Christians across the world when he said, "In line with the values of the civilization to which we belong, we consider the existence of different religions and cultures as a richness" (TRT World 2022b). He added, "This understanding, which is the basis of the peace and security, unity, and solidarity of our nation, is our most important power that will enable us to live together peacefully in the future." These two quotes point to a recognition of heterogeneity as a key part of Turkish identity, but recent political developments are hardly conducive to DEUCE.

Political Islam and the AKP

Like other political doctrines, Islamism – in its contemporary shape – is a non-secular form of government and ideology that places an interpretation of Islamic principles, however understood, at the forefront of Turkey's national fabric (Mozaffari 2007: 17). At the very least, Islamism is a form of social and political activism grounded in an idea that public and political life should be fused by a set of Islamic principles. As such, Islamist activism is a public manifestation of an Islamically informed political will, often expressed as resistance to diverse types of secular ideas, lifestyles, and policies (Poljarevic 2015).

The recent Islamist revitalization in Turkey has accelerated since Erdoğan arrived on the Turkish political scene. He was elected mayor of

Istanbul on the ticket of the Welfare Party (WP) in 1994. As the mayor of Istanbul, he governed as a charismatic and smart technocrat, albeit an Islamist one. His 1994 victory shook the Turkish secular establishment – created by Turkey's emergence as a state in 1923 – to its core. As the WP mayor of Istanbul, he organized the commemoration of the conquest of Constantinople by Sultan Mehmed, a popular Ottoman ruler among Islamists in Turkey. He also was convicted and sentenced to ten months in prison for inciting "religious hatred" after reciting a poem comparing mosques to barracks, minarets to bayonets, and the Muslim faithful to an army. Erdoğan subsequently resigned as the mayor of Istanbul. Years later, he broke with the Welfare Party to help form the Justice and Development Party, or the Adalet ve Kalkinma Partisi. Better known as the AKP, it won the Turkish parliamentary elections in 2002, but Erdoğan – its leader – was banned from serving as the prime minister. His fate was altered by a December 2002 constitutional amendment, which removed his disqualification. The following year, he won a by-election and formed a new government as the new prime minister of Turkey. Despite the AKP's orientation towards Islamism, the party committed itself to advancing economic and political reforms to bring Turkey closer to the democratic standards of the EU and the core principles of DEUCE.

Over the years, however, the AKP chipped away at the strict separation of religion and state ushered in by Kemal, the founder of the Turkish republic, who I return to later in this chapter. While campaigning for parliamentary elections in early 2011, the AKP pledged to replace Turkey's constitution with a new one that, it claimed, would strengthen democratic freedoms, but the West was skeptical of its commitment to these values.

Turkey's Islamist turn means that it is increasingly unlikely that the country will soon re-enter negotiations to join the EU, despite public opinion polls showing that the Turkish public sees the European Union as an important ally in dealing with issues pertaining to international relations. Almost 60 percent of Turkish respondents in a German Marshall Fund survey felt that European Union membership would be positive for Turkey (Ünlühisarcıklı, Tastan, and Canbilek 2022). On the other hand, when asked in 2022 about the biggest threat against Turkey's national interests, 58 percent mentioned the USA, the highest of any other country (Ünlühisarcıklı, Tastan, and Canbilek 2022). Only 39 percent of Turks in 2022 trusted NATO, the Western military alliance that Turkey is part of. These polls are concerning to those interested in strengthening ties between the West and Turkey.

Domestic politics in Turkey have also discouraged a DEUCE-like culture from emerging between Christians and Muslims. A Turkish corruption scandal incriminating Erdoğan in 2013 led to protests in Gezi Park, which Erdoğan quelled with an "iron fist" (Sanderson 2018). Not only did he respond to the protestors with violence, resulting in 22 deaths, but he also accused Fethullah Gülen, an Islamic philosopher and his former ally, of trying to overthrow the Turkish government by supporting the protestors. Gülen was framed at this time by Erdoğan as a subversive Islamist and an enemy of the state who was fashioning a "state within a state," or a "parallel state" (Sanderson 2018) that was subservient to Western nations and interests, and thus to Christians and Christianity. I return to Gülen later in the chapter.

Soon thereafter, in a 2017 nationwide referendum, Erdoğan granted himself new powers like control over the judiciary, the broad power to make law by decree, and the abolition of the office of the prime minister as well as Turkey's parliamentary system. In other words, he had absolute power (Filkins 2017). Today, some see him as a dictator and a promoter of what scholars have termed "neo-Ottomanism," which is symbolic of the Clash of Civilizations and Turkey's rejection of heterogeneity.

The Rise of Neo-Ottomanism and the Muslim Brotherhood

Neo-Ottomanism is driven by a desire to revive the Ottoman Empire through cultural, economic, military, and political power (Maziad and Sotiriadis n.d.). It has been characterized as a misguided vision of international Islamism that evokes cultural hegemony and militancy (Maziad and Sotiriadis n.d.). One scholar described the AKP's embrace of neo-Ottomanism this way:

> *[Erdoğan] is asserting a fake messianism based on a skillfully crafted cosmetic image of "defender of Muslims" or even "commander of the faithful," signaling his "caliphetic" ambitions. By adopting a highly populist language of intercivilizational antagonism, Erdoğan is making the best use of Islamophobia for his*

platform at home and abroad. For Erdoğan, Islamophobia is not an ill to be erad-icated. It is rather a source of free political adrenalin to be used as a smokescreen to cover his corrupt and antidemocratic enterprise at home and a pretext to pose as human rights defender abroad. Hence his inflammatory rhetoric against the West and disdain for any meaningful dialogue with non-Muslims. Erdoğan's reckless West-bashing on grounds of Islamophobia is not a solution oriented approach but rather a deliberate choice to keep the tension high. This puts Muslims in further trouble as the term Islamophobia is abused for short term political ends instead of being recognized [as] a universal human rights threat just like Anti-Semitism (Anli 2019).

This passage fits with the idea that Turkey has prioritized – and been born out of the idea – that it is religion and not the nation that counts. Religion, in this case Islam, is used as a political tool to garner support among the Turkish electorate. Barriers to recognizing Turkey's diversity inevitably arise out of this position. Religious harmony also is hampered because of Islamist interests and Turkish nationalism.

Much of the neo-Ottoman vision of Turkey is said to be influenced by *Stratejik Derinlik*, or *Strategic Depth*, a book by Ahmet Davutoğlu, the former Minister of Foreign Affairs and later prime minister of Turkey. Davutoğlu called for establishing deeper ties with former Ottoman terri-tories in the Balkans and Middle East at the expense of Turkey's allies in the West (Ergin and Karakaya 2017: 38). Advocates of neo-Ottomanism regularly stoke irredentist sentiment by questioning the Treaty of Lausanne (1923), the agreement between the West and Turkey that set the boundaries of Turkey's borders (Brown 1924: 113–16). Others imply that Kemal made unnecessary territorial concessions to the West and that Turkey has the right to demand a return to the national borders envi-sioned by the Misak-i Millî, or the National Pact.[6]

Neo-Ottomanism also is evident in the emerging alliances between Turkey and other Sunni countries around the world (Lappin 2020). Though Ankara insists it only backs Palestinians politically, Turkey has been accused of supporting Hamas, the Gaza-based group designated as a terrorist organization by the EU and USA. President Erdoğan himself has hosted Ismail Haniyeh, a Hamas leader, in Istanbul as a guest of honor in 2020 and again in 2024.[7] Evidence suggests that Hamas's military lead-ership set up a secret cyberwarfare and counter-intelligence headquarters in Istanbul in the year 2018 (Pfeffer 2020). Turkish authorities stated that they are unaware of the headquarters' existence, or Hamas operatives in Turkey.

Hamas's archenemy – Israel – also is in the crosshairs of the neo-Ottomans, particularly after the 7 October Hamas attack on Jewish communities in southern Israel. Under the AKP government, Turkey's relationship with Israel has soured over the years. AKP members have championed Palestinian nationalism and publicly advanced anti-Israel views. Erdoğan accused Israel of "terrorism" against the Palestinians in Gaza in July 2021, stating that "[Israelis] are murderers, to the point that they kill children who are five or six years old. They only are satisfied by sucking their blood" (France 24 2021). His words followed the Anti-Semitic canard – known as "blood libel" – which falsely accuses Jews of murdering people to use their blood in the performance of Jewish rituals. The recent Israeli counterattack on Hamas in the Gaza Strip has further enforced "blood libel," a phrase which unfortunately represents the Clash of Civilizations and the denial of DEUCE as well as heterogeneity.

The plight of secularism in Turkey and the emergence of neo-Ottomanism is further evident in its relationship with Pakistan, a country that was also originally founded as a secular state, but one that has gradually slipped into Islamism. The Turkish government has relied on the network of the Muslim Brotherhood, especially its offshoots in Pakistan, to encourage "Islamic solidarity" worldwide (Yilmaz 2022: 45). Together, Erdoğan and Imran Khan, the former prime minister of Pakistan, pushed foreign policies driven by "Muslim nationalist emotions" (Yilmaz 2022: 45). Both leaders used anti-Western populist rhetoric by focusing on Islamophobia in the West while ignoring "Christophobia" in their own countries. Turkey also strengthened its soft power by helping Khan implement his Islamist populist vision via Turkey's highly industrialized film industry, which has effectively recreated past glories [of the Ummah] and projected current affairs into historical events to promote Islamist initiatives (Yilmaz 2022: 45–6).

The Gulf state of Qatar also has been linked to Turkey's neo-Ottoman enterprise. It, too, has a sympathetic approach toward the Muslim Brotherhood. Qatar has been viewed as a "closeted Islamist actor" because of its support of groups that are offshoots of the Muslim Brotherhood (Roberts 2019: 1). The two states also feel jointly targeted by the anti-Muslim Brotherhood approach emanating from states like the UAE and, to some degree, Saudi Arabia (Roberts 2019: 6). The latter are advocating the acceptance and evolution of DEUCE in their respective countries.

For Turkish Muslims, and Muslims worldwide, neo-Ottomanism might rejuvenate memories of Islamic grandeur and the sense of responsibility of being stewards of a more glorious past (Yavuz 2016: 443). For Christians in and around Turkey, however, neo-Ottomanism rejuvenates painful memories of cultural destruction, forced deportations, and genocidal campaigns (Yavuz 2016: 445). From both of these perspectives, neo-Ottomanism constitutes a frontal challenge to Turkey's foundational Kemalist narrative, one that rejects the country's Islamic and imperial past in exchange for a secular and Western-oriented society.

Cyprus – An Island Divided

Cyprus, an island and European Union state – and nation of concern to NATO members – is another battleground in the conflict between the West and the Ummah. The Cypriotic people were included in the Book of Acts as an influential group within the wider Church of Antioch. The island became the home of Saint Barnabas, the early Christian missionary mentioned in the New Testament as one of the Apostolic Fathers.[8] Cyprus also is recognized as the first country in the world to be governed by a Christian. Today, Christianity is the largest religion on the island, which is currently partitioned between North Cyprus – a Turkish territory – and the Republic of Cyprus.

As of 2024, a United Nations (UN) peacekeeping force is stationed on the border between North Cyprus and the Republic of Cyprus. The UN is there to monitor a buffer zone – known as the Green Line – which segregates Christian Cypriots, who now live in the south of the island, and Muslim Turks, who live in the north (Psaropoulos 2022). Recent reports have claimed that local authorities are trying to evict UN peacekeepers from their bases in Northern Cyprus, which could trigger another crisis between the West and Islam (Psaropoulos 2022).

There is no doubt that relations between the Christian Cypriots and the Muslim Turks on Cyprus are impacted by memories of conquest and colonization. The Ottoman Empire invaded Cyprus in the year 1570.

After 300 years of Ottoman rule, Cyprus was effectively placed into the control of the UK, which annexed the island in 1914 following its victory over the Ottoman Empire in World War I. The secular Turkish republic that arose out of World War I renounced all claims to Cyprus by signing the Treaty of Lausanne in 1923. Following several decades of British rule, the island emerged as an independent republic after the signing of the Treaty of Guarantee in 1960, which was signed by Cyprus, Greece, Turkey, and the UK. The agreement stated that all four countries were committed to the independence and territorial integrity of Cyprus. The treaty banned any of the countries from engaging in economic or political unions with other states. This agreement was violated when Turkey invaded Cyprus in 1974, around the time when Turkey started waning from its secular foundation.

Turkey named its Cyprus operation – "the Attila Plan" (Bulut 2022b) – after Attila the Hun (d. 453), the leader of the Hun Empire.[9] The battle evoked images of his conquest, which stretched as far west to the Ural River in modern-day Germany and the Netherlands, to the Danube River in modern-day Poland and Estonia. Attila invaded the Balkans on two occasions, besieged Constantinople – the capital of the Byzantine Empire – and marched through Gaul, which comprises modern-day France. His nickname was "the sacker of cities." In other words, he represented Muslim expansion into Europe, the blatant disregard for Christian acceptance within the realm of Turkic-speaking territories, and the antithesis of DEUCE. The Permanent Representative of Cyprus to the United Nations described the Attila Plan invasion in the following manner:

> *Turkey – in unchallenged command of the air and the sea and illegally using armaments and sophisticated weapons in her possession strictly for purposes of defense under a relevant alliance agreement – launched a full-scale aggressive attack against Cyprus, a small non-aligned and virtually defenseless country, possessing no air force, no navy, and no army except for a small national guard. Thus, Turkey's overwhelming military machine embarked upon an armed attack including napalm bombing of open towns and villages, wreaking destruction, setting forests on fire, and spreading indiscriminate death and human suffering to the civilian population of the island . . . The landing of the Turkish forces on the territory of Cyprus became from its inception no less ferocious in inhumanity towards*

the civilian population, in violation of all principles of international law and accepted concepts of a civilized society (United Nations Security Council 2006: 9).

Soon after the invasion, Cyprus was partitioned, and the Republic of Cyprus emerged. The northern part of the island, now belonging to Turkey, is said to have experienced "almost the total obliteration of the local [Greek and Christian] heritage" (Tzoitis 2021). The consequences of Turkey's takeover have been described as "forced Islamization."

Following its seizure of Northern Cyprus, Ankara transferred 150,000 "Turkish settlers" from the inner Anatolia region of Turkey to their new territory. These Turkish settlers are said to have replaced approximately 170,000 Greek Cypriots. The transference has been criticized as an attempt to alter the demographic balance of the island. Other commentators have claimed that Turkey engaged in a deliberate "ethnic cleansing" and "replacement scheme" that not only transferred Muslims onto Christian lands, but also largely destroyed both the Christian and Jewish cultural heritage of the area. According to one report:

The churches [in occupied Cyprus] have been subject to the most violent and systematic desecration and destruction. More than five hundred churches and monasteries have been looted or destroyed – more than 15,000 icons and saints, innumerable sacred liturgical vessels, gospels, and other objects of great value have literally vanished. A few churches have met a different fate and have been turned into mosques, museums, places of entertainment or even hotels, like the church of Ayia Anastasia in Lapithos. At least three monasteries have been turned into barracks for the Turkish army (Ayious Chrysostomos in the Pentadactylos Mountains, Acheropoiitos in Karavas, and Ayos Panteleimonas in Myrtou). Marvelous Byzantine wall-paintings and mosaics of rare artistic and historical value have been removed from church walls by Turkish smugglers and sold illegally in America, Europe, and Japan. Many Byzantine churches have suffered irreparable damage.

Turkey officially declared the so-called "Turkish Republic of Northern Cyprus" (TRNC) in the occupied north of Cyprus in 1983. The TRNC was recognized only by Turkey and remains unrecognized by the international community to this day. The Turkish regime in occupied Northern Cyprus has recently been accused of driving neo-Ottomanism by erecting in 2022 a mausoleum of Pertev Mehmed Paşa (d. 1572), a Muslim commander involved in the Ottoman invasion of Cyprus in the sixteenth century (Bulut 2022b). Around 80 percent of Cyprus's main capital-producing resources lie under Turkish occupation. The Turkish military presence in Cyprus is believed to be somewhere between 35,000 and 40,000 soldiers, vastly outnumbering Christian Cypriot forces.

Relations between Christian Cypriots and Muslim Cypriots were further complicated in September 2022, when the USA removed an embargo on arms sales to Cyprus, which had been enforced since 1987 to prevent further violence on the island (Al-Jazeera 2022). Nicos Anastasiades, the former President of Cyprus, welcomed the decision by Washington, calling it "a landmark decision reflecting the burgeoning strategic relationship between the two countries, including in the area of security" (Al-Jazeera 2022). Erdoğan responded by stating that Turkey will reinforce its military presence in Northern Cyprus (Reuters 2022). The emerging Cyprus–USA allyship is said to be driven by worsening tensions between Turkey and Greece, a conflict the Cypriot Foreign Minister Ioannis Kasoulides is weary of getting drawn into (Tugwell, Georgiou, and Johnson 2022).

It is likely that Cyprus will experience an insecure existence as events in the Gaza Strip between Hamas and Israel may engender an ongoing stand-off between Greece and Turkey near the island of Cyprus. Any attempts to initiate basic DEUCE tenets is likely to be a huge challenge in Cyprus in the near future.

Greek Angst in the Aegean Sea

Greece, which neighbors Cyprus, has a long and complicated history with Turkey. The Ottoman Empire invaded Greece for the first time in the 1350s. Subsequent centuries witnessed additional invasions and the further Ottoman colonization of the Greeks. Starting in the nineteenth century, however, the Ottoman Empire struggled to govern Greece's population. Ethno-nationalist movements arose on the periphery of the Ottoman Empire, which proved – like in the case of the Greeks – to impact the degree to which Ottoman authorities were forced to recognize the aspirations of Christians and the need to acknowledge heterogeneity.

Groups of social bandits – referred to as the *klephts* – emerged as symbols of resistance against Ottomanism in the nineteenth century.[10]

Revolutionary Greeks like Adamantios Korais (d. 1833), Anthimos Gazis (d. 1828), and Rigas Feraois (d. 1798) resisted Ottoman rule by promoting civic nationalist ideas arising out of the French Revolution. These ideas culminated in the Greek War of Independence between the years 1821 and 1832. Driven mainly by the *Megali Idea* – the Greek term for the "Great Idea" – the newly independent Greece was to be cemented in the Greek language and Orthodox Christianity. It officially gained its independence in 1829, from which point it expanded its territory via multiple forays into Ottoman lands.

Today, Turkey fears that Greece is trying to "strangulate Turkey" by making the Aegean Sea a "Greek sea" and by militarizing key islands that are closer to Turkey. The Turkish government has accused Greece of deploying troops and weapons on Aegean Sea islands, which Turkey claims is in violation of treaties requiring the islands to be non-militarized (Becatoros and Fraser 2022). The Greeks, on the other hand, fear that Turkey is trying to seize Greek islands to exploit oil and gas and thus to reduce its dependence on imported energy. Tensions over energy rights also have been intensified by Turkey's claim to the Greek island of Kastellorizo, an island in the Eastern Mediterranean Sea. Turkey has recently sent energy exploration ships, naval auxiliary ships, and warships in its direction (Lappin 2020).

Relations between the two neighboring countries hit a boiling point in December 2022 over Greece's reported cooperation with the USA in the Aegean Sea. While addressing a group of Turkish youth in the northern Turkish city of Samsun, Erdoğan mentioned that Turkey had begun making its own short-range ballistic missiles called Tayfun, which, he said, was "frightening the Greeks." He told the youth, "[The Greeks] say 'It can hit Athens'" (Becatoros and Fraser 2022). Nikos Dendias, the Foreign Minister of Greece, responded by stating, "It is unacceptable and universally condemnable for threats of a missile attack against Greece to be made by an allied country, a NATO member."

The angst in the Aegean Sea between Turkey and Greece has gained the attention of Western powers. France, led by President Emmanuel Macron, came to Greece's aid in 2020 after the Greek and Turkish militaries nearly came to blows over a dispute about energy exploration rights (Gehrke 2021). Turkey responded by using a cutting-edge Russian anti-aircraft missile system, purchased in defiance of American sanctions, to track F-16 fighter jets flown by Greece, France, and Italy during a joint military exercise with the UAE (Gehrke 2020). It is for these reasons that experts have called Turkey "neither a friend nor foe" of the West. Unlike the immediate post-World War II era, Turkey, and the West – particularly the USA – no longer appear to share overarching interests that can bind them together (Cook 2018). Turkey and the West have effectively gone from ambivalent allies to DEUCE antagonists.

Relations between Greece and Turkey can be improved if the two countries engage in cross-cultural contact, economic cooperation, and tourism (Heraclides 2011: 6), which are paramount to DEUCE's effectiveness. This approach would mirror what the Emirates and Israelis have managed to accomplish with the Abraham Accords, as explained in chapter 1. It is anticipated that the acceptance and promotion of DEUCE in the UAE, Saudi Arabia, and Israel may result in a groundswell movement to follow suit, but it will take time.

PART TWO – THE DIALOGUE OF CIVILIZATIONS

While the previous section made it clear that Turkey has been a battleground site in the Clash of Civilizations, its unique geographic location in Asia Minor has made it a center of the Dialogue of Civilizations. In addition to the Ottoman Empire's relative tolerance of Christianity, modern leaders and movements have promoted and implemented DEUCE concepts in Turkey as well as the Turkish diaspora. Underlying the Dialogue of Civilizations, however, is the ability of the Clash of Civilizations to pop up and pull Christians and Muslims back into conflict and division.

The Gülen Movement

On the night of 15 July 2016, Turkish military personnel attempted a coup d'état by occupying streets and seizing various facilities, including television stations and bridges, in both Ankara, the Turkish capital, and Istanbul, the largest Turkish city. The coup d'état attempt has been described as badly organized and executed because it failed within 12 hours (Sanderson 2018). Nevertheless, a total of 265 Turks died in the street violence (Commission on Security and Cooperation in Europe 2016). The Turkish government immediately claimed that Fethullah

Gülen, a Muslim Turkish philosopher and scholar who has lived in exile in Saylorsburg, Pennsylvania, since 1999, was behind the attempted coup d'état.[11]

Gülen is widely considered to be a liberal thinker when it comes to Islam's relationship with the West. He is the de facto founder and leader of the Gülen movement – also known as the Hizmet movement – a transnational, cultural, religious, and social movement that emphasizes education, interfaith dialogue, and community service, all of which are critical to the success of DEUCE. Gülen's early years were shaped by Sufism – the mystical form of Islam – and later Said Nursi (d. 1960), who believed that Islam had a positive role to play in the public sphere. One of Gülen's primary teachings – interfaith dialogue – is one of the faces of the international network of private and public schools inspired by his teachings (Harvard Divinity School n.d.d.). The movement's active promotion of both dialogue and education – the first two components of DEUCE – could be used as a model for other communities seeking to be enriched by diversity.

It is important to note that the Gülen movement is not a centralized or formal organization with membership rosters, but rather a set of loosely organized networks of people inspired by Gülen. It includes people of many religions and is widely viewed as a peaceful movement promoting a moderate version of Islam that sidesteps forming official alliances with any political party. Personally, I have worked extensively since 2020 with the movement's various outlets. Over the course of the last several years, I have traveled across the USA to give talks at dozens of Gülen-affiliated interfaith and intercultural organizations. I am struck by the movement's commitment to DEUCE concepts and their expression of Turkish hospitality, which is second to none. Its affiliates have opened their businesses, cultural centers, schools, and places of worship to me and provided me with a snapshot of the community that is rarely – if ever – fairly represented in Turkish society.

The Turkish public has mixed perceptions of Gülen and his followers. While many are sympathetic to Gülen's teachings, they have been criticized by Turkish secularists and some Turkish Muslims as lacking in transparency (Harvard Divinity School n.d.d.). They have also been accused of being "terrorists," but this label is widely rejected in the West.

In the weeks that followed 15 July 2016, the Gülen movement was described by one leading Turkish journalist as being involved in a "tremendous attack of a deep state" (Başaran 2016). The *Hurriyet Daily News* accused Gülen of building a secret network, nested mainly in the Turkish judiciary and security apparatus, to gain power (Başaran 2016). The article added that Gülen's followers are more loyal to him than the institutions they work for. These kinds of accusations greatly reduce any chance of DEUCE being used between the Gülen movement and the wider Turkish population.

These kinds of anti-Gülen sentiments also seeped into other societies around the world. *Der Spiegel*, the prominent German media outlet, referred to the Gülen movement as a "secretive and dangerous cult." Some critics have claimed that he is working for the Vatican (Commission on Security and Cooperation in Europe 2016: 5). In previous years, puppets representing Gülen were hanged and burned in public rallies by protestors in Turkey. Signs calling Gülen "a dog of Zionism" and "Abu Jahil" – the archenemy of Prophet Muhammad – have also been seen on the streets of Turkey (Commission on Security and Cooperation in Europe 2016: 5).

Such depictions of Gülen make it easier for the Turkish authorities to justify their persecution of his followers. After the coup d'état, Erdoğan proceeded to carry out a massive purge of the Gülen movement by removing tens of thousands of civil servants, police officers, soldiers, and teachers from their jobs, most of whom were linked to the Gülen movement.[12] He also imprisoned thousands for their alleged sympathies with the coup d'état and seized assets from everyday Turks who had built businesses and lives through years of hard work (Commission on Security and Cooperation in Europe 2016: 3).

Since the coup d'état, the Gülen movement has been officially classified by the Turkish government as FETÖ, standing for "Fethullahist Terrorist Organization."[13] Pakistan, as well as the Gulf Cooperation Council (GCC), have aligned with Turkey in designating the movement "FETÖ." Media outlets in Turkey and around the world, along with everyday Turkish citizens, followed suit. In addition to blaming Gülen for the coup d'état, Erdoğan asked the American government to extradite Gülen. Michael Flynn – the retired US army Lieutenant General and former National Security Advisor during the Trump Administration – was offered $15 million to forcibly remove Gülen from his residence in

Pennsylvania. Turkish authorities cited the US government's refusal to extradite Gülen as evidence of the Turkish claim that the USA is working with the Gülen movement to undermine both Turkey and the Ummah (Robinson 2022).

Independent experts are skeptical of Turkey's accusations and point to the idea that Turkey is "fertile soil" for a range of conspiracy theories regarding the Gülen movement, the USA, and NATO. One journalist claimed that there can be "no doubt that conspiracy theories claim an important place in Turkish mainstream media," which, he said, pointed to a "deep [Turkish] distrust against foreign political powers and against religious minorities," thus making it harder for the Turkish people to integrate Christians in Turkish society (Häde 2015: 187). These kinds of claims make it difficult to recognize heterogeneity as a positive aspect of Turkish society, as opposed to hybridity, which entails a deeper engagement – or synthesis – with diversity.

Western media narratives focus on Turkey's drift away from Western values and towards an increasingly dictatorial approach to governing. What Western media narratives ignore, however, are the nuances surrounding Turkey's promotion of neo-Ottomanism. Turkey today is in a constant state of change with Erdoğan's authoritarianism entrenched in power. The country will remain in the spotlight as he displays overt Islamist rhetoric and dictatorial tendencies. Any attempt in moving toward DEUCE is a huge challenge under Islamist governments.

The Millet System and Eastern Christians Under Ottoman Rule

Coincidentally, elements of DEUCE and principles of the Dialogue of Civilizations appeared to flourish throughout the Ottoman Empire, which lasted from 1300 to 1922. The Ottoman Empire has been described as "the last great cosmopolitan empire that came after the Roman Empire" (Yavuz 2016: 442). This description may come as a surprise to some Westerners given that Islamic civilization is rarely associated with tolerance in the West. Some scholars have long admired the Ottoman Empire for its DEUCE-like governing philosophies toward religious minorities.

Christians, as *Ahl Al-Kitab* – the Arabic term and Islamic concept meaning People of the Book – were afforded a significant degree of tolerance by the Ottoman sultans through a system known as *millet*, which translates to "religious community" or "nation" in English. While Ottoman identity was rooted in Sunni Islam, the second biggest *millet* or community was that of the Orthodox Church. Under the *millet* system, Albanians, Arabs, Armenians, Bulgarians, Greeks, Romanians, and Serbs each had the relative ability to govern over their communal structures. There were also smaller Catholic, Jewish, and Protestant *millets* around the empire. The Ottoman state also recognized sectarian differences within each *millet*. Evidence of this is found in the different Armenian *millets* – the Catholic Armenians, Georgian Armenians, and Protestant Armenians.

The Ottoman Empire ensured that members of each *millet* had freedom of religion and security of life and property, providing that they did not interfere with Ottoman governance or promote the supremacy of Christianity over Islam. Each Christian *millet* was granted the legal right to collect their own taxes, develop their own educational institutions, establish their own courts, and use their own language (Weinholtz 2021). They were also granted rights pertaining to matters of family law, such as birth, death, inheritance, and marriage.

A number of Greeks enjoyed privileged positions in the bureaucracy of the Ottoman state. In terms of their own sovereignty, Greeks controlled the affairs of their Orthodox Church by means of the higher clergy led by the Ecumenical Patriarchate of Constantinople. Some Greek merchants and sailors became wealthy and used their wealth to build libraries and schools, publish books and pamphlets in Greek, and send Greek students to European universities to study, all of which led to the "modern Greek Enlightenment." Education, the second principle of DEUCE, was clearly an important element of Turkey's nineteenth-century reforms of religious tolerance.

Scholars typically conclude that the Ottomans were far more tolerant of Christians than Western European nations were of Muslims between the fourteenth and twentieth centuries. As proof, in 1492, the Kingdom of Spain issued the Alhambra Decree, which ordered all "Jews and Jewesses of our kingdoms to depart and never to return or come back to them." In response, Sultan Bayezid II (d. 1512) sent the Ottoman navy to rescue some of the Jews who were expelled by the Alhambra Decree. He also ordered his officials to ensure that Jews were welcomed into

Ottoman territories, another sign of the Ottoman Empire's acceptance of heterogeneity.

The tolerance displayed toward Christians by the Ottoman Empire, however, is a bit more complex than these optimistic depictions. Despite the advantages of the *millet* system, Christians were disadvantaged in a number of ways in comparison to Muslims. While Christians (and Jews) were considered *dhimmi*, meaning "protected" people, under Ottoman law, Christians were not allowed to bear arms, serve in the Ottoman military, or marry Muslims, unless they converted to Islam. Ottoman courts also considered the testimonies of Muslims as more "authentic" than the testimonies of Christians. Clearly, there is a difference between theory and reality when some religious groups are treated as more equal than others.

Perhaps the most overt form of discrimination toward Christians came in the form of the *paidomazoma*, or the "Janissary levy." Christian families in the Balkans were required, at irregular intervals, to deliver to the Ottoman authorities a given proportion of their most handsome and intelligent male children to serve as civil servants or elite troops of the Ottoman Empire (Britannica n.d.b.). These men were forcibly converted to Islam. Such harsh measures are a far cry from accepting heterogeneity of the principles of DEUCE.

PART THREE – THE SYNTHESIS OF CIVILIZATIONS

While not perfect, the Ottoman Empire and Turkey – its successor – have had moments which reflect a commitment to move beyond dialogue and mere peaceful coexistence to an environment much more collaborative and enriching for its Christian population. But, yet again, the Clash of Civilizations consistently rears its ugly head as Christians and Muslims work together to achieve the "civic synthesis" that is at the center of the Synthesis of Civilizations.

Tanzimat Tolerance in the Ottoman Empire

Revolts against the Ottoman Empire by the Greeks and other Christian territories, as discussed previously, convinced successive generations of Ottoman leaders that they had to change their philosophy and policies. The Ottomans turned not to their own history of governing religious minorities, but rather to the "European model" (Toksöz 2022).

Tanzimat, the Turkish word that translates to "reorganization," was the name given to the empire's liberal policies in relation to its Christian subjects. Undertaken by Sultan Abdülmecid I (d. 1861) and Sultan Abdülaziz (d. 1876) between the years 1839 and 1876, the Tanzimat reforms promoted freedom of religion in the Ottoman Empire. A civil code of rights was issued to ensure that all Turkish citizens, regardless of ethnicity or religion, had the same equal rights. A modern secular court system, rather than older "religious courts" of the *millet* system, also were introduced. Christians living in the Ottoman Empire were gradually permitted by law to bear arms and serve in the Ottoman military. More specifically, the Rescript of Gülhane (1839) and the Rescript of Reform (1856) guaranteed security of life, honor, and fortune, a standardized system of taxation, and a fairer method of military conscription and training. In the Rescript of Reform, Abdülmecid I pushed for "the formation of roads and canals to increase the facilities of communication and increase the sources of the wealth." In essence, he pushed for DEUCE facilitation by means of traveling, just as Israel and the UAE has done in opening flights to and from cities like Tel Aviv and Dubai.

Mustafa Reşid Paşa (d. 1858), the Ottoman diplomat and statesperson, was the chief architect of the Tanzimat reforms. He created new state courts that were independent of the *Ulema* (the Islamic religious council) and developed reforms that reorganized the Ottoman army based on the Prussian conscript system. Paşa also created provincial representative assemblies and a new secular school system. The latter two initiatives were modeled after the laïcité approach of France, which I return to later in this chapter. These reforms coincided with a restoration project of the Hagia Sophia during the reign of Sultan Abdülmecid I. Between the years 1847 and 1849, he hired Gaspare Fossati (d. 1883)[14] and Giuseppe Fossati (d. 1891) – two brothers and architects of Swiss nationality and Italian descent – to supervise the project. With the help of hundreds of workers, the Fossati brothers documented a large number of Byzantine mosaics, which were later archived in Swiss libraries. They also built the Church of Saint Peter and Saint Paul between 1841 and 1843, along with several other secular and Islamic buildings. The fact that Abdülmecid I chose the

Fossati brothers to engage in these endeavors suggests that he embraced diversity as a means to achieve civilizational progress.

Despite these improvements for Christians, the decline of the Ottomans in the nineteenth century could not be reversed. This decline is related to its struggle in managing the Empire versus managing local Turkish nationalist interests. By the mid-1870s, the positive impact of Tanzimat started to gradually wane due to the Clash of Civilizations. The Serbian-Ottoman War (1878), the Bulgarian-Ottoman War (1908), and the Balkans Wars (1912–13) were sparked by revolts of Christian nations – Serbia and Bulgaria, in the above cases – on the borderlands of Europe and the Ottoman Empire. Things spiraled downward again in 1912, when Bulgarian troops advanced toward Constantinople in 1912. Upon their arrival, Tsar Ferdinand (d. 1948) of Bulgaria was said to have prepared his regalia for a triumphal entry into Constantinople, to be followed by mass in Hagia Sophia, envisioning himself as Emperor of a Christian empire (Ousterhout 2020). The *New York Times* responded by publishing a long article captioned, "Bulgars May Plant Cross on [the Hagia Sophia]" (see Ousterhout 2020). A similar article was written by William T. Ellis, a fervent Presbyterian from Swarthmore, Pennsylvania, and news correspondent for the *New York Herald*, who wrote about the Clash of Civilizations a few years prior to Bulgaria's invasion of Ottoman land in Europe:

> *The Turkish problem, which engrosses the attention of European diplomats and is intertwined with the future of Greece, Crete, Bulgaria, [Serbia], Montenegro, and [Romania] . . . is essentially a problem of Islam versus Christianity. Greeks, Russians, Armenians, and Syrians see it all typified in the cross coming back to the mosque of Saint Sophia at Constantinople . . . For nearly five centuries [the Hagia Sophia] has been in the hands of the [Muslims]. But the belief is strong in millions of hearts that "the cross is coming back." When it does, the Turkish empire will have fallen (see Ousterhout 2020).*

Tensions between the Christians on the borderlands of the Ottoman Empire reached their zenith during World War I, which coincided with the Armenian genocide of 1915. The Ottoman Empire killed more than 1.5 million Armenians, a mostly Christian minority that the Ottomans viewed as a threat to the state (Robinson 2022). At the time of World War I, the Armenian population in the Ottoman Empire numbered approximatcly two million. The number of Armenians living in Turkey today numbers only around 60,000.

To this day, the Turkish government denies that the Ottoman Empire's treatment of the Armenians constitutes a genocide. Turkey has long lobbied the USA and EU nations against using "genocide" to describe what happened. Turkey's ally – Pakistan, the subject of the next chapter – is one of a handful of countries that also denies the Armenian genocide was in fact a genocide. Such spinning on the part of the Turkish government is an impediment to any acceptance of DEUCE with the Armenians and other local Christian populations in Turkey.

Kemalism and the Separation of Religion and State

The Ottoman Empire lasted for 623 years until its defeat at the end of World War I. The Sultan at the time – Mehmed V – was forced by Western powers in 1920 to sign the Treaty of Sèvres.[15] This agreement abolished the Ottoman Empire itself and reduced the Ottoman territory to a small portion of Anatolia.[16] Two years later, following the Turkish War of Independence, Mustafa Kemal – popularly referred to as Atatürk (translated to "Father of the Türks") – abolished the institution of the caliphate and the title of Caliph held by the Ottoman Sultanate since 1517. He used some of the empire's secular leanings and took them much further by creating a secular constitution. His approach to governing, popularly referred to as Kemalism, encompassed a series of sweeping reforms to secularize the Turkish public sphere and to transform Turkey into a "Western nation." He viewed the Ottoman-Islamic tradition as part of an "archaic past" and as "obstacles to progress" (Yavuz 2016: 446).

Kemalism, the founding ideology of the Turkish republic, refers to the revolutionary reforms instituted by Kemal himself. Not only did Kemal institute a separation of religion and state, but he created an outright separation of religion and society in the realms of education, jurisprudence, politics, and the public sphere. He renounced the idea that Turkey had a "pan-Islamic" and "pan-Ottoman" vision for its foreign policy. His own version of Turkish nationalism was driven by six primary principles, which were enshrined in the Republican People's Party (CHP) program of 1931, which was then written into the Turkish constitution in 1937. The six principles were nationalism, populism, republicanism, revolution, secularism, and state-controlled economic development. Secularization was officially introduced by the Constitution of the Republic of Turkey, issued on 29 October 1923. Turkish laicism – or *laiklik* as it is known in the Turkish language – calls for the separation of religion and state, but also for the government's "active neutrality" in ensuring that one religion does not dominate politics. Enshrined in the Turkish Constitution of 1937, *laiklik* is typically described as freedom *from* religion, meaning that political affairs should be devoid of religious influences, a key ingredient in developing the Synthesis of Civilizations. At the same time *laiklik* gives the Turkish government the ability to control the practice of all religions within the borders of Turkey.

When Kemal was proclaimed Atatürk in November 1934, the Turkish Council of Ministers decreed that the Hagia Sophia should be a museum:

Due to its historic significance, the conversion of Ayasofya Mosque, a unique architectural monument of art, located in Istanbul, into a museum will please the entire Eastern world; and its conversion to a museum will cause humanity to gain a new institution of knowledge (see Ousterhout 2020).

In turning the Hagia Sophia into a museum, the Turkish government presented its vision of the New Turkey as a hub for dialogue, education, and understanding. Perhaps most importantly, the government committed itself to secularization and a civic-oriented national identity. To stamp Kemal's point home, a 1928 amendment officially removed the provision declaring, the "Religion of the [Turkish] state is Islam." He replaced Sharia laws with secular laws, and religious courts and schools were officially abolished. However, these changes were coupled with the banning of the dervish Sufi orders and religious symbols in the public domain. These policies were seen by proponents of freedom of religion as restrictive of their human right to freely and openly practice their faith.

The current Turkish Constitution of 1982 mirrored the secular sentiments outlined in the constitution of 1923. Article 24 – titled "Freedom of religion and conscience" – stated, "No one shall be compelled to worship, or to participate in religious rites and ceremonies, or to reveal religious beliefs and convictions, or be blamed or accused because of his religious beliefs and convictions." The Turkish Constitution neither recognizes an official religion nor promotes any, which is helpful in fostering the Synthesis of Civilizations. It defines the country as a secular state that provides freedom of conscience, freedom of conviction, freedom of expression, freedom of religion, and freedom of worship (United States Department of State 2022). The Turkish Constitution also prohibited discrimination on religious grounds and exploitation or abuse of "religion or religious feelings, or things held sacred by religion." This overt recognition of heterogeneity paved the way for the potential application of DEUCE, but the rise of neo-Ottomanism has stunted the embrace of heterogeneity and thus prevented a deeper synthesis from emerging between Christians and Muslims, thus complicating any movement toward DEUCE.

There is no doubt that Kemalism had a pronounced impact on the emergence of the Turkish republic and the everyday lives of citizens in Turkey. The abandonment of Ottoman nationalism in favor of Turkish nationalism, with its overt secular orientation, represented another turn to civic governance and state-building. But only decades after Kemal's death, Turkish society started seeing Kemalist nationalism as a failed ideology. Kemalism was replaced by neo-Ottomanism, which, as noted several times throughout this book, is an impediment to DEUCE and the Synthesis of Civilizations.

Transcending Neo-Ottomanism

Like it has throughout history, present-day Turkey and its neighboring nations are fertile grounds for the Clash of Civilizations, the Dialogue of Civilizations, and the Synthesis of Civilizations. Some scholars say that the country itself does not belong entirely to one civilization or one country, but rather to several civilizations simultaneously (Yavuz 2016: 449). At the present time, Turkey appears to be operating in the realm of the Clash of Civilizations by shunning its heterogeneity in favor of neo-Ottoman nationalism that denigrates – and even excludes – Christian populations within Turkish borders and in the West. Moving forward, Turkish leadership should integrate Christianity into Turkish identity, or else it runs the danger of sliding further into Islamism and away from DEUCE. The leaders of Turkey could start by converting the Hagia Sophia back to an intercivilizational museum for all of humanity.

CHAPTER 4

Honor

Pakistan and Its Neighbors

Honor – or the act of maintaining a moral code of conduct in one's personal actions and treatment of others – is at the center of various controversies surrounding the treatment of Christians in Pakistan. In Urdu, one of the official languages of Pakistan, *izzat* is the term that refers to the esteem, respect, and social standing associated with individuals or entire families. It is often negotiated in Pakistani society through the *biraderi*, the Urdu term for the social network and system based on kinship group or extended family ties. Acting in ways that are embarrassing, immoral, indecent, or socially inappropriate brings shame – or *sharma* in Urdu – upon a person and an entire family. Maintaining honor – the "H" of this chapter – is widely viewed in Pakistani society as paramount to upholding one's personal integrity, but also to the well-being of the Pakistani nation as a whole.

PART ONE – THE CLASH OF CIVILIZATIONS

The following sections outline some key challenges endemic to Pakistan that complicate day-to-day life for Pakistani Christians, Pakistan's cultural identity, and its relationship with other countries. Historically, Pakistan has had a complex, but oftentimes close relationship with the USA and other major Western powers. Despite their commitment to one another in the realms of military cooperation and trade, the relationship has not been particularly fruitful when it comes to relations between Christians and Muslims.

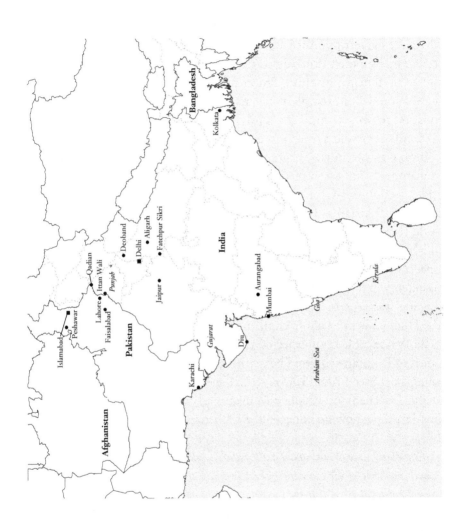

The Case of Asia Bibi

A low point for Christian and Muslim relations in Pakistan occurred in 2010 in Ittan Wali, a village in the Sheikhupura District in the Punjab province of Pakistan. A Pakistani Christian woman named Asia Bibi courted controversy after being surrounded by a group of Muslim women who were harvesting fruit with Bibi. The Muslim women accused her of contaminating their drinking water by drinking from their bucket. They also accused her of insulting Prophet Muhammad, who Muslims believe is a role model of exemplary character and conduct. Due to their reverence and respect for him, any kind of perceived disrespect toward him or his family is viewed as dishonorable by many Pakistani Muslims.

Bibi was eventually charged with committing blasphemy against Muhammad, an act punishable by life imprisonment or even death under section 295-C of the Pakistani Penal Code 1860.[1] Scholars typically view Pakistan as having the most draconian blasphemy laws in the world (Marshall and Shea 2011). These laws have been described as "mad" and "perverse" because they lead to the justification of mob violence, especially against Christians (Rahman 2021). Bibi appealed the charge of blasphemy in front of the High Court of Lahore, but her case was denied, and she was sent to prison (British Broadcasting Corporation 2020a). The High Court of Lahore confirmed her death sentence in 2014.

Bibi's fate took an unexpected turn in 2018, the year that the Supreme Court of Pakistan acquitted her, citing a lack of evidence. In his acquittal ruling, Asif Saeed Khan Khosa – the Chief Justice of the court – referred to the Covenant of Prophet Muhammad with the Monks of Mount Sinai[2] to show how he honored the Christians in his midst:

> *[Christians] were [Muhammad's] allies and he equated ill treatment of Christians with violating God's covenant. [The Christians that Muhammad encountered] were not required to alter their beliefs, they did not have to make any payments and they did not have any obligations. The Charter was of rights without any duties, and it clearly protected the right to property, freedom of religion, freedom of work, and security in person (Supreme Court of Pakistan 2018: 54–5).*

In Bibi's case, a previously maligned Pakistani Christian received an honorable reprieve from the Pakistani court system. However, this kind of reprieve is an exception – and not the rule. Jurisprudence in Pakistan is far from being consistent and it is questionable whether the Pakistani government is committed to furthering DEUCE.

Bibi spent a total of eight years in prison. Her lawyers announced in 2019 that she had arrived in Canada, where two of her daughters were granted asylum. Before her arrival, she had to be kept at a secret location out of fear that extremists would murder her (Graham-Harrison 2020). In Canada, she and her family members were given assumed identities to protect them from death threats.

The Pakistani Supreme Court's verdict was hailed by some as a rejection of the Islamist ideology that is at the core of Pakistan's blasphemy laws, but not all critics were pleased with the verdict (Rahman 2018). One critic claimed that it appealed too much to Islamic values and not enough to the secular values outlined in the Constitution of Pakistan (Darr 2018). Other critics lambasted the ruling because it had no immediate impact on the legal rights or political inclusion of Pakistani Christians (Ahmed 2021a: 274). What is clear, nonetheless, is that Bibi's case highlights the increasing danger posed by Islamism towards Christians and the quest to more fully honor followers of Christianity.

Dishonoring Pakistani Christians

Dishonoring a person or group of people can be done through disrespectful and insulting words, but also through acts of violence, which Pakistan is not immune to. It became the subject of international headlines in September 2013, when two suicide bombers attacked the All-Saints Church in Peshawar, a city located in the Khyber Pakhtunkhwa province in northwest Pakistan. The attack killed 85 Christians.[3] The Tehrik-i-Taliban Pakistan (TTP), an Islamist group known as the Pakistani Taliban, claimed responsibility for the attack, and said it was revenge for American drone strikes in Khyber Pakhtunkhwa, one of the four provinces of Pakistan on the border with Afghanistan. Ten years later – on 16 August 2023 – an attack on an even larger scale occurred in Faisalabad, a city located in the province of Punjab. A mob of Muslim men attacked a Christian settlement after two Christians were accused of committing blasphemy. The mob – armed with sticks and stones – vandalized several churches and destroyed dozens of houses. It also vandalized Christian graves in a community cemetery. Human rights organizations responded to the incident by calling on the Pakistani government to take immediate action to protect Pakistani Christians from further violence (Human Rights Watch 2024). Many Christians of Faisalabad expressed their concern that local and federal authorities would not prosecute the perpetrators, due to entrenched discrimination against Christians in Pakistani society. The aforementioned incidents suggest that the pursuit of DEUCE in these parts of Pakistan is not on the horizon anytime soon.

The dishonoring of Pakistani Christians might remind readers of the treatment – or should I say mistreatment – that immigrants often face when putting down roots in a new country. Christians in the Indian subcontinent, however, are not a new immigrant group. In fact, Christianity has had a long presence there. Thomas (d. 72) – the apostle of Jesus and India's patron saint – established a church in Kerala, a city in the southernmost part of India, around the year 52. Centuries later, Christians from Portugal and Great Britain reshaped the subcontinent's Christian landscape through colonization and imperialism. Toward the end of the fifteenth century, the Portuguese Empire started trading in cities like Goa, on the southwestern coast of today's India, which saw the spread of Roman Catholicism. At the beginning of the eighteenth century, the British arrived in the subcontinent and introduced Protestantism there. By the nineteenth century, British Protestant missionaries accompanied British expansion. Cities like Lahore, the ideological and intellectual center of the Punjab, underwent a strong process of Christianization, which hit the poor and rural "untouchable" communities particularly hard.

Today, the Pakistani Christian population consists mainly of the descendants of lower-caste Hindus who converted to Christianity over the last few centuries.[4] It is the country's largest minority religious population. Pakistani Christians are primarily Protestants, but a significant Catholic population resides in the provinces of Punjab and Sindh. As of 2024, there were approximately three-to-four million Christians living in Pakistan, amounting to slightly less than two percent of the country's population of more than 242 million people.

While it is true that the lived experiences of Pakistani Christians vary based on factors like geographical location and socioeconomic background, it is widely believed that being Christian in Pakistan comes with a certain set of challenges – discrimination, lack of legal recognition, and a lack of community support. These three issues suggest that it is dishonor – rather than honor – which best describes the current state of Pakistani Christians.

Advocates for religious freedom around the world have identified Pakistan as a country of concern. Open Doors, an organization that tackles the international persecution of Christians, ranked Pakistan the seventh most difficult country in the world to live in for Christians. The US State Department, under its International Religious Freedom Act of 1999, also has repeatedly identified Pakistan as a "Country of Particular Concern." These classifications point to a wider global consensus that Pakistani Christians are treated like second-class citizens (Open Doors USA n.d.b.). Many of them find themselves relegated to dirty jobs and grim fates as sewer cleaners and street cleaners.[5] They receive little to no salary, often wait between weeks and months for paychecks, and even find themselves being entirely cheated out of their pay (International Christian Concern 2022b). In terms of their employment background, many jobs in Pakistan are not allocated on merit, but rather by means of *sifarish*, an Urdu term referring to introductions, recommendations, and connections inside the *biraderi* system (Ballard n.d.). Given that most Muslim *biraderis* are far larger, more prosperous, and better connected than their Christian counterparts, young Muslims of upper-caste status are in broad terms far better off in the Pakistani job market than Christians (Ballard n.d.: 5). Pakistani Christians also are occasionally forced to use different drinking fountains from Muslims and have been reported as suffering from the "silent epidemic" of abductions, forced conversions,[6] and forced marriages of Christian girls and women (International Christian Concern 2022b).

Dishonoring Pakistani Christians is antithetical to the spirit of DEUCE, to the Dialogue of Civilizations, and to civic nation building. It is anticipated that Pakistan's adoption of such tenets will be a challenge to the nation in the future. However, the emerging support for religious tolerance by countries like the UAE and Saudi Arabia will continue to put pressure on Pakistan to ameliorate their treatment of Christians.

Islamism and Pakistani National Identity

Pakistanis in general – not just Pakistani Christians – are currently going through a challenging time, even by the standards of Pakistan's reputation as a country prone to coups and military rule. Since gaining its independence in 1947, Pakistan has had three coups.[7] Though it is not a failed state or a rogue state, it has – to varying degrees – tendencies of both (Hussain 2005). Its most recent crisis occurred in April 2022, when Imran Khan – the country's former prime minister – was forced out of office. He claimed that a foreign conspiracy led by the USA was created to topple his government. Critics responded by accusing him of tapping into anti-American sentiments, particularly among the younger Pakistani population (Mogul and Saifi 2022). In the months after his ouster, Khan called for a new *jihad* to rid Pakistan of Western influences, a move that played straight into the Clash of Civilizations. For Christians – a group often associated with the West in Pakistan – his words were worrisome.

Khan's veering to Islamism is paradoxical in light of his biography and lived experiences. He was born into an affluent Pashtun family from Lahore and received an education from the University of Oxford, where he studied economics, philosophy, and politics. He entered Pakistani politics as an outspoken critic of government corruption and the founder of the Pakistan Tehreek-e-Insaf (the Justice Movement or the PTI), a political party, in 1996. Around the 2008 national elections, Khan criticized the Pakistani government's policy of supporting the USA in its war against Al-Qaeda and the Taliban, who had strongholds along the border between Afghanistan and Pakistan. At the same time, he attacked the economic and political "elites" of Pakistan, whom he accused of being "too Westernized" and out of touch with "Islamic norms." Ten years later, in the 2018 elections, the PTI emerged as the largest party in the National Assembly and Khan formed a coalition government. While in office, he lambasted the West for being Islamophobic, but rarely issued statements condemning the persecution of Christians in his own country (Shahid 2022). He also shocked the West when he identified Osama Bin Laden – the former Al-Qaeda leader and mastermind of 9/11 – as a martyr of Islam. The early years of his administration coincided with the USA withholding $300 million in military aid to Pakistan. The Americans claimed that Pakistan was not doing enough to combat terrorism and thus deepening anti-Western sentiment and undermining the faith and trust in the Dialogue of Civilizations and DEUCE.

Khan is quite the enigma in his own right with his public comments, some of which have further complicated any softening in relations between the West and Pakistan. In 2020, Khan personally endorsed *Diriliş: Ertuğrul*, a Turkish historical television series that translates to "Resurrection: Ertuğrul." The series depicts the life of Ertuğrul Bey – the father of Osman I (d. 1326) – the founder of the Ottoman Empire in 1299. The series frames the Ummah as under the control and whims of Western crusaders and pagans, whom the series depicts as "barbaric" and "nefarious" (Yilmaz and Shakil 2021). The Ummah is only saved from defeat because of its strong Islamist ideals, which were embodied in both the higher and lesser forms of *jihad*. He instructed the nation to watch *Diriliş: Ertuğrul* in April 2020, when the series first aired on Pakistan Television Corporation (PTV), the country's state-owned media platform. He remarked about it:

> Turkey has made this film or drama series which they call Resurrection . . . And for the first time, they depict how the Turks progressed and how they conquered half of Europe as one of the greatest forces of time . . . [The] Western culture and civilization has hijacked us to such a great degree that we are unaware of our own past.

In summary, Khan stressed that *Diriliş: Ertuğrul* should be used to educate the aloof and Western-inspired younger Pakistanis about the Muslim world's military triumphs so that Western civilizational hegemony is broken (Yilmaz 2022: 46). The success of the television drama is proof that Islamism[8] is an attractive political ideology among Pakistanis, as it has been for decades, and that education – the second principle of DEUCE – can be misconstrued for indoctrination.

For Khan, the success of the series reaffirmed his goal of making Pakistanis feel part of the Ummah and victims of Western colonialism (Yilmaz 2022: 46). For Erdoğan, his partner in Turkey, its success reaffirmed his country's neo-Ottoman cultural influence in Pakistan and the AKP's soft power in promoting "civilizational Islamism" (Yilmaz 2021). These developments are a distinct challenge to honoring Christians under Islamist governments. DEUCE may be fatally delayed in Pakistan.

PART TWO – THE DIALOGUE OF CIVILIZATIONS

Culture and religion are at the forefront of questions surrounding Pakistani national identity and the country's relationship with other countries in the world. The key to its growth revolves around creating opportunities for DEUCE and improving internal and external collaborations between the West and the Ummah. This will be a challenge for Pakistan, unless they acquiesce to external pressures from more progressive Muslim countries. At stake is Pakistan's reputation as a country committed to honoring freedom of religion, a value enshrined in the Constitution of Pakistan, as many Muslims in the region have done in previous centuries.

Sir Sayyid and Maududi – The Search for a "Modern Muslim Country"

The importance of honoring one's country can be viewed from multiple viewpoints. Honoring one's country could be tied to civic nation building in that citizens are equal under the law and granted democratic rights. It can also be seen from the perspective of honoring one's country by preserving its cultural heritage and traditions. Preservation, in this context, operates in two ways: it reinforces hegemony of the dominant ethnicity and helps to provide unity to the ethnic group by means of customs and common historical experiences. These two perspectives – the civic nation and ethnic nation – are a useful framework in exploring the role that honor played as the harbinger of the Indian nationalist movements in the nineteenth and twentieth centuries, which led to the creation of the Republic of India and the Islamic Republic of Pakistan.

One must explore the history of Western colonization to understand the development of Indian national identity and Pakistani national identity in the twentieth century. In 1455, Alfonso V (d. 1481) – the king of Portugal – received a papal bull[9] authored by Pope Nicholas V (d. 1455), who started Portuguese colonization on the Indian subcontinent. In 1498, Vasco de Gama (d. 1524) – the Portuguese explorer – conquered the island of Diu – on the southern coast of Kathiawar Peninsula – and Goa, a state located on the western coast of India, along the Arabian Sea. The Portuguese established lucrative trading spots in both locations. Simultaneously, the Portuguese colonial authorities funded and supported Catholic missionaries throughout the subcontinent. Some of these missionaries made their way to the court of Akbar the Great – the sixteenth- and seventeenth-century emperor of the Mughal Empire, who I return to later in this chapter.

The British also had a large presence on the Indian subcontinent. In 1600, the East India Company – the English trading company created by Queen Elizabeth I (d. 1603) – arrived in India in the final days of the Mughal Empire. There, the British established trade links and secured profitable goods, such as spices and textiles, and established their head-quarters in Calcutta (modern-day Kolkata), the capital of the Indian state of West Bengal in east India. Over the following decades, the British faced competition from Dutch and Portuguese companies as they all sought to establish dominance over India's lucrative trading routes. In doing so, these Europeans placed profit and power above safeguarding the rights of the indigenous populations.

The East India Company expanded its influence in the eighteenth century by signing treaties with Indian rulers. It gradually became a political power and established colonial rule over the Indian subcontinent. As its territory expanded, it created the British Raj, the period of Britain's colonial rule over the Indian subcontinent from 1858 to 1947,[10] which lasted until India gained independence in 1947. The British Raj arose in 1857, the year of the Indian Mutiny. This widespread, but unsuccessful, rebellion by the indigenous population set the stage for British direct rule over India.

During and immediately following the mutiny, a young Muslim – Sayyid Ahmad Khan (d. 1889) – emerged as a voice of moderation, a bridge between the West and the Ummah, and a historic proponent of the first three principles of DEUCE.

Sir Sayyid, as he is commonly known, was conferred the title of "Sir" in 1888 by Queen Victoria (d. 1901), the former queen of Great Britain and Ireland and the Empress of India, who valued his contributions to education and social reforms on the Indian subcontinent. Sir Sayyid served as a magistrate for the East India Company for almost 30 years before the start of the Indian Mutiny. In 1858, he published *The Cause of the Indian Revolt*, a book which gave a critical account of British colonization on the Indian subcontinent. Although he challenged and questioned the policies and practices of the British, he did not call for their removal from the Indian subcontinent. He called, instead, for equal representation for Hindus and Muslims in the British colonial government. In doing so, he was effectively promoting cross-cultural encounters, higher levels of proficiency in the English language and sciences, and more educational opportunities for Indians, which, for some Muslims, meant that he was honoring the West more than Islam.

Like bridge-builders before him, Sir Sayyid had his fair share of critics. Some accused him of being "too modern" and "too Western." He, however, believed that the West and the Ummah could be in dialogue and coexist with one another. While he favored Western educational systems and the West's promotion of science, Sir Sayyid wanted to integrate them into indigenous South Asian Muslim identities. In other words, he believed that human beings and communities can honor one another by honoring both their own and others' traditions while simultaneously preserving their unique identities.

To engage in the Dialogue of Civilizations, Sir Sayyid founded the Muhammadan Anglo-Oriental College – or simply the Aligarh Muslim University – which is located in Aligarh, a city in the northern Indian state of Uttar Pradesh. Founded in 1875, it set out to replicate the quality of British universities like Cambridge and Oxford without dishonoring Islamic values or Westernizing completely (Aligarh Muslim University n.d.). Its aims were to uplift the Muslim community by means of education and understanding, the second and third principles of DEUCE. The university's overall philosophy was not purely Western or Islamic. It was a combination of both.

Sir Sayyid's legacy in Pakistan today is a bit of a mixed bag (Ahmed 2021b). One academic described him as a modernist who embodied brotherhood, humanity, tolerance, and tranquility (Azeemuddin 2017: 1). Others see him as a dangerous reformer who dishonored the Ummah by making it more Western.

One critic of Sir Sayyid's work in fostering the Dialogue of Civilizations was Abul A'la Maududi (d. 1979), an Islamic theologian and politician. Maududi grew up in Aurangabad, a city in west-central India. As a youth, Maududi asked his father – Ahmed Hassan – to send him to Aligarh Muslim University to follow in the footsteps of Sir Sayyid. Although he distrusted the West, Ahmed reluctantly sent his son to Aligarh. Much to his chagrin, Maududi assimilated by playing cricket – a popular British sport – and wearing Western clothing. This erosion of his cultural identity, and his desire to change, was viewed by some – including his father – as being dishonorable. In the context of DEUCE, Maududi – according to his father – had too much exposure to it.

Afraid for his family's honor, Ahmed withdrew his son from Aligarh and sent him to be educated by the *Ulema* – or Islamic scholars of religious authority in Islam (Paracha 2014). The young Maududi's education in the *Ulema* was rooted in a similar philosophy to Wahhabism, a puritanical interpretation of Islam that you learned about in chapter 1. He graduated as a scholar from Darul Uloom Deoband, a prominent Islamic seminary located in Deoband, Uttar Pradesh, in 1926. Deoband is known for its conservative positions and strict adherence to the Hanafi school of Islamic jurisprudence. He later became active in Indian colonial politics. At first, he advocated for a united India that was both Hindu and Muslim in character, but he concluded that Hindu nationalism was a threat to the well-being of Muslims (Harvard Divinity School n.d.a.). To represent the interests of Muslims, he started the Jamaat-e-Islami, an Islamist political organization which later shaped the emergence of the Islamic Republic of Pakistan in 1947. The party's aims were to Islamize the various sectors of Indian society and to establish a fully Islamic country. Maududi's ideas and writings went on to influence several global movements, including Al-Qaeda, the Muslim Brotherhood, and the Taliban.

The legacies of Sir Sayyid and Maududi offer two competing narratives on the civilizational interplay between the West and the Ummah. Despite their differing philosophies, the notion of honor was paramount in their efforts toward the eventual creation of the Islamic Republic of Pakistan. The quest for honor is the conduit in the quest for some semblance of dialogue and synthesis, which will likely remain a significant impediment for Pakistanis in the twenty-first century.

The *Quaid-i-Azam* and the Politics of Theocracy

One of Maududi's contemporaries – Muhammad Ali Jinnah (d. 1948) – was born in Karachi to a wealthy merchant family. From an early age, he was exposed to English customs and norms, as well as British legal, philosophical, and political texts. As a young man, he enrolled in the Christian Mission School in Karachi and later moved to London.[11] In that city, he joined Graham's Shipping and Trading, a company that did business with his father, a prosperous Muslim merchant from Karachi. His educational background and professional experiences gave him an advantage in furthering the Dialogue of Civilizations in his hometown and beyond. Jinnah was a visionary for his time and played a big part in establishing the foundation of Pakistan.

Not long after moving to London, Jinnah left his family's business to join Lincoln's Inn, one of the four Inns of Court, the professional associations for lawyers in the English legal system. Jinnah is said to have admired it for a mural in the building's main dining hall, which honored Prophet Muhammad as one of the most influential lawgivers in history (Ahmed 1997). When he returned to Karachi in 1896, he applied his Western education to the Indian independence movement by joining the Indian National Congress, one of the major political parties during the Indian independence movement. He then served in Delhi as the representative of Mumbai (formerly Bombay) to the Legislative Council of India (Ahmed 1997). Curiously, Jinnah resisted joining the Muslim League – the political party that played a significant role in the creation of Pakistan – until 1913, seven years after its founding. He was then elected in 1916 as president of the Lucknow Session of the Muslim League, which played a crucial role in shaping the course of Indian politics.

While serving in these political roles, Jinnah maintained his upper-class English professional lifestyle. His identity is said to have combined "Anglo-Indian" traits with Muslim Indian traits. In the early 1930s, he had a large house in Hampstead, an affluent London neighborhood favored by academics, artists, and media figures. He even had an English chauffeur who drove his Bentley and an English staff to serve him (Ahmed 1997). Like Sir Sayyid, he embraced elements of British culture even as his opponents accused him of being too Westernized.

By 1940, Jinnah was presiding over the Muslim League, which passed the Lahore Resolution – a call for a new and separate Muslim homeland on the Indian subcontinent. Its leaders feared that Muslims would be second-class citizens in a united India dominated by Hindus. He and his colleagues envisioned a new country, which they called Pakistan – meaning "Land of the Pure" – to secure the rights of Muslims while still honoring religious diversity within its citizenry. Jinnah laid out his vision for Pakistan in his first speech to the new nation in 1947:

[Pakistanis] may belong to any religion or caste or creed. That has nothing to do with the business of the state. We are starting with this fundamental principle that we are all citizens and equal citizens of the state. We should keep that in front of us as our ideal and you will find that in the course of time Hindus will cease to be Hindus and Muslims will cease to be Muslims, not in the religious sense because that is the personal faith of each individual, but in the political sense, as citizens of the State.

Here, Jinnah advocated for a "civic synthesis," which you read about in chapter 2. Like Roger II, the Sicilian king, Jinnah committed himself to the idea of building a multicultural and multi-religious identity. For his efforts, Pakistanis refer to him as the *Quaid-i-Azam*, the Urdu term which translates to "Great Leader."

Despite what appears to be his preference for secularization, some scholars debate whether Jinnah advocated for Islamization. They point to a speech he made to Americans, when he said that Pakistan was committed to defending democracy and secularism:

The constitution of Pakistan has yet to be framed by [the] Pakistan Constituent Assembly. I do not know what the ultimate shape of this constitution is going to be, but I am sure that it will be of a democratic type, embodying the essential principles of Islam. Today, they are as applicable in actual life as they were 1,300 years ago. Islam and its idealism have taught us democracy. It has taught [the] equality of man, justice, and fair play to everybody. We are the inheritors of these glorious traditions and are fully alive to our responsibilities and obligations as framers of the future constitution of Pakistan (Sherwani 2005: 463).

The Pakistani government ratified its constitution on 23 March 1956, the year of the formal establishment of the Islamic Republic of Pakistan as a parliamentary democracy.[12] While the original Pakistani constitution does not explicitly refer to Pakistan as a "Muslim nation," it does identify it as an "Islamic republic" (Rahman 2021). It clearly stated that the Qur'an and the Sunnah inform the nation's laws. Yet, it also offered democratic rights, although the guarantee of those rights is a matter of controversy.

Despite promoting civic nationalism at times, Jinnah also invited Maududi to deliver a series of lectures on the foundations of Islamic civilization and forming an Islamic state (Qazi 2017). These lectures, which were broadcast from official state-run radio channels, called for the Islamization of Pakistan's economy, politics, and society. Jinnah also championed the Islamization of South Asia in November 1942 while addressing students at Aligarh Muslim University. He told them, "Let me live according to my history in the light of Islam, my tradition, culture, and language, and you do the same in your zones [of activity]" (Ahmad 1960: 458–9). In another speech two years earlier, he said that "Pakistan does not mean just independence and sovereignty. It means [an] Islamic ideology that we have to safeguard; it has been conveyed to us as a valuable gift and a treasure [to honor]" (Ahmad 1960: 175). Given the complexities related to Jinnah's vision and its impact on the foundation of Pakistan, it is no wonder that any interfaith initiatives driven by DEUCE are so challenging for Pakistanis.

Jinnah's vision of an "Islamic democracy" slowly waned upon his passing in 1948. Pakistan started to gradually move closer to a theocracy during the rule of Muhammad Zia Ul-Haq (d. 1988), the Four Star general and sixth prime minister of Pakistan. Ul-Haq became the Pakistani president following a coup d'état in 1977. Upon seizing the Pakistani government, he declared martial law and imprisoned Zulfikar Ali Bhutto (d. 1979), the president of Pakistan.[13] Ul-Haq's rule coincided with the rising influence of the *Ulema* (the Islamic clergy) and Islamist parties, especially the Jamaat-e-Islami, which Maududi founded. The number of madrassas, or Islamic schools, also increased under Ul-Haq's reign. Most of the madrassas were either directly or indirectly affiliated with Deobandism. Where one finds Deobandism, one does not typically find DEUCE. One would also be hard pressed to find an honorable treatment of Christians within societies governed by theocratic leanings.

Ul-Haq amended the Pakistani constitution in 1980 to establish the Federal Sharia Court, a special Islamic institution charged with deciding whether or not a Pakistani law was "repugnant to the provisions of Islam" (Darr 2018). Each Pakistani court was given a special "Sharia branch" to judge legal cases according to the Qur'an and the Sunnah. The ultimate goal of his system was to prevent the Pakistani parliament from enacting laws that were deemed "un-Islamic," or those that dishonored the sanctity of Islam.

It is no surprise, then, that Ul-Haq's time in office has been described as a period of intensified Shariaization. Freedom of the press and freedom of speech were weakened when his government amended the Pakistani Penal Code and the Criminal Procedural Code in 1980, 1982, 1984, and 1986. Ordinance 20, which was adopted in 1984, included amendments to Sections 295 and 298, which are viewed as enabling the abuse and targeting of Christians and other religious minorities.[14]

As you learned about in the case of Asia Bibi, the Pakistani penal code has been the subject of controversy and criticism by international bodies and Western governments. They appear to violate Article Nineteen of the United Nations Universal Declaration of Human Rights, which reads, "Everyone has the right to freedom of opinion and expression; this right includes freedom to hold opinions without interference and to seek, receive, and impart information and ideas through any media and regardless of frontiers." Similarly, the Commission on International Religious Freedom (USCIRF) of the USA claims that blasphemy laws are detrimental to freedom of religion because of the human right to embrace a full range of thoughts and beliefs and the right to speak or write about them publicly. Ul-Haq's clampdown on the human rights of Pakistani Christians contributed to the Clash of Civilizations. It also stifled honor and the ability to participate in DEUCE.

Some Pakistanis today hail Ul-Haq as a "hero" who defended the Ummah by protecting the honor of Prophet Muhammad. Other Pakistanis denounce him as a "villain" who eroded the country's original secular vision. Accordingly, the quest for honor in the Pakistani context can be perceived both as a positive and negative. As of 2024, Pakistan is neither theocratic nor democratic, which is quite the juxtaposition. It is somewhere in-between as it tries to honor Christianity and Islam at the same time.

"Love For All, Hatred For None" – The Ahmadiyya Muslim Community

When I was a PhD student at Trinity College Dublin in 2013, I read a newly published book on the state of freedom of religion in Pakistan. The book details the author's familial experiences with persecution and violence. Given the details and stories covered on previous pages, one might think that the author of the book is a Christian. The author, however, is Qasim Rashid – an Ahmadi Muslim and an American citizen.

The title of Rashid's book – *The Wrong Kind of Muslim – An Untold Story of Persecution and Perseverance* – reminds us of the sensitive debates surrounding Muslim identity.

Ahmadi Muslims believe in the 1889 appearance of Mirza Ghulam Ahmad (d. 1908), an Indian Muslim born in Qadian, a village in the Gurdaspur District of Punjab. He claimed the title of the "Promised Messiah" – or the metaphorical second coming of Jesus and the Mahdi – whose advent was foretold by Prophet Muhammad (Al-Islam n.d.). Ahmadi Muslims – his followers – believe that God sent him to condemn bloodshed, end religious wars, restore justice, and bring peace to the world (Al-Islam n.d.). It is the only Islamic organization worldwide to endorse the separation of mosque and state. My own experiences with them have convinced me that they are some of the world's torchbearers for the DEUCE model.

Part of the persecution of Ahmadi Muslims in Pakistan and around the Ummah is tied to their views on prophethood. Many Muslims perceive their view that Ahmad was the Promised Messiah as blasphemous and "un-Islamic." Controversy also surrounds Ahmadi Muslims on whether they view Prophet Muhammad as the *Khatam-un-Nabiyyin* (Seal of the Prophets), or the last in a line of Abrahamic prophets like Abraham, Moses, and Jesus. Ahmadiyya Islam, however, recognizes Ahmad as a subordinate to Muhammad and a non-law-bearing prophet. For some Muslims, these are dishonorable and un-Islamic positions.

Seeking education – the second layer of DEUCE – was also paramount to Ahmad's worldly mission. He called on Muslims to engage in *jihad bil qalam* – the "*jihad* by the pen" – to dispel allegations and misinformation about Islam (Considine 2019: 15). He penned over 80 books and tens of thousands of letters, delivered hundreds of lectures, and engaged in scores of public debates (Al-Islam n.d.). He was an avid proponent of interfaith dialogue and recognized the important teachings of Abraham, Buddha, Confucius, Guru Nanak, Jesus, Krishna, Lao Tzu, Moses, and Zoroaster. Honoring leaders from other faith traditions helps to foster cooperation and understanding between civilizations. It also helps to promote education, strengthen social cohesion, and advance peace.

The plight of Ahmadi Muslims in Pakistan might surprise readers given that they played a significant role in the formative years of the Islamic Republic of Pakistan.[15] Despite their nationalist efforts, large-scale anti-

Ahmadi riots broke out in Lahore in 1953. In later years, the tombstone of Dr. Abdus Salam (d. 1996), an Ahmadi Muslim, was desecrated by vandals who blotted out the reference to his Muslim faith. Dr. Salam, it should be noted, is the first Muslim in history to win the Nobel Prize, which was awarded to him in 1979.

It is unfortunate that Dr. Salam's faith is the reason why he is not celebrated in Pakistan (Thames 2021). Textbooks do not honor him or tell his impressive story. Salam was a self-taught math genius who went to Oxford University to undertake research on physics. One would think that any country would be proud to honor such a distinguished citizen of their country.

Today, Ahmadi Muslims are similar to Pakistani Christians in that they face threats from the authorities and extremist groups. Ahmadi Muslims are banned from selling Ahmadiyya religious literature, referring to their places of worship as mosques, or holding national identification cards, like driver's licenses and passports (United States Department of State 2021). They are banned from representation on the National Commission for Minorities within the Ministry of Religious Affairs (United States Department of State 2021). They are also not allowed by law to use the standard "Islamic greeting" of *as-salamalaikum*, or "peace be with you." According to the Pakistani Constitution and the Pakistani Penal Code, Ahmadi Muslims are forbidden to identify themselves as "Muslims" or assert that they are rightful adherents to the Islamic faith. As per Section 298-C of the penal code:

> *Any person of the Qadiani Group or the Lahori Group (who call themselves "Ahmadis" or by any other name), who directly or indirectly, poses as a Muslim, or calls, or refers to, his faith as Islam, or preaches or propagates his faith, or invites others to accept his faith, by words, either spoken or written, or by visible representations, or in any manner whatsoever outrages the religious feelings of Muslims shall be punished with imprisonment of either description for a term which may extend to three years and shall also be liable to fine.*

Pakistan's blasphemy laws, in short, bans Ahmadi Muslims from identifying as Muslims, using Islamic terminology in their speech, proselytizing or preaching Islam, or insulting the religious feelings of Muslims (United States Department of State 2021: 5). There is said to be an entire "cottage industry" that castigates them, encourages boycotts of their business, excludes them from society, and even calls for violence against them (Thames 2021). These are the dishonorable norms in Pakistan despite the progressive tenets of Ahmadiyya Islam.

While the future for Ahmadi Muslims in Pakistan looks bleak, the community is flourishing around the world. The Ahmadi population worldwide spans over 200 nations with membership exceeding tens of millions (Al-Islam n.d.). It is the world's largest Islamic community under one spiritual leader – His Holiness Mirza Masroor Ahmad – the fifth caliph of the Ahmadiyya global community who currently resides in the UK. Under his leadership, the Ahmadiyya Muslim Community has built over 16,000 mosques, 600 schools, and 30 hospitals around the world (Al-Islam n.d.).

The official motto of the Ahmadiyya Muslim Community – "Love for All, Hatred for None" – was coined by Hazrat Mirza Nasir Ahmad (d. 1982), the third spiritual leader of the Ahmadiyya Muslim community. Mirza Masroor Ahmad explained the significance of the motto in a sermon delivered on 9 May 2014:

> [Ahmadis] use this slogan (Love for All, Hatred for None) to make it clear to the world that Islam teaches love, peace, and kindness and it is not correct to associate cruelty and viciousness with the faith of Islam. We employ this slogan to signify that we wish to live together by breaking down walls of hatred. When we serve humanity in any way at all or when we disseminate the message of Islam we do so because we have love for every person in the world and we wish to remove hatred from each heart and instead sow the seeds of love. We do so because this is what our master, the Holy Prophet [Muhammad] (peace and blessings of Allah be on him) taught us (True Islam 2021).

My experiences over the years have taught me that Mirza Masroor Ahmad lives up to the high ideals of Ahmadiyya Islam. I first met him in 2018 when he visited Houston, Texas. Our private discussion touched on the importance of knowledge, interfaith dialogue, and pluralism in the West. I met him again in 2022 in Zion, Illinois, for the inauguration of an Ahmadi Muslim mosque (Ali 2022). This more private discussion was significantly longer than our previous one in Houston. For me, it was a refreshing experience despite all the negative commentary about

Ahmadi Muslims. It remains puzzling to me why many Muslims have hatred toward them. Ironically, they are flourishing in the West and are doing their part to enact DEUCE.

The Ahmadiyya Muslim Community USA also invited me to speak at their annual Jalsa convention in Harrisburg, Pennsylvania, in 2016. At one point in my speech, I shared my affinity for "Love for All, Hatred for None," which was followed by a rupture of loud applause and thousands of smiles among attendees. My message was one of pluralism and peace. These values, ultimately, are at the heart of the Ahmadiyya Muslim community. Paradoxically, these values could help Pakistan bring more honor to Pakistani communities. However, without sufficient openness to DEUCE, the struggle for religious equality in Pakistan will remain precarious.

PART THREE – THE SYNTHESIS OF CIVILIZATIONS

The first two components of DEUCE – dialogue and education – represent the initial stages of the quest toward the Synthesis of Civilizations. The quest to actualize the synthesis is just as important as the ultimate attainment of that synthesis. In this section, I explore the quest of one Muslim leader and make the important distinction between religious syncretism and civic synthesis.

"Peace With All" at Akbar the Great's Court

The Letter of Paul to the Romans – a work by Saint Paul – is the longest and most significant of Saint Paul's writings in the New Testament. In the letter, he encouraged people to support and love one another and to repay evil with good. He specifically wrote about the importance of the "Golden Rule" – or the command of treating others how one wishes to be treated:

> If someone has done you wrong, do not repay him with a wrong. Try to do what everyone considers to be good. Do everything possible on your part to live in peace with everybody. Never take revenge, my friends, but instead let God's anger do it. For the scripture says, "I will take revenge, I will pay back, says the Lord." Instead, as the scripture says, "If your enemies are hungry, feed them; if they are thirsty, give

them a drink; for by doing this you will make them burn with shame." Do not let
evil defeat you; instead, conquer evil with good (Romans 12:17–21).

Paul's words remind me of the life and legacy of Jalal Ud-Din Muhammad Akbar (d. 1605) – popularly known as Akbar the Great – the founding emperor of the Mughal Empire (1526–1858), which encompassed present-day India, Pakistan, and parts of Bangladesh. He is known for developing the *Sulh-i-kul,* a philosophy translating to "universal peace" or "peace with all." Sixteenth-century texts describe him as a man who found pleasure in philosophical and religious deliberations, with a tendency toward mysticism (Kuczkiewicz-Fraś 2011: 76–7). According to one scholar of the Mughal Empire, he was by far the most "pluralist" of the Mughal rulers (Varadarajan 2022). Some scholars have even claimed that he is one of the most "pluralist" oriented rulers in history (Varadarajan 2022).

Akbar the Great's vision for Mughal society was rooted in moderation and tolerance. He was driven by a desire to honor all Mughal subjects with equal status and rights and to limit the influence of the *Ulema* in his court (Kuczkiewicz-Fraś 2011: 77). His reign witnessed the abolition of the *jizya* (the poll tax levied on non-Muslims), the lifting of restrictions on erecting Hindu temples and Christian churches, and the appointing of Christians within Akbar the Great's administration.[16]

In 1569, Akbar founded a new capital city – Fatehpur Sikri – which is located near Agra in present-day Uttar Pradesh. On that site, he built the Buland Darwaza – also known as the Gate of Magnificence or the Door of Victory – after a successful military campaign in Gujarat. The arch of the building includes an inscription that reads, "Jesus, on whom be peace, has said: 'The world is a bridge. Pass over it. But build no house upon it'" (Ahmed 2003: 27–8). While the quote is actually attributed to Akbar the Great rather than Jesus, it nevertheless points to a metaphorical vision of life being like a bridge – a passage across to different times, spaces, and even groups of people.

Building bridges was a primary objective in Akbar the Great's pursuit of civilizational excellence. In the late 1570s, he sent a letter to Portuguese Jesuit missionaries living in Goa requesting that they send learned priests to bring the Bible to the Mughals so they could educate themselves on Christianity (Monserrate 1922: 2). He stated in the letter:

Let the priests understand that I shall receive them with all possible kindness and honor. Their arrival will be a great delight to me – and when I have learnt what I long to know about the law and its perfection and salvation it offers, they shall be allowed to return as soon as they like. I shall send them back again dignified with very many honors and gifts. Let them have no fear in coming. For I take them under my own protection and guarantee (Monserrate 1922: 2).

The Portuguese authorities accepted Akbar the Great's invitation. Father Rodolfo Acquaviva (d. 1583), the son of the Duke of Atri in the Abruzzo region of Italy, served as the head of the mission (Rochford n.d.). Father Antonia Monserrate (d. 1600), Acquaviva's deputy and the chronicler of their journey, joined him. They both arrived in Fatehpur Sikri around 1580. Akbar the Great welcomed them to his court alongside his two sons – Jahangir and Murad – who both wore Portuguese hats and scarlet cloaks with golden fastenings to honor their Christian guests.

Upon their arrival to the Mughal court, the Christians were offered a considerable amount of gold, but they rejected the gift because of their Christian vow of poverty (Kuczkiewicz-Fraś 2011: 81). Acquaviva and Monserrate, in turn, offered Akbar the Great a copy of *Biblia Regia*, a Bible commissioned by Philip II (d. 1598), the king of Spain.[17] Akbar the Great received the Bible and treated it with reverence, taking it into his hand and kissing it, after which he placed it on his head (Du Jarric 2004: 10). He understood that honoring other religious traditions contributes to inclusivity and tolerance. He also understood that embracing religious diversity can strengthen social cohesion.

What did Acquaviva and Monserrate think about their experiences in the Mughal court of Akbar the Great? One scholar put it this way: "There is no doubt that the [Christian] missionaries were amazed by the tolerance of the Mughal ruler – they were coming, after all, from Europe, dominated at that time by the raging Inquisition" (Kuczkiewicz-Fraś 2011: 82). Even though the priests took issue with Akbar's tendency to veer toward religious syncretism, there is little doubt that they were honored by his hospitality and his court's willingness to engage in dialogue, education, and understanding, the first three stages of DEUCE.

Similarly, what did Akbar the Great think about his experiences with Christian priests? He later entrusted Jahangir, his son, to the Christians to learn the Portuguese language and to be raised in the Catholic faith.

Jahangir is said to have covered the walls of his bedroom with frescoes of Christian saints, a custom that spread among other notables in the Mughal Empire. Numerous murals featuring Jesus and Mary, as well as other Catholic saints, were painted on the walls of Mughal mausoleums and palaces around this time (Kuczkiewicz-Fraś 2011: 87). Moreover, Murad – Akbar the Great's eldest son – was entrusted to Monserrate to learn the Portuguese language and principles of Christian ethics (Monserrate 1922: 52). The fact that Jahangir and Murad were raised in the Christian tradition suggests that Akbar the Great and the priests had deeply meaningful experiences, which often evoke the feeling of being honored.

Acquaviva and Monserrate's three-year mission to Fatehpur Sikri ended in 1583, but Christian missions carried on over the next three centuries. Christians continued studying astronomy and geography in the observatories of Delhi and Jaipur, where they produced research and provided a steady supply of books, often richly illustrated with European paintings (Kuczkiewicz-Fraś 2011: 86–7). Christian priests also published books, one of which – *Mesihname*, or "Book of Jesus" – was published in 1602. It focused on the similarities between Hinduism, Islam, and Sufism. Another book, the *Hamratu'l Falasife* – "The Fruit of Philosophy" – was published in 1603 by a Muslim named Abdulsattar with the help of Jeronimo Xavier, a relative of Francis Xavier (d. 1552), the Spanish missionary (Bulut 2022a). These events are all illustrative of attempts to achieve the Synthesis of Civilizations, which is not possible without engaging in DEUCE.

The Christian-Muslim encounter at Akbar the Great's court included other interfaith conversations, some of which were critical, and even tense. The Christians broke the etiquette of the Mughal court by "blaspheming" against Islam and Muhammad, which led to discontent and even hostility among the courtiers of the Mughal court (Kuczkiewicz-Fraś 2011: 83). The Christian missionaries, on the other hand, were frustrated that Akbar the Great leaned more toward religious syncretism than the monotheism found in Christianity and Islam (Kuczkiewicz-Fraś 2011: 84). The Christians showed that they were willing to engage in dialogue, but they were not interested in "blending" their faith or theology with that of Akbar the Great. The Mughal emperor, on the contrary, believed that narrow-minded interpretations of religion were shallow forms of worship which dishonored the transcendent nature of God.

Religious Syncretism and the House of Worship

To achieve his goals as the ruler of the Mughal Empire, Akbar the Great created – in addition to the *Sulh-i-kul* – an unorthodox way of thinking about religion as a whole (Kuczkiewicz-Fraś 2011: 76–7). While in power, he constructed the *Ibidat Khana* – or House of Worship in English – in Fatehpur Sikri. Originally, he hoped it would serve as a space for the *Ulema* to discuss Islamic law. However, he quickly realized that the *Ulema* were not engaging in civil discourse or seeing eye-to-eye on issues pertaining to religion. Out of frustration, he turned the prayer chamber into a hall of philosophical debates for all people and all levels of society – not just Muslim scholars. He even personally invited a diverse group of representatives to engage in DEUCE.

Before diving deeper into this matter, let us pause to distinguish civic synthesis and religious syncretism. In the examples above, he clearly advocated for a civic-oriented culture where DEUCE was welcomed as a tool to increase social harmony. They do not point to blending or combining different religious beliefs, practices, or traditions in a harmonized or unified system. This is a key part of this book's thesis – that civic synthesis at the communal and social level is different from religious syncretism, or the doctrinal fusion of faiths.

By 1582, Akbar had established what some scholars have referred to as a "new religion." He called it the *Din-i Ilahi*, which translates to the "Divine Faith" or the "Religion of God." The *Din-i Ilahi* has been described as an "elite eclectic religious movement" and "personality cult," which never numbered more than 19 adherents (Britannica n.d.a.). The religion had no priestly hierarchy or sacred scriptures, but its adherents did adhere to the saying *Allahu Akbar*, or "God is most Great." Members were handpicked by Akbar the Great himself. It was generally regarded by his contemporaries as *biddah*, the Arabic term referring to an innovation or heretical doctrine that opposed the fundamental tenets of Islam.

Accusations that Akbar the Great was a "heretic" continue into the current time. Opposition to his views on religious syncretism primarily come from Wahhabi scholars. These scholars identify him as a *kafir*, an Arabic word meaning "disbeliever," because he fused Western philosophy and Islamic principles. Critics also see Akbar the Great as an "enabler" of Western cultural imperialism (Tomlinson 2012). One prominent academic journal referred to the *Din-i Ilahi* as a heretical movement in South Asian Islam (Ahmad 2012). Another critic said that the Divine Faith was born from the "dangerous" and "twisted ideology" of Christian priests, who followed *philosophia perennis*, or perennialism (Bulut 2022a). According to Agostino Steucho (d. 1549), a perennialist is someone who believes that all world religions are part of some "ancient wisdom" (see Schmitt 1966). Perennialists might affirm the unity of all religions without dishonoring their own spiritual uniqueness (Bano et al. 2023: 3).

Regarding perennialism, my own experiences suggest that there is a wider distrust of the concept among religious supremacists, some of whom condemn me as an "enemy" of Christianity and Islam because, they claim, I am dishonoring God by creating a new religion, which they have dubbed "Abrahamism," a term that I have highlighted several times in this book.

The Future of Honor in Pakistan

Pakistanis have plenty of historical examples to use for inspiration in undertaking the noble endeavor of honoring its citizens. The likes of Sir Sayyid, Jinnah, and Akbar the Great all provide direction in successfully balancing Western and Islamic principles. Pakistan does not have to choose either the West or the Ummah. Rather, it can honor both civilizations, as these role models did in their respective lives.

The West also plays a significant role in Pakistan's future. Shadowy wars and dishonorable tactics of violence will only add mistrust between Westerners and Pakistanis. While the West should avoid foreign misadventures that give credence to the Clash of Civilizations, it should also push back, when necessary, against the idea that Western values are the root of all of Pakistan's problems. Pakistanis must engage in introspection as much as they do in finger-pointing at foreign adversaries.

Another challenge for Pakistan in the future is resisting the ability of Islamists to push groups like Christians even further into second-class citizenship status. The Islamization of Pakistan, or any country for that matter, will always raise the concern of how, if at all, Christians fit into the social fabric of the nation. If Pakistan were to continue with the Islamization process, then Pakistanis need to rethink what it means to be an "Islamist." Will it mean draconian blasphemy laws that target Christians, or will it be similar to the Covenant of the Prophet Muhammad with the monks of Mount Sinai? Will it be shame, or will it be honor? As a Christian and humanist, I hope it is the latter.

CHAPTER 5

Harmony
West Africa and Egypt

As a native of Boston, Massachusetts, I became a fan at an early age of the Boston Celtics, the winningest franchise in the history of the National Basketball Association (NBA), the American professional basketball league. In the early-to-mid 1990s, I went to countless games with my family members. The Celtics, unfortunately, were not fielding particularly good teams at the time, having fallen on challenging times. The last time they had won the championship was in 1986, when I was only a one-year-old. It was not until the 2007–2008 season that the Celtics returned to their former glory days, having won the championship in that year.

The 2007–2008 Celtics team had a motto – *Ubuntu*. The origin of the idea was at the behest of Doc Rivers, the coach of the Celtics at the time. *Ubuntu* is an African philosophical word that translates to "I am because we are" (Boston Celtics History n.d.). Desmond Tutu (d. 2021), the former Anglican archbishop of Cape Town, said the following about it:

> *In my culture and tradition the highest praise that can be given to someone is "Yu, u nobuntu," an acknowledgement that he or she has this wonderful quality – Ubuntu. It is a reference to their actions toward their fellow human beings, it has to do with how they regard people and how they see themselves within their intimate relationships, their familial relationships, and within the broader community. Ubuntu addresses a central tenet of African philosophy – the essence of what it is to be human.*
>
> *The definition of [Ubuntu] has two parts. The first is that the person is friendly, hospitable, generous, gentle, caring, and compassionate. In other words, someone who will use their strengths on behalf of others – the weak and the poor and the ill – and not take advantage of anyone. This person treats others as he or she would be treated. And because of this they express the second part of the concept, which*

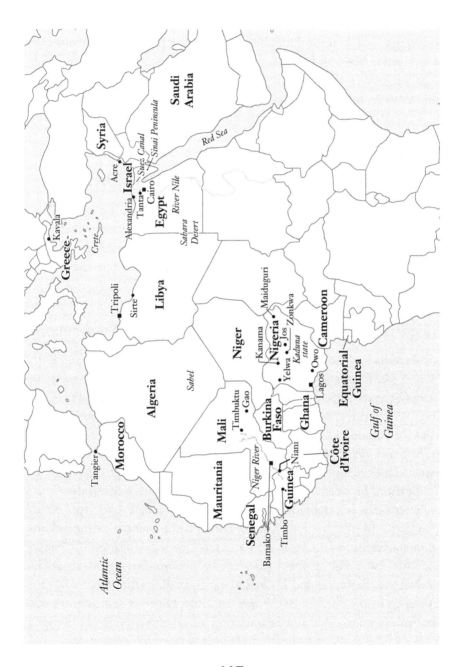

concerns openness, larger heartedness. They share their worth. In doing so my humanity is recognized and becomes inextricably bound to theirs (Tutu 2007: 3).

Ubuntu – or, as I have condensed it to, harmony – is a useful concept in resolving conflicts around the African continent, particularly in countries like Nigeria, Mali, and Egypt, where Christians and Muslims are struggling for power and searching for cooperation, interdependency, and solidarity. In those countries, *Ubuntu* is desperately needed, especially in West Africa, as countries contemplate their potential interest in the pursuit of DEUCE.

PART ONE – THE CLASH OF CIVILIZATIONS

The country of Nigeria imposes many challenges to the concept of *Ubuntu*. Nigeria has been referred to as the "eye of the storm" when it comes to Christian persecution in the world. To understand the lived experiences of Nigerian Christians, one must be educated on the history of Islam in West Africa.

Nigeria – The Eye of the Storm of Christian Persecution

Islam's roots in West Africa stretch back to the ninth century, when North African Muslims made contact with the Sahel (meaning the "border" in Arabic), the transitional region located between the Sahara Desert in the north and the savanna woodland regions in the south. The Sahel stretches from the Atlantic Ocean to the Red Sea. While it is not entirely located in the Sahel region, Nigeria – the most populous country in Africa – has part of its territory on the Sahel borderland, a hotspot in the Clash of Civilizations between Nigerian Christians and Nigerian Muslims.

Present-day interreligious conflicts in Nigeria date back to Usman Dan Fodio (d. 1817), a Fulani herdsman and the founder of the Sokoto caliphate.[1] Between the years 1804 and 1808, he waged war on the Hausa State of Gobir and annexed parts of the present-day region of northern Nigeria (Barkindo and Dyikuk 2022: 1). Fodio's army eventually met resistance in the Middle Belt States and into Nigeria's southern region. His rule is known for the Islamization of northern Nigeria. Tensions between Christians and Muslim have been fermenting ever since.

118

Fodio, as noted, was a Fulani herder, a transnational group with a significant population in West African countries like Nigeria, Niger, Mali, Guinea, and Senegal. The Fulani adopted Islam as their official religion in the early eleventh century. In the sixteenth century, they participated in local "holy wars" and established themselves as a powerful military force in the region. Since then, Fulani Muslims have been targeting Christian farming communities on the borderlands of northern Nigeria and southern Nigeria. Their raids are driven by several factors including competition with Christians over scarce resources and a desire to Islamize the area. Nuhu Bitrus, a Christian rights activist in Jos – the capital of Plateau State in the central part of the country – claimed that Fulani Muslims are never prosecuted for the atrocities they commit because Muhammadu Buhari, the former Nigerian president, was a Fulani Muslim himself. His administration posed many challenges for Christians and the promotion of interreligious harmony, as well as DEUCE.

One of those challenges, Boko Haram – the terrorist group whose name translates to "Western education is forbidden" in the Hausa language – is known for attacking Nigerian Christians. Since the late 1990s, it has displaced millions and killed thousands of Nigerians – both Christians and Muslims – primarily in the northeastern region of the country. In the early 2000s, the group clashed with the police in Maiduguri – the capital of Borno State – and indiscriminately killed Christians and Muslims. There, they built a mosque and named it after Ibn Taymiyyah (d. 1328), an Islamic theologian who influenced the development of Wahhabism, the puritanical form of Islam that you read about in chapter 1. By 2004, Boko Haram moved its headquarters to Kanama, a village in Yobe State – near the border with Niger, the northern neighbor of Nigeria. In that location, it set up a "state within a state" with its own government and military force that enforced Wahhabism, the antithesis of *Ubuntu*.

While Boko Haram's state in Maiduguri existed for only a few years, it returned to the city in the middle of 2010 and unleashed a campaign of assassinations in neighboring Borno State and Yobe State. On Christmas Eve in 2010, it detonated bombs near churches in markets in two districts of Jos, Plateau State. Dozens of Christians were killed in the bombings (Walker 2012: 5). On Christmas Day the following year, the group once again detonated bombs in three states – Niger, Plateau, and Yobe – which, combined, killed 45 people (Walker 2012: 6). It also conducted a

2011 attack by planting a car bomb at the UN headquarters in Abuja, the Nigerian capital, located in the central part of the country. That bomb killed at least 23 people and injured more than 80 (Director of National Intelligence n.d.). Four years later, in March 2015, Boko Haram pledged allegiance to the Islamic State in Iraq and the Levant (ISIL) and started publicly using the name "ISIL–West Africa Province." The US State Department responded in November 2014 by classifying Boko Haram as a "Foreign Terrorist Organization" (Director of National Intelligence n.d.).

It is no surprise that countless international organizations monitoring the well-being of Christians have identified Nigeria as "the eye of the storm" for Christian persecution in the world (Barkindo and Dyikuk 2022: 1). The number of deadly attacks – which occur primarily in the northern territories and the Middle Belt States – points to severe persecution. Between 2009 and 2023, at least 52,250 Nigerian Christians were killed in "religiously motivated violence" (see Chimtom 2023b). The violence has been particularly bad in recent years. Between October 2020 and September 2021 alone, approximately 4,303 Christians were killed in jihadist-related contexts (see Warren 2022).

Violence against Nigerian Christians hit a high point in June 2022, when Saint Francis Xavier Catholic church – in Owo, Ondo State – was attacked by Muslims during Mass on Pentecost.[2] An estimated 70 Christians died and dozens more were injured (Morning Star News and Casper 2022). A few weeks after the Saint Francis Xavier Church massacre, Fulani Muslims attacked two more churches – Maranatha Baptist Church and Saint Moses Catholic Church – in Kaduna, a state in northwest Nigeria (International Christian Concern 2022a).

And yet, Joe Biden – the 45th president of the USA – removed Nigeria from its November 2021 list of "Countries of Particular Concern" (CPC). Critics of his decision, like the United States Commission on International Religious Freedom (USCIRF) – an independent federal government commission[3] – said that it was "appalled" at the failure to designate Nigeria as a CPC. Other critics of President Biden described his soft approach on Nigeria as a "political move" to appease Nigeria, an emerging strategic partner to the USA, and Nigerian Americans, who make up a sizeable portion of the Nigerian diaspora (Toosi 2021).

Violence and *Ubuntu* can be considered opposites, as they represent contrasting states – one of physical force with the intent to damage or injure, and the other cooperation, peace, and understanding. Seemingly, some Nigerian Muslims have weaponized Islam, which is a bit of a dichotomy itself. The basic tenets of Islam suggest that it is a tolerant religion that seeks to integrate, understand, and support interfaith dialogue for the benefit of all. Islam, however, has been hijacked and redefined by Islamists, to the contrary of the religion's tenets.

Managing Religious Diversity in Nigeria

The emergence of the present-day country of Nigeria is intertwined with the spread of Christianity and Western colonization on the African continent. Although Portuguese traders introduced it to West Africans in the late fifteenth century, Christians were not a dominant feature in the region until the late nineteenth and early twentieth century, when Christian missionaries assisted European nations in their colonization of West Africa.

England was one of several European nations – among them Belgium, France, Germany, Italy, and Portugal – that engaged in the "Scramble For Africa," the period of Western colonization during the late nineteenth and early twentieth century. The period is marked by Christian missionaries, the economic exploitation of Africa's natural resources, and the creation of arbitrary national borders by European powers. These European goals certainly did not contribute to *Ubuntu* or the promotion of DEUCE principles.

The "Scramble For Africa" had a lasting impact on the health of Christian and Muslim relations. In 1914, Lord Frederick Lugard – a British colonial administrator – merged Northern Nigeria (populated mainly by Muslims) and Southern Nigeria (populated mainly by Christians) into a single entity, the Colony and Protectorate of Nigeria. By 1960, Nigeria gained its independence from the British. It officially became a Western-style republic on 1 October 1963. Its educational, governmental, and legal systems were all based on Western principles. Today, Nigeria is the most populous country on the African continent with a population of 220 million people. It is known for its diversity and dynamism – with over 250 ethnic groups – but also its complexity and divisions, as its various groups seek recognition and representation in the Nigerian government.[4]

It might seem that the poor state of Christian and Muslim relations in Nigeria connotes civilizational differences between the West and the Ummah, but it is centered around politics and the unfinished wars of religion brought to Africa as Western powers encountered Islam in Africa (Walker 2012: 2). The population of Nigeria is split in two – half of the population identifies as Christian and the other half as Muslim. The Christians live primarily in the southern states of Nigeria and are largely Roman Catholics and Anglicans, the members of the Anglican Church of England. A diverse group of Protestant churches are also active in Nigeria.[5] The northern areas of Nigeria are populated predominantly by Sunni Muslims, who comprise diverse ethnic groups, among them Fulani, Hausa, and Yoruba. There is also a significant Sufi presence across the northern states.

There is a growing concern today that the Nigerian government – whose secular constitution separates religion and state and guarantees freedom of religion for all citizens – is turning into an Islamist state that is dangerous for Christians (McGarvey 2022). Reverend Jacob Kwashi, the Anglican bishop of Zonkwa Diocese, summarized his views thus:

We have never seen an evil government in [Nigeria] like the one of today. The [Nigerian] government is fully in support of the bloodshed in Nigeria. We are being killed just because we are not Muslims. These evil Fulani jihadists are enjoying the backing of the government to go about killing people, destroying their houses and farmlands, yet when we try to defend ourselves, the government will go about arresting our people. What kind of justice is this? (Morris 2021).

Similar sentiments were offered by Goodluck Jonathan, the former president of Nigeria, who claimed in January 2012 that Boko Haram was being used by Muslim politicians from northern Nigeria to overthrow his government. Critics like him claimed that Muhammadu Buhari – the former Nigerian president – was an Islamist who ignored the persecution of Christians (see Chimtom 2023b). One critic said that he made lopsided appointments of Muslims to key positions in the executive, judiciary, and legislative arms of the Nigerian government, as well as to key positions in the military and security apparatuses (McGarvey 2022).

Nigerian Christian leaders have additionally criticized their country's leaders for failing to establish an environment that fosters *Ubuntu* – especially in the northern region. Matthew Man-oso Ndagoso, the archbishop of Kaduna State, claimed that the Kaduna government had not given permission to any Christian community to build a church in the last 60 years, with the exception of a church built under the administration of a Catholic leader in the early 1990s. He stated that Christians in Kaduna are not able to freely practice their faith as guaranteed by the Constitution of Nigeria (Chimtom 2023a). Another critic – Sir Henry Yunkwap, the president of the Catholic Laity Council of Nigeria – called on Nigerian leaders to arrest and prosecute more perpetrators of terrorism. He claimed that they "must see the life of every Nigerian as very important" (Samasumo 2022).

The ethics of *Ubuntu* (harmony) and DEUCE are needed in Nigerian society today to ameliorate perceived political and religious differences. A key aspect of achieving harmony is to have a state of political balance as a means to counter a state of hegemony, where one group dominates another. The same kind of imbalances that are found in Nigeria are also found in Egypt, which I shift to next.

An Eternal Struggle – The Copts in Egypt

Like the West and Turkey, as you read about in chapter 3, the West and Egypt have always been bounded by civilizational building, geography, and history, which goes back thousands of years. The ancient Greeks traded with – and entered wars against – the ancient Egyptians. Alexander the Great (d. 323 BC) conquered Egypt in 323 BC. In the following generations, the Greeks built the Great Library of Alexandria,[6] a major center of scholarship during the Ptolemaic Kingdom of Egypt, a Hellenistic kingdom of Macedonian and Greek royal lineage that stretched from 305 BC to 30 BC. The Roman Empire conquered Egypt in 30 BC at the Battle of Alexandria, after which Christians spread their religion with the arrival of Saint Mark (d. 70), the author of the Gospel of Mark, to Alexandria in the middle of the first century. Diocletian (d. 311), the emperor of the Eastern Roman Empire, conquered Egypt in the early fourth century. In the ancient world, Alexandria was one of the five episcopal sees of Christendom.[7] The Byzantine Empire ruled over Egypt until the Islamic conquest of Egypt in 641. Of all the countries covered in this book, Egypt might serve as a pre-eminent borderland in discussing the Clash of Civilizations between the West and the Ummah.

The majority of Egyptian Christians today are Coptic Christians, or Copts. They are members of the Egyptian Orthodox Church, or simply the Coptic Church, founded by Saint Mark in Alexandria around the year 64, during the reign of Nero (d. 68), the Roman emperor known for persecuting Roman Christians. The Coptic Church played a significant role in early Christological debates. It separated from Constantinople, the center of Christendom at the time, following the Council of Ephesus, which convened in 431 to debate the relationship between the divine and human natures of Jesus. At Ephesus, Nestorius (d. 451) – the archbishop of Constantinople – argued that Mary – Jesus's mother – should be regarded as *Christokos*, the Greek term meaning "Birth-giver of Christ." Saint Cyril (d. 444), the Patriarch of Alexandria, counterargued that Mary should be regarded as *Theotokos*, the Greek term meaning "Birth-giver of God," which meant that Jesus's divine and human natures were inseparable. In the end, the Council of Ephesus ruled in favor of Patriarch Cyril and declared that Nestorius was a "heretic." He was deposed and sent into exile.

The council's ruling in favor of *Theotokos* contributed to the formulation of Orthodox Christology within the Coptic Church. For Christians on the opposite sides of the debate, the division represented the opposite of moderation or unity, an important reminder that *Ubuntu* is just as important within civilizations as it is between them.

Coptic history witnessed another notable change with the arrival of Islam to Egypt in the seventh century. The Arab Muslims, only ten years removed from Prophet Muhammad's death, conquered Egypt in 641, when Amr Ibn Al-As (d. 664), a military commander and companion of Prophet Muhammad, defeated the Byzantines at the Battle of Heliopolis, near present-day Cairo. Two years later, the Muslims conquered Alexandria. Under Islamic rule, Egyptian Christians were granted a significant degree of autonomy and freedom in their own religious affairs. Under the Fatimid dynasty rule of Caliph Al-Hakim (d. 1021), however, the Copts fell victim to discrimination and violence. Their conditions improved when the Ottoman Turks conquered Egypt in 1517. The Ottomans integrated the Copts into the *millet* system, as you read about in chapter 3, which helped to restore a semblance of *Ubuntu* in Egyptian society.

Today, the Copts represent about 10–15 percent of Egypt's total population of 110 million people. They are Egypt's largest minority group and the largest sect of Christianity in the entire Middle East. Although they are granted freedom of religion, the Copts face restrictions on building churches, running for political office, and proselytizing in the Egyptian public sphere. Coptic activists claim that their tax money is used for "Islamic initiatives" like building mosques, schools, Islamic universities, and training imams. The same taxes, the Coptic activists claim, are rarely – if ever – delegated to similar Christian initiatives (Marshall 2021). The Copts have also campaigned to remove religion from the Egyptian identification card system, as a means to avoid discrimination, but to no avail (Rohan 2017). These recent developments suggest an absence of *Ubuntu* and diminishing protections when it comes to Egyptian Christians.

Violence – the antithesis of DEUCE – has been a concern in recent years for the Copts of Egypt. In April 2017, a Muslim suicide bomber attacked Saint Mark's Coptic Orthodox Cathedral in Alexandria. The attack killed 17 people. On the same day, a Muslim suicide bomber attacked Saint George's Church in Tanta, a city along the Nile Delta. Twenty-one Christians were killed there, and 59 others were injured (Middle East Monitor 2017). The Muslim suicide bombers conducted their attack on Palm Sunday, the Christian feast day commemorating Jesus's final entry into the city of Jerusalem in the year 33.

The international community once again reacted with shock after the release of a February 2015 video that showed the execution of 21 male hostages on a beach near Sirte, a city located on the Mediterranean Sea in northern Libya. The video showed black-clad masked members of ISIS condemning them to death for being "followers of the hostile Egyptian church" (Arab News n.d.). All but one of them were Coptic Christians. One week after their execution, Pope Tawadros II – the leader of the Coptic Orthodox Church of Alexandria – declared them "martyrs."

Bombing churches obviously runs counter to *Ubuntu*, which has a counterpart term – *Maat* – in ancient Egyptian religions. *Maat* is the name of an Egyptian goddess who oversaw legal matters to ensure balance, harmony, honesty, and justice (Virtue 2003: 121). She was also responsible for the arrangement of the constellations and seasons, which upheld cosmic order against chaos (Mufila 2023). Ancient Egyptian pharaohs were expected to embody *Maat* in their governance, a reminder of the deep roots of *Ubuntu* on the African continent.

It is important to add that Egypt is not in the same category as highly restrictive countries, such as Saudi Arabia, when it comes to freedom of religion for Christians. According to the Egyptian government, there are almost 3,000 churches in the country (see Osama 2016). There is not a single church in Saudi Arabia. In a sign of their desire to engage with Christians, the Egyptian government officials visited the main Coptic Cathedral during the Christmas season of 2021 and assisted the main construction of a Cathedral of the Nativity of Christ in Egypt's new administrative capital (Marshall 2021). These symbolic acts and gestures – which reflect the broader principles of commitment and engagement in DEUCE – help to build a culture of *Ubuntu* in Egypt.

PART TWO – THE DIALOGUE OF CIVILIZATIONS

The civilizational interplay between the West and the Ummah in Egypt is rooted in conflict, but it is also rooted in cross-cultural collaboration, a process that has significantly impacted the development of the modern-day country of Egypt.

The Europeanization of Egypt

In what might surprise readers, the founding father of Egypt – Muhammad Ali (d. 1849) – is in fact an ethnic Albanian born in Kavala, Greece. He arrived in Egypt in 1798 as a general of an Albanian-led army of the Ottoman Empire. His mission in Egypt was to recover it for Selim III (d. 1808) – the Ottoman sultan – after it had fallen to Napoleon Bonaparte (d. 1821), the Emperor of France, during the French occupation of Egypt (1798–1801). The Ottoman-Egyptian forces were triumphant in Egypt and Ali quickly rose to fame as a political figure. Selim III granted him the title of *wali* – the viceroy of the Ottoman Empire in Egypt – and the rank of *pasha*, an honorary title similar to a British knighthood.

Scholars typically view Ali's efforts as an attempt to "Europeanize" Egypt. To clarify, my use of the term Europeanize refers to making something more European in terms of knowledge productions, languages, and culture. This can refer to the adoption of artistic styles and architectural designs.

Beginning in the 1820s, Ali encouraged young Egyptians to study at European universities, in the hope that they would translate Egyptian literature and military manuals into Arabic. The Egyptians who answered his call ushered in the *Nahda* – the Arabic term given to the Arab Renaissance. As an extension of the *Nahda*, Ali's government founded Bulaq Press, the Arab world's first indigenous press, and also built a palace – the Muhammad Ali Pasha Palace – which is famous for its European influences. Some drawings and decorations in the palace were painted in the leading Italian and French styles of the nineteenth century. Other parts of the palace exhibit a fusion of European decorative motifs with the spirit of Islamic architectural planning (Marie 2022). To achieve such marvels, Europeans and Egyptians involved themselves with dialogue, education, understanding, commitment, and engagement – the five principles of DEUCE.

Ali's relationship with the Ottoman sultan, Mahmud II (d. 1839), came to fruition around the time of the Greek War of Independence, which I covered in chapter 3. To appease Ali's rising influence, Mahmud II offered him the island of Crete – located in the Mediterranean Sea – if he squashed the Greek rebellion. He accepted the task, but his forces suffered a stunning defeat. The Greeks – backed by Great Britain, France, and Russia – sunk Ali's entire navy at the Battle of Navarino, off the west coast of the Peloponnese Peninsula in Greece, in 1827. As compensation for the loss of his navy, Ali asked Mahmud II for the territory of Syria. When the Ottoman sultan rejected the request, Ali built an entirely new navy and invaded Syria, which started the First Turkish-Egyptian War (1831–3). These kinds of clashes remind readers that the Clash *within* Civilizations is relevant to any comprehensive understanding of the Clash of Civilizations, both of which are impediments to DEUCE.

Starting under the rule of Queen Victoria (d. 1901), the British gradually established control over Egypt. They offered Ali hereditary rule of the country if he withdrew from Syria, but he declined the offer. He thought that France would support him in a war against the British, but France never came to his aid. The British navy – with the help of the Austrian navy – proceeded to establish a naval blockade over the coastline of the Nile Delta, which allowed them to also capture the city of Acre, in present-day Israel. Ali agreed to the terms of the Convention of London in 1840, which stripped him of his claim over Crete. He also was forced to downsize his navy and reduce the size of his army in exchange for his hereditary rule over Egypt.

Ali's endeavors undoubtedly brought Egypt closer to Europe, but it also led to conflict with Europe. He led his life in accordance with the Dialogue of Civilizations, knowing well that each civilization had certain strengths that other civilizations might be able to benefit from. On the other hand, he engaged in the Clash of Civilizations by entering wars against European powers. While his legacy may be difficult to understand, it nevertheless provokes intrigue on the civilizational interplay between the West and the Ummah.

Following Ali's death in 1848, Egypt was a self-governing vassal state of the Ottoman Empire. His sons and successors – Abbas I (d. 1854) and Sa'id (d. 1863) – halted several of his European reforms. Isma'il Pasha (d. 1895), another of his successors, sold Egypt's shares of the Universal Company of the Maritime Canal of Suez, the company that owned the 99-year lease to manage the Suez Canal. Isma'il's decision was viewed across Egypt as an embarrassment and humiliation. The British then purchased Isma'il's shares of the Suez Canal in 1875, a move that significantly enhanced Britain's influence in Egypt. With the help of other European powers, the British eventually deposed Isma'il and installed his son – Tewfik Pasha (d. 1892) – as the Egyptian ruler. Tewfik was considered by many to be a "puppet" of British interests in Egypt, making efforts to promote harmony (*Ubuntu*) more challenging due to mistrust and politics.

The official British occupation of Egypt started in 1882, nearly 40 years before the start of World War I. Together with the French, it ended the Egyptian nationalist uprising in the Anglo-Egyptian War in 1882, which was sparked in 1881 by Ahmed 'Urabi, an Egyptian army officer who mutinied on the grounds that Tewfik was too closely tied to British and French financiers. Britain and France responded by issuing a "Joint Note" to Egyptian authorities declaring that Tewfik was the "rightful" leader.

'Urabi's rebellion exacerbated resentment for Egyptian Christians and European Christians in Egypt in general. It also led to the Bombardment of Alexandria, which had a rippling effect on Egyptian Christians. During that event, more than 50 Christians were killed in anti-Christian riots. Most Europeans fled Alexandria due to anti-European sentiment. Following the incident, William Ewart Gladstone (d. 1898), the British prime minister at the time, portrayed 'Urabi as a self-seeking tyrant who massacred Christians. Gladstone tried to put him on trial, but he was instead sent into exile.

When World War I started, the British government declared itself the "protectorate" of Egypt. The British conscripted over one and a half million Egyptians into the Labor Corps and stationed thousands of British soldiers in Egypt to fight against the Ottoman Empire. Following the Ottoman Empire's collapse at the end of World War I, Egyptian nationalists were preparing for self-government and total independence, as promised by the "Fourteen Points" of Woodrow Wilson (d. 1924), the then president of the USA.

The Europeanization or Westernization of Egypt was both good and bad for the country. On the positive side, it served to once again bring Egyptians into international relevance. Perhaps a better term would be "modernization" given the considerable downsides to Europeanization. Specifically, the richness of Islam had many positive attributes that were wrongly rendered second-class status by the Europeans in Egypt. Instead of interfaith unity, the religious divide became more contentious, which came to the surface during the Egyptian Revolution, the focus of the next few pages.

"Religion is For God, and Egypt is For All"

In 1919, relations between Christians and Muslims in Egypt made a noted turn after the end of World War I. The two populations viewed each other as allies in Egypt's struggle for independence from the British. The Egyptian Revolution, which coincided with the end of the war, led to the formation of the Wafd Party, a democratic and secular political group that represented Egypt at the Paris Peace Conference (1919–20) after the end of World War I. The founder of the party is Saad Zaghloul (d. 1927), an Egyptian activist, lawyer, and graduate from Al-Azhar University – widely regarded as one of the most prestigious Islamic universities in the Ummah. He also worked for a French law school in Cairo. These experiences enabled him to acquire the necessary skills to promote harmony amongst Egyptians.

The Wafd Party won the majority of seats in the Egyptian parliamentary elections in 1924. The party's official flag had the Coptic cross and the Islamic crescent on it, a symbol of their commitment to freedom of religion. Similarly, the party's official motto – "Religion is For God and the Nation is For All" – points to an Egyptian identity grounded in civic nationalism and secularization. When asked about the Copts in Egypt, Zaghloul declared, "Copts have the same rights and duties as Muslims and are on the same footing" (see El-Faki 2018: 60). He also appointed Copts to major political positions within the party, which encouraged the integration of Christians and Muslims at the civil and political levels of society. It did so while simultaneously honoring the distinct differences between Christianity and Islam, thus avoiding religious syncretism. It did not concern itself with synthesizing the two religions. Rather, it focused on creating a civic nation, which helps to promote bonds between Christians and Muslims.

Following their victory in the 1924 Egyptian elections, the Egyptian Christians gradually experienced a worsening of relations with Egyptian Muslims. Critics of the Wafd Party accused it of sheltering a Coptic conspiracy against Muslims, a charge which one scholar claimed was "unfair and unprovoked" (Bowie 1977: 106). They also claimed that its politicians used too much "Islamic sentiment" in politics, which, at times, led to the persecution of the Copts (Bowie 1977: 106). In Egyptian schools, the history of Christianity in Egypt was gradually erased. The number of Coptic civil servants also slowly declined, and the independent Coptic court system – initiated during the Ottoman Empire's *millet* system – was terminated. By 1955, the Egyptian government created a Ministry of Islamic Affairs, which started waging a "land war" against the Coptic Church by confiscating land and by delaying building permits to build new churches.

The decline of the Wafd Party – and its promotion of DEUCE principles along with the Dialogue of Civilizations – marked the end of a high point in Christian and Muslim relations in Egypt. Its loss of support among Egyptians, and the Egyptian government's persecution of its supporters, were gifts to the more Islamist-oriented political parties in Egypt.

The Muslim Brotherhood and the Politics of the Arab Spring

In the formative years of the Egyptian state, the Wafd Party developed an uneasy relationship with the Muslim Brotherhood, a political party and Islamist movement founded in 1929 by Hassan Al-Banna (d. 1949), an Egyptian Muslim. Al-Banna critiqued the influence of Western culture in Egyptian society, rejected European political influence, and denounced the encroachment of American and European cultural norms (Harvard Divinity School n.d.c.). He viewed Islam as a "complete system" to govern all aspects of both private and public life (Vidino 2015: 5). One of his inspirations – Rashid Rida (d. 1935) – was a student of anti-colonialist Muhammad 'Abduh (d. 1905), an influential Islamic scholar who argued that Islam should be the primary reference point – and organizing force – in modern societies. While the Wafd Party had secular intentions for Egypt's future, the Muslim Brotherhood wanted an Islamic society and state, in which all aspects of Egyptian law were subject to the Sharia.

For Egyptian Christians, this triggered a fear of Islamism – which indicates hegemony – or dominance of one group over another. Hegemony is the opposite of the balance, cooperation, and peaceful coexistence that accompanies *Ubuntu* and DEUCE.

By the end of the 1940s, competition between the Wafd Party and the Muslim Brotherhood reached a climax. The former had overtaken the latter's long-standing dominance in Egyptian politics (Jadaliyya and Ahram Online 2011). After Al-Banna's assassination in 1949, it changed its strategy and joined forces with Gamal Abdel Nasser (d. 1970), the leader of the Free Officers Movement, a nationalist group of military officers who sparked the Egyptian Revolution of 1952. Both the Muslim Brotherhood and the Free Officers Movement viewed the West and the Egyptian monarchy as a "common enemy." After the latter toppled King Farouk Bin Abdulaziz Al-Saud (d. 1965), the Egyptian monarch, in a bloodless coup d'état, Nasser terminated the Egyptian Constitution of 1923. In 1954, the Muslim Brotherhood organized an assassination attempt on Nasser, who proceeded to ban the Muslim Brotherhood and the Wafd Party in his attempt to turn Egypt into a single-party state.

In this period, Copts and other Egyptian Christians viewed Nasser as a secular reformer who used pan-Arab rhetoric to further Egyptian nationalism. While he did not overtly condemn the Copts or Christianity in his speeches, he was nevertheless critical of the West, especially its ally-ship with Israel, a country that I return to in chapter 7.

Following Egypt's defeat against Israel in the Six-Day War (1967), Nasser resigned but quickly returned to power after popular demonstrations for his return. He relaunched a military conflict with Israel to regain control of the Sinai Peninsula, which was occupied by Israel. His successor, Anwar Sadat (d. 1981) – the third president of Egypt – allowed the founding of the New Wafd Party,[8] which described itself as a centrist party standing for democratic rights like freedom of speech and independence of the judiciary. Following the Egyptian Revolution of 2011, the New Wafd Party joined the National Democratic Alliance voting bloc, which was then led by the Freedom and Justice Party, an offshoot of the Muslim Brotherhood. Leaders of the New Wafd ended up leaving the alliance before the parliamentary elections in 2012. It came in third in the elections with almost 10 percent of the vote, making it the most successful non-Islamist party in Egypt.

The spirit of the New Wafd Party – along with the Dialogue of Civilizations and DEUCE concepts – was invoked in 2011 at Tahrir Square, the public square in the heart of Cairo, during the Arab Spring – the series of demonstrations and protests across the Arab world. While there are incidents of clashes between Christians and Muslims during the Arab Spring, there were instances of harmony (*Ubuntu*) and unity among followers of Christianity and Islam. To show solidarity with Muslims who had clashed with the Egyptian military, a group of Coptic protestors made a human chain around Muslims while they were performing their after-noon prayers on *jummah*, the holiest day in the week in Islam (Alexander 2011). A Western journalist who witnessed the human chain said that nearby graffiti showed the Muslim crescent embracing the Christian cross. Attached to the symbol were the words, "We are all against the regime," which suggests that Egyptian Christians and Egyptian Muslims were committed to the same political cause.

Two days later, on the Christian holy day of the week (Sunday), Muslims returned the favor by constructing a human chain as Christians celebrated Mass in Cairo's central plaza (Cole 2011). After forming the ring, the crowd of Christians and Muslims chanted "one hand" – mean-ing "we are one" – and held up a cross and the Qur'an side-by-side

(Kennedy 2011). The "one hand" is a symbol of unity in that Christians and Muslims committed themselves to engaging together in civic spaces.

Another Islamist party in Egypt – the Freedom and Justice Party – was declared the winner of the Egyptian elections in 2012. Mohamed Morsi (d. 2019), the party's leader, campaigned on applying the Sharia to "all walks of life, as it is the source of wisdom and divine mercy" (Dunne and Hamzawy 2017). While critics claimed that Morsi had theocratic leanings, he maintained that Egypt – under the rule of the Muslim Brotherhood – would be a "civil state," albeit with an Islamic flair. After winning the presidency, he resigned as head of the Muslim Brotherhood to demonstrate, at least symbolically, that he is no longer the head of a political movement. "I am president for all Egyptians," he said in a post-election victory event (Shehata n.d.).

But for Copts and other Egyptian Christians, the Muslim Brotherhood's victory fed the fear that Christians would slide deeper into second-class citizenship. Some even feared that the new government would shut down churches and impose the *jizya* (Soliman 2022). It is therefore unsurprising that Pope Tawadros II, the Coptic Pope, and the Copts in general quickly sided with Abdel Fattah El-Sisi, the Egyptian general who led a coup d'état in July 2013, in the counter-revolution to the Arab Spring. El-Sisi removed Morsi from office and banned the Muslim Brotherhood from participating in Egyptian politics. It remains banned to this day. The Copts and Egyptian Christians supported El-Sisi out of the common fear that they may both be persecuted under an Islamist government (Soliman 2022). Since taking office, El-Sisi has taken steps to build bridges between the Egyptian government and the Coptic population. He has attended important Coptic church celebrations, established a high-level committee to fight sectarianism, visited a cathedral, and supported the construction of a new cathedral in Egypt (Bonesh 2021).

Despite that, President El-Sisi's relationship with Egyptian Christians – as well as with the West – is a complicated issue. As the previous examples show, he has committed himself to protecting the rights of Christians and has engaged with them in the public sphere. However, critics believe that he has not done enough to protect Egyptian Christians from discrimination, persecution, and violence, all of which indicate an affront to DEUCE.

PART THREE – THE SYNTHESIS OF CIVILIZATIONS

The Synthesis of Civilizations, as noted in the previous chapter while exploring Akbar the Great's life, is pushing for a civic synthesis at the level of civil society rather than religious syncretism between Christianity and Islam. An important part of developing civic synthesis is to protect knowledge as well as the safety of vulnerable members of a given community. In this section, we journey first to Mali – the West African nation – which has emerged as a battleground in the civilizational interplay between the West and the Ummah. I then return to the Nigerian context to offer insight into relevant acts of *Ubuntu*.

The Mali Empire and the Manuscripts of Timbuktu

The Lion King, the animated musical drama produced by Walt Disney in 1994, focused on the life of Simba, a lion cub and the pride and joy of his parents – King Mufasa and Queen Sarabi. The plot is centered on Simba's journey to becoming the "rightful" king of his homeland. It is also a coming-of-age tale with elements of *Ubuntu* like community building, compassion, humanity, and interconnectedness.

Sundiata Keita (d. 1255), the founder of the Mali Empire known as the "Lion King," is said to be the inspiration behind *The Lion King*. The capital of Keita's empire – Niani – is located in the present-day country of Guinea, but his territory was comprised mostly of the present-day country of Mali, a landlocked country bordering Algeria, Burkina Faso, Guinea, Côte d'Ivoire, Mauritania, Niger, and Senegal. Mali emerged as an epicenter for Islamic civilization in West Africa. Muslim city-states within the empire – like Gao, a city along the River Niger in northeastern Mali – served as hubs of Islamic education and centers of trade along the trans-Saharan trading routes.

One of Keita's successors – Mansa Musa (d. 1337) – ruled the Mali Empire for 25 years. He doubled the empire's territory and made significant strides in cultural advancements, particularly in architecture and education. After returning from his famous pilgrimage to Mecca in 1324, Musa built the Great Mosque of Djinguereber, and a royal residence, the Madugu. He also built the Sankore mosque, around which the University of Sankore was established. During the medieval period, the University of Sankore served as a key site of learning for West Africans.

Musa incorporated Timbuktu – the ancient city founded by Buktu, a Tuareg woman in the eleventh century – into his empire. He chose the city because of its strategic location where the River Niger borders the southern edge of the Sahara Desert (Quick 2019). The city is a natural meeting place for Arabs, the Fulani, the Songha, the Soninke, the Tuareg, the Wangara, and other West African nations (Quick 2019). It is thus fertile ground for *Ubuntu*, but also for the Synthesis of Civilizations.

As Mali rose in influence, so did Timbuktu. An elite group of Muslim judges and Muslim scholars, who were educated in the city's pre-eminent schools, led the local government (Singleton 2004: 1). Many of Timbuktu's universities were operated out of mosques and were run by influential families. The city's libraries were filled with books and volumes on topics like astronomy, government, medicine, philosophy, and religion (Worrall 2016). In the fourteenth century, it became known locally as a "university town" with a fervent reputation for scholastic activity. By the sixteenth century, it was a global center of learning, as one scholar described:

> *Imagine a city in sixteenth century West Africa where thousands of Black African students pondered over the latest ideas in science, mathematics, and medicine. A fabled town in the middle of the scorching desert, overflowing with countless valuable books, wonderful crafts, exquisite fabrics, and unrivalled gold jewelry! Imagine a community of highly cultured, wealthy people whose famed city was the subject of legends, its prosperity and mystique behind ochre walls attracting some of the greatest adventurers of the time. Timbuktu gives solid proof of a powerful African past and an unbroken chain of African scholarship (Quick 2019).*

At the height of Timbuktu's golden age in the sixteenth century, the city boasted over 150 schools (Quick 2019). Even the great European travelers of the Renaissance described it as a thriving commercial center with camel caravans and traders on boats along the River Niger (Worrall 2016).

Timbuktu's existence as the center of a West African civilization is proof that Islamic civilization is capable of fostering education, multiculturalism, and pluralism, all of which are central to the DEUCE ethos. Its reputation as a center of education pushes back against the notions of Islamic inferiority, Black inferiority, educational backwardness among

Muslims, and a lack of record-keeping or public archives – such as libraries or universities – within African civilization (Quick 2019). These facts also push back against the artificial East (Islam) versus West (Christian) binary that erases the possibility of the Synthesis of Civilizations, and therefore the implementation of DEUCE.

Preserving the Manuscripts of Timbuktu

Timbuktu houses a priceless collection of historic manuscripts that have been preserved in private scholarly collections or stored in documentation centers over the years.[9] The manuscripts are a living embodiment of West African scholarship dating back to the twelfth century (Huddleston 2009: 129). According to the Library of Congress in the USA, the collection is "indicative of the high level of civilization attained by West Africans during the Middle Ages and early modern period" (Library of Congress n.d.a.). The Library of Congress added that "[s]cholars in the fields of Islamic studies and African studies are awed by the wealth of information that these manuscripts provide."

The Timbuktu manuscripts made international headlines in 2012 when they were targeted by Islamist militant groups who had recently conquered the northern part of Mali, including Timbuktu.[10] These groups – led by the National Movement for the Liberation of Azawad (MNLA) – started the Azawad separatist movement by launching a rebellion after a coup d'état in Bamako, the capital. Following the MNLA's declaration of independence, Islamist militant groups – including Ansar Dine and Al-Qaeda in the Islamic Maghreb (AQIM) – seized control of the territory of Azawad, which is closely tied to the Tuareg people – a Berber ethnic group with a distinct cultural and linguistic presence in several Saharan countries, including Algeria, Burkina Faso, Libya, Niger, and Mali. The Tuareg have cited grievances related to cultural identity, economic disparities, and political marginalization as the reasons for their violence.

Azawad's goals were to destroy Timbuktu's ancient Sufi shrines, impose a rigid interpretation of the Sharia over Mali, and overthrow Mali's secular constitution. Several of the Islamist militant groups, like Ansar Dine, viewed Timbuktu's manuscripts – as well as the city's historic religious artifacts and monuments – as "idolatrous" and thus worthy of destroying. They also viewed them as anathema to their violent worldview (Worrall

2016). In power, the Ansar Dine governed harshly. They conducted amputations and whippings of opponents in Timbuktu's public places.

Given the precarious state of the manuscripts, local Muslim leaders joined together to stop Azawad from destroying the collection (Worrall 2016). Their rescue operation in 2012 had three stages over the course of several months. The first stage started when Abdel Kader, a local scholar, moved the manuscripts out of Timbuktu's main libraries and into people's basements, safe houses, and storage rooms. In the second stage, the preservationists removed the manuscripts from the city by vehicles and transported them across 600 miles of desert, passing through checkpoints and bluffing their way all the way to Bamako, the capital in the south. The third stage started in 2013 after France intervened in the Malian civil war. It was too dangerous at that time to transport the manuscripts by vehicle on the roads of Mali, so the preservationists ended up transporting the manuscripts by boat up the River Niger toward Bamako. Once they were offloaded from the boats, they were put into taxis and eventually placed into safe spaces.

Not only did the rescue operation successfully save the manuscripts, but it also reinvigorated the notion of *Ubuntu* in Timbuktu. By preserving the manuscripts, Muslims and their partners were committed to accommodating a diversity of cultures, opinions, and religions.

The fate of Timbuktu today is unclear. It has been described as having an "uneasy balance" between its past tradition of education and potential Islamist changes (see Boissoneault 2015). In June 2023, a referendum on whether Mali should remain a secular state raised concerns for Reverend Mohamed-Ibrahim Yattara, a Malian pastor, who argued that the Islamization of Mali would endanger the practice of *Ubuntu* among Malians:

[The Constitution] defines what is freedom of religion. For us, this is a crucial issue. Many people are pushing to remove the word "secular" from the Constitution. Many Muslims who go to Mecca or visit an Arabic country want to start a new mosque. Bamako is full of mosques, and there is a new Islam at large. It is a stricter and less tolerant Islam than the one we Christians lived alongside for so many years. I know many moderate Muslims feel the same way. Religion has entered into the public domain in a new way and that has changed everything. My fear, and the fear of many of my fellow [Christians] is that we could end up living in a

hard-line Islamic state, which enforces Sharia law. It will make every Christian in Mali fear for their future. [The Malian] constitution, for all its other faults, is our best chance of avoiding this (Christianity Today 2023).

Whatever its fate, Timbuktu's legacy as a legendary crossroad of civilizations seems likely to endure indefinitely (Boissoneault 2015). Preserving its knowledge can serve as the foundation for dialogue and education, the first two stages of DEUCE. It can also lead to more understanding (stage three of DEUCE) and respect of different beliefs, customs, and cultures, all of which fosters *Ubuntu*. In our increasingly interconnected world, preserving knowledge – and sharing it – fosters a commitment (stage four of DEUCE) to address global challenges and enables engagement (stage five of DEUCE) across national borders.

A Guardian Angel in Plateau State

Ubuntu, as we have seen throughout the chapter, calls on human beings to protect one another and see each other as interconnected and mutually dependent. While the term has no specific link to the notion of a "guardian angel," readers should know that they are related and relevant to building bonds between Christians and Muslims.

In both Christianity and Islam, angels are portrayed as messengers of God who offer divine guidance and protection. Psalm 91:11, for example, states, "[God] will command his angels concerning you to guard you in all your ways." Islam also recognizes the presence and power of angels, known in Arabic as *Kiraman Katibin* – or the Noble Recorders. Angel Gabriel, or *Jibreel* in Arabic, initiated the Qur'an's revelation to Prophet Muhammad at Mount Hira in the year 610. As I noted in *People of the Book – Prophet Muhammad's Encounters with Christians*, Gabriel gives Muhammad protection on many occasions throughout the course of his life (Considine 2021). In fact, he is said to have visited the prophet of Islam more than any other human being throughout history.

Imam Abubakar Abdullahi, a Nigerian Muslim imam, is a living embodiment of a "guardian angel." His heroism is the perfect example of *Ubuntu* in practice.

On 23 June 2018, a group of Fulani Muslim herders attacked a Christian community in Nghar, a village in Gashish District in Plateau

State (Obiejesi 2018). The incident started in Yelwa, a village about one-half mile away from Nghar. The Christians of Yelwa, upon seeing the attack, ran to Nghar in fear for their lives. There, they encountered their guardian angel, Abubakar Abdullahi.

As the Fulani Muslims shot indiscriminately around Nghar, Imam Abdullahi opened the doors of his mosque and allowed dozens of Christians to shelter there. He then locked the doors so that the Fulani Muslims would not enter, but they ended up demanding entry into the mosque. Imam Abdullahi, however, refused to let them in. He told them that they would have to kill him first. When asked why he had saved the Christians of Yelwa, Imam Abdullahi said that they were his allies and friends. Forty years before the attack, they had helped him and his fellow Muslims build a mosque in Nghar, a clear sign that Christians and Muslims in Nigeria are committed to each other's well-being.

Imam Abdullahi's heroism appeared in local and international media outlets. He said in one interview that he was inspired by Prophet Muhammad, who engaged with diverse groups of people and stood for our common humanity. He stated that the Prophet of Islam had "a cordial and peaceful relationship with everybody regardless of their religion," and added, "So long as I am alive, I am ready to save lives, whether that of an animal or human beings. So long as it has life, I will save that life" (Ojoye 2018). For his life-saving efforts, Imam Abdullahi was honored by the US State Department in July 2019. He was given the International Religious Freedom Award for selflessly risking his own life to save members of another religious community who, without his intervention, would have been killed (see Adebayo 2019).

Imam Abdullahi's actions show us that *Ubuntu* is a "living law." This law is based on recognizing the oneness and wholeness of humanity (Nabudere 2005: 6). It is a natural partner to Christians and Muslims who are working for balance and reconciliation in Nigeria and beyond.

Ubuntu in Action

Today, the notion of *Ubuntu* (harmony) is critically important to Christian and Muslim relations on the continent of Africa. Without it, several of Africa's most important nations – Nigeria, Egypt, and Mali – will continue dealing with centuries-long conflicts and struggles. These three countries all have the potential to be leaders in the adoption of the principles of DEUCE. To engage in it, their leaders must first address the discrimination and violence faced by Christians. Peace is not merely the absence of violence, and no genuine peace can be achieved if violence continues.

CHAPTER 6

Healing
The United States of America

The history of the USA is replete with legacy stories about slavery and religious persecution and their related impact on American society. This chapter will review some key moments, while simultaneously outlining key initiatives undertaken by Christians and Muslims to ease and relieve what has transpired in history.

One example is my own experience on Sapelo Island, an island off the coast of Georgia, in January 2008. I visited there while directing *Journey into America*, the documentary film produced by Dr. Ahmed – my former professor who has popped up throughout this book. Our journey to Sapelo Island started with a guided tour of Hog Hammock, a West African-looking settlement dotted with wood-framed, one-story houses with gabled roofs. It is one of the fifteen Saltwater Geechee settlements on the island. The Geechee are descendants of enslaved West Africans brought to work on southern plantations in the present-day USA.

Our tour guide and host – Mrs. Cornelia Walker Bailey (d. 2017) – was the direct eleventh-generation descendant of Bilali Muhammad, a well-documented enslaved West African Muslim. After finishing the tour, Mrs. Bailey invited Dr. Ahmed and his team for a fireside chat in the living room of her home. I listened as she shared her family stories that were passed down through the generations. They described how local practices of the historic Baptist churches were influenced by Islamic rituals and traditions. She said that Christian worshippers used to take their shoes off before entering the prayer hall; women covered their heads while praying; and Christian men and women engaged in prayer in separate locations – one on the left side of the prayer hall for the men and the other on the right for the women, as if it were a traditional mosque. Mrs. Bailey also talked about her community's long Christian tradition

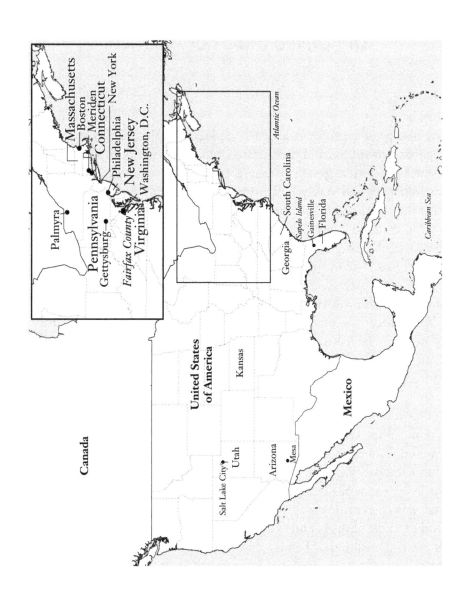

of washing their feet and hands, with its source being the *wudu*, the cleansing ritual performed by Muslims before praying. She also recalled that her grandmother refrained from eating pork and that her Christian grandmother prayed five times per day, both of which are traditional Islamic practices (Ahmed 2010: 164–6).

Our cozy, fireside chat took a serious turn as Mrs. Bailey described the horrors of slavery on Sapelo Island. One story related to a pregnant mother who had her belly split open – and the fetus trampled under – by the boots of an enraged slaveowner.

Related stories about the horrors of slavery were published by Samuel Wood, a Quaker abolitionist and printer. In 1805, he published a graphic text titled "Injured Humanity," which showed seven vignettes of the treatment of slaves in the Caribbean islands. Wood's publication also had written descriptions of the horrors of slavery – a slave woman dying of miscarriage due to ill treatment; a slave girl dying of wounds inflicted during a whipping carried out by a slaveowner; a slave woman being forced into prostitution by her slaveowners; slaves being forced to eat the carcasses of animals; and even a slaveowner dropping hot lead on the head of a rebellious slave. Slaveowners, according to Wood, showed "as little concern [toward the enslaved] as sheep and lamb by the butcher."[1]

America's seminal "national wound" is undoubtedly slavery. During the Transatlantic Slave Trade (1525–1866), approximately 400,000 Africans were shipped to the present-day USA (Gates n.d.). Anywhere from 10 to 50 percent of this population were Muslims (The Pluralism Project – Harvard University n.d.). Slaves came from lands as far north as the present-day country of Senegal, down to the Gulf of Guinea, and further southwards toward the present-day country of Cameroon.[2] The largest African nations represented in the enslaved population were the Yoruba and Igbo (of present-day Nigeria), Akan (of present-day Ghana and Côte d'Ivoire), Mande (of present-day Guinea), and Wolof (of present-day Cameroon) (Hall 2007).

Subsequent wounds in American society were opened in the ensuing generations. These wounds include Islamophobia, which – like slavery – is deeply rooted in the Clash of Civilizations. This chapter explores these "unhealed wounds," from the days of slavery up until the present day. More importantly, I provide theoretical "medicine" to heal such wounds later in the chapter. The medicine includes humanity, integration, knowledge, moderation, and unity, which are all integral to the concept of DEUCE.

PART ONE – THE CLASH OF CIVILIZATIONS

America's reckoning with slavery is a necessary reckoning because it accounts for the silence of the history of enslaved people, which included Muslim Americans. In this regard, resolution with slavery and other forms of discrimination (like Islamophobia) is part of the healing process in the present-day USA and with America's relationship with the Ummah.

Bilali Muhammad and the War of 1812

One of the best known enslaved West Africans is Bilali Muhammad. Born in 1770 into the Fulbe nation of Timbo – a city in present-day Guinea – Bilali was enslaved in his early thirties and brought to the Bahamas, where he was sold to Thomas Spalding (d. 1851) of Sapelo Island. Bilali served as the imam of approximately 80 men while living there. He is reported to have prayed five times daily, fasted during Ramadan, and regularly wore a *fez*, the flat-topped hat worn by Muslims in the late eighteenth century and throughout the nineteenth century. He and Phoebe – his wife – had twelve sons and seven daughters, three of which were named Fatima, Medina, and Yoruba. He was buried with a Qur'an and prayer rug.

Around the year 1806, Spalding made Bilali the head slave manager of over 400 slaves that included both Christians and Muslims. His six years as the head slave manager prepared him well to accept the most significant task of his life – serving in the Sapelo Island militia during the War of 1812, which is sometimes called the USA's Second War for Independence against Great Britain.

When a British attack on Sapelo Island seemed imminent, Spalding appointed Bilali to the position of captain of Sapelo Island's militia. He armed Bilali and 80 of the slaves with muskets. This decision suggests that he had a distinctive level of trust in Muhammad (Lowcountry Digital History Initiative n.d.). Given that he was a Muslim – an identity often depicted as "anti-American" in popular discourse – it is noteworthy that Bilali defended Sapelo Island, even as an enslaved person who reportedly criticized his Christian peers. Bilali is said to have told Spalding that the "loyal" Muslims under his command would protect Sapelo Island from the British, but he added that he could not vouch for the loyalty of the so-called "Christian dogs" among Spalding's slave population. Bilali's use of "Christian dogs" suggests that Christian and Muslim slaves on the island engaged little in DEUCE and were divided along religious and ethnic lines (Lowcountry Digital History Initiative n.d.). These kinds of old wounds are still present in American society, which I will explore further as the chapter progresses.

Sometime in the 1820s, Bilali hand-wrote a 13-page text in Arabic about his knowledge of the Sharia. The "Bilali Document," as it is commonly known, begins with a phrase used daily by Muslims worldwide – "In the name of God, the Beneficent, the Merciful." Bilali then referred to Prophet Muhammad as his "true master," an ironic twist given his enslaved status. The Bilali Document also includes a description of the *adhan* – the Islamic call to prayer – and the *wudu* – the Islamic ablution before praying. It is currently held in the Hargrett Rare Book and Manuscript Library at the University of Georgia.

Bilali's journey from slave to captain reminds us of the complexities and contradictions involved in discussions about healing America. On the one hand, Bilali was stripped of his freedom, denied his dignity and honor, and prevented from returning to his ancestral homeland in present-day Guinea. On the other hand, he faithfully served his community members by leading them through an existential crisis, even as he sacrificed for Christians who did not act or think like him.

Islam at Mount Vernon

The healing process continues as we turn to George Washington (d. 1799), the first US president. He was the grandson of Lawrence Washington (d. 1698), an English aristocrat and planter who was born in Sulgrave, a village in Northamptonshire, England. George Washington inherited his first slave at the age of 11, the year his father – Augustine Washington (d. 1743) – passed away. By the time of his death, he owned 500 slaves.

Several generations of Washingtons engaged in the Transatlantic Slave Trade from Mount Vernon, their family's primary residence in Fairfax County, Virginia. The plantation's property records – as documented on the official Mount Vernon website – show elements of Islamic heritage. The tithe tables listed the names Fatimer and Little Fatimer, who were mother and daughter. Fatimer is a derivative of the name Fatima, the daughter of Prophet Muhammad. Another enslaved woman – Nila – is an adaptation of Naailah, a name taken by some Muslim women.

Sambo Anderson also is listed on Washington's tithe tables. He served as Washington's top assistant at Mount Vernon. Sambo is said to have had facial cuts, gold rings around his ears, and tattoos that suggest a royal lineage of the Hausa, a nation that spans the present-day countries of Niger and Nigeria. The Hausa bear an Islamic influence dating back to the days of the Mali Empire, as you read about in the previous chapter. In an 18 January 1876 article titled "Mount Vernon Reminiscence," an anonymous older citizen of Fairfax County contended that Sambo was a "great favorite of the master [Washington]; by whom he was given a piece of land to build a house on."[3] The older citizen claimed that Sambo owned a boat or skiff that allowed him to freely travel the area, a rare privilege given to a slave in the American colonies. Washington also reportedly granted Sambo permission to own a gun, another rare privilege for a slave at that time.

It is impossible to understand how Washington could profess to love liberty and yet also own human beings. His predicament has been referred to as "Enlightenment racism" (Monticello n.d.c.). He knew that slavery was wrong, but he rationalized the ownership of slaves with a sense of paternalism. Thomas Jefferson (d. 1826), a contemporary of Washington and a slave owner himself, captured the essence of Enlightenment racism best when he wrote that freeing slaves was like "abandoning children" (Monticello n.d.c.). These vestiges of slavery haunt American society to this day, as African Americans – as well as Native Americans – have little to no knowledge of their ancestral legacies. Needless to say, this is clearly the antithesis of the concept of DEUCE that is emerging today in the USA and on the world stage.

While Washington never lobbied publicly for ending slavery, his personal letters show his moral concerns about its practice. He knew that the USA would have to reckon with the original wound of slavery. He made this view clear in a 1786 letter, in which he wrote, "there is not a man living who wishes more sincerely than I do, to see a plan adopted for the abolition of [slavery]." To his credit, when he died in 1799, Washington freed 123 slaves working on five different farms across 8,000 acres (Mount Vernon n.d.a.). Jefferson also raised his moral concern over the institution of slavery. In *Notes on the State of Virginia*, he wrote, "I tremble for my country when I reflect that God is just – that his justice cannot sleep forever" (Monticello n.d.a.).

America's first serious reckoning with slavery occurred during the Civil War (1861–5), which was followed 100 years later by the Civil Rights Movement in the 1960s. While the Union victory freed the enslaved population, Southern Reconstruction and the rise of the Jim Crow laws prevented African Americans from experiencing a genuine freedom and liberty, as promised in the Declaration of Independence. The Civil Rights Movement made strides in terms of voting rights, but the coming of Black Lives Matter in 2020 reminded the American public that the legacy of slavery had never been completely reconciled, and that the nation is far from healed from its past wounds.

The original wound of slavery was compounded in the twenty-first century when the nation witnessed the opening of a new wound – Islamophobia, which represents a major challenge for the success of DEUCE.

"Creeping Sharia" and Islamophobic Hate Crimes

When it comes to Americans' knowledge of Islamic civilization, the Sharia is the most misunderstood concept. It is unsurprising that it is part of the ongoing "culture war" in the USA (Hummel 2020: 317). In 2010 – the same year that Reverend Terry Jones held the "International Burn the Qur'an Day" in Florida – a number of American state legislatures introduced bills prohibiting the application of "foreign laws" across the country. While the bills rarely included the actual word "Sharia" – a term I defined and described in chapter 1 – they were widely regarded by Muslim Americans as bills that targeted everyday "Muslim life," as well as Islamic principles.

One of the more well-documented anti-Sharia bills was passed in the state of Kansas. In May 2012, Sam Brownback – the Republican governor of Kansas – signed a bill aimed at keeping state courts from using Islamic or other "non-American" influences when making laws (Murphy 2012). Supporters said that the law would reassure foreigners in Kansas that state laws and the Constitution would protect them, but opponents of the bill said it "singled" out Muslims for ridicule and suspicion. On these grounds, organizations like the Council on American-Islamic Relations (CAIR), a Muslim American organization, claimed that the bill was illegal because it infringed on constitutionally protected religious rights (see Radiance Weekly 2022 for the quote). CAIR's legal counsel called it "un-American bigotry."

Most of the nationwide anti-Sharia efforts overlook the simple fact that courts across the country have long considered Sharia to be compatible with the Constitution (Considine 2019: 152–3). Issues like commercial disputes, custody decrees, divorces initiated in other countries, and other religious matters, have long been considered "valid" by American courts (Awad 2012). In validating aspects of the Sharia, American judges are protecting the First Amendment,[4] which guarantees freedom of religion and freedom of conscience for people of all faiths – and even those who profess no faith.

While American courts might be able to protect Muslims from religious infringements, they are unable to prevent more serious harm. Hate crimes against Muslim Americans have been well documented since 9/11 (Considine 2019: 71–4; Shanmugasundaram 2018). In October 2023, the Federal Bureau of Investigation (FBI) released their annual statistics on hate crimes. Muslim Americans continued to be overrepresented among the victims. President Joe Biden responded to the FBI's data by saying it is "a reminder that hate never goes away, it only hides" (White House 2023). He added, "Any hate crime is a stain on the soul of America."

Even non-Muslims who are racialized as Muslim can fall victim to Islamophobic hate crimes (Considine 2017b; Considine 2019: 143–5). The first fatal act of Islamophobic violence after 9/11 was Balbir Singh Sodhi, a Sikh American who owned a Chevron gas station in Mesa, Arizona. He was murdered on 15 September 2001 by Frank Silva Roque, who mistook Sodhi – who had a beard and wore a turban in accordance with his Sikh faith – for an "Arab Muslim." Roque, who shot Sodi while he was arranging American flags in front of his gas station, told authorities that he shot him because he wanted to "kill a Muslim" in retaliation for 9/11. Roque was convicted of first-degree murder and sentenced to life in prison (Sikh American Legal Defense and Education Fund n.d.). Given the deep-rooted racism in the USA, there are many geographical areas that will be averse to any acceptance of DEUCE.

Islamophobia in the USA does not just manifest in anti-Islam legislation or hate crimes against Muslim Americans, or those perceived to be Muslim. Evidence also shows that Muslim American communities have been – and continued to be – subjected to systematic surveillance.

An Associated Press investigation, which earned a Pulitzer Prize, revealed that the Intelligence Division of the New York City Police Department (NYPD) ran a counterterrorism surveillance campaign that involved mapping, photographing, video recording, and infiltrating over 250 mosques and 31 Muslim organizations across New York. One scholar summarized the program by calling it "racialized state surveillance of Muslims" (Alimahomed-Wilson 2019). The opening of this wound left a generation of Muslim Americans struggling with feelings of alienation, distrust, fear, and isolation (Khan and Ramachandran 2021), all of which make healing that much more difficult.

An important part of any healing process is admitting when an injustice has occurred. The NYPD admitted in court that it ran a spying program on mosques, student groups, and restaurants to collect intelligence on Muslims (Pilkington 2018). It also admitted that the program did not produce credible evidence of "terrorist" activities or networks in New York City. As part of its settlement in court, the NYPD created a new set of guidelines for intelligence gathering. It also had to submit a new policy for its "counter-radicalization" efforts (Considine 2019: 32). For many Muslim Americans, the NYPD's adjustment was a welcome decision. For others, the mistrust was still there. Sundry Muslims and their allies feared that the mistrust might persist in future generations, which could throw salt on unhealed wounds.

Making amends for injustices also is part of the healing process. Consider the story of Ted Hakey Jr., a former US Marine turned activist. In November 2015, Hakey Jr. was arrested after firing 30 shots into the Ahmadiyya Baitul Aman Mosque in Meriden, Connecticut. Thankfully, no Muslims were injured in the attack.

What followed Hakey Jr.'s hate crime is a quintessential story about the benefits of DEUCE. Before his sentencing in court, Hakey Jr. sat down with the mosque leaders to apologize for his crime. Zahir Mannan, a local Ahmadi Muslim leader, described meeting him:

This huge bodybuilder-type guy comes in and to see tears coming down his face and red cheeks, it humbled us . . . It was a genuine connection that you cannot fabricate . . . He became my brother when he prayed next to me . . . He prayed with me, and he did not have to do that (Grant 2017).

Hakey Jr. considered himself a changed man after praying with the members of the Ahmadiyya community. While he did not convert to Islam, he became an activist against Islamophobia. He went on to travel around the country in the hope of inspiring others to embrace the community that taught him the true meaning of forgiveness, which is crucial for genuine healing.

While the Constitution of the USA established a basic humanistic foundation to heal from the legacy of racism and slavery, the implementation of these concepts has been anything but easy. Part of the challenge is because of the "melting pot" of humanity in the USA, a country that has long been a haven for immigrants escaping oppression and religious discrimination. Over time, the sheer size of the "melting pot" – and its changing diversity – impinges on efforts to heal the nation and may impinge on promoting dialogue, education, understanding, commitment, and engagement (the five elements of DEUCE) between Christians and Muslims. The complexities associated with healing are such that this challenge will be with Americans for the foreseeable future.

PART TWO – THE DIALOGUE OF CIVILIZATIONS

The USA's relationship with its own Muslim population is confounded by additional complexities that emerge when we consider the worldwide relationship between Americans and Muslims. While the historical and contemporary contexts point to a Clash of Civilizations, it also points to positive interreligious understanding and constructive transnational engagements between Christians and Muslims, both of which point to the frequency of the Dialogue of Civilizations.

"Islam Hates Us" or Pinckney's Oath?

Islamophobia in the USA reached a historic peak during the first presidential campaign of Donald Trump. In 2014, the chief strategist of

Trump's campaign – Steve Bannon – claimed that Western civilization was entering the beginning stages of a bloody and brutal war against "jihadist Islamic fascism" (Feder 2016). One year later, Michael Flynn – who went on to be Trump's national security advisor – tweeted that "Fear of Muslims is RATIONAL." In the same year as Flynn's tweet, Trump called for a ban on Muslims entering the country on the grounds that the nation's security was at risk due to Islamic terrorism. His proposed policy became popularly known as the "Muslim Ban." It was widely perceived by Muslim Americans and their allies as being anti-Muslim or Islamophobic.

Matters were aggravated in March 2016, when Trump appeared on CNN and said, "I think Islam hates us" (Schleifer 2016). He added that it is difficult to separate Muslims from ISIS because "you don't know who's who." His comment drew a swift rebuke for not distinguishing between the religion of Islam and radical groups like ISIS. Trump, in essence, intensified old wounds and impeded healing 250 years after slavery was abolished. Some critics claimed that he sent the country back decades and impeded any remediation efforts that have been undertaken to employ the methodology of DEUCE.

While Trump's comments played into the hands of those promoting the Clash of Civilizations, he is certainly not the first Christian American leader to depict the West and Islam as enemies. Following 9/11, President George W. Bush – an Evangelical Christian – vowed to "rid the world of evildoers" and cautioned Americans by stating, "This crusade, this war on terrorism, is going to take a while." In strict usage, the word "crusade" describes the wars between Christians and Muslims that you read about in chapter 2 (Waldman 2001).

Several of President Bush's advisors used similar Clash of Civilizations rhetoric. Reverend Franklin Graham, who offered the invocation at his first presidential inauguration, described Islam as a "very wicked and evil religion" (Ahmed 2003: 36). Reverend Jerry Falwell (d. 2007), the Baptist American leader and founder of Liberty University, called Prophet Muhammad a "terrorist." Reverend Jerry Vines, the former leader of the Southern Baptist Convention – the largest Protestant denomination in the USA – called Prophet Muhammad a "demon-possessed pedophile." For Muslim Americans and Muslims around the Ummah, these kind of characterizations of Islam and Prophet Muhammad throw salt on the unhealed wounds that were opened during the Crusades.

The Clash of Civilizations in America again came to a head in September 2010, when Reverend Terry Jones of the Dove World Outreach Center in Gainesville, Florida, organized an event called "International Burn the Qur'an Day." He appeared on media outlets across the world issuing statements like "Islam is of the Devil" and "Islam is fascist." While Reverend Jones never actually held the event, his actions angered Muslims around the world, with counter-protests emerging around the Ummah.

On a personal note, it is hard to comprehend how any purported religious leader could advocate such inhumanity. From an Islamic perspective, a sizeable portion of the Ummah perceives the actions and comments of the aforementioned Christian American leaders as constituting a "War on Islam" and a rejection of religious pluralism in the USA, a country whose founding generation created a constitution that protects freedom of religion. During the Constitutional Convention on 20 August 1787, Charles Pinckney (d. 1824) – a representative of South Carolina – proposed the idea of eliminating "religious tests" as a requisite to serving in the newly formed American government. His proposition was approved by his colleagues. Any person – regardless of their religious persuasion – was granted the right to serve in a state or federal office.

Today, many US politicians take their oath of office by placing a hand on a religious text. While the Bible is by far the most common text in swearing-in ceremonies, the Constitution[5] – by Pinckney's design – makes no requirement that the Bible, or any other religious text, must be used.

It seems like events in the twenty-first century have done little to heal the endemic social and political divisions in the USA. The negative comments and questionable actions by public servants at the state and federal levels have done more to divide Americans than to heal them. Educators have an opportunity to be leaders in the promotion of DEUCE and the moderation that is at the heart of the Dialogue of Civilizations. This needs to be started early in the education of young Americans to at least establish a recovery foundation for accurate and validated learning.

The Controversy over Jefferson's Qur'an

What would happen if the Qur'an – the Islamic holy text – was used by a Muslim American politician in their oath of office ceremony in the House of Representatives?

In 2007, Keith Ellison, an African American Muslim representing the state of Minnesota, found out by placing his hand on a Qur'an[6] owned by Thomas Jefferson during his oath of office ceremony. Ellison said that Jefferson's Qur'an represented the pluralist vision of the Founding Fathers, who, he said, "believed that knowledge and wisdom could be gleaned from any number of sources, including the Qur'an" (Library of Congress 2007). Ellison's detractors took issue with his decision and subsequent comments to the media. In fact, his oath ceremony erupted into a national controversy and a wider discussion on the relationship between the West and Islam.

Dennis Prager, the popular radio show host, claimed that he – and any other Muslim Americans for that matter – should be banned from taking their oath on the Qur'an. Prager even accused Ellison of "undermining American civilization" (Prager 2006). Similarly, Virgil Good – the former Republican Party member of the House of Representatives – responded by stating, "When I raise my hand to take the oath on Swearing in Day, I will have the Bible in my other hand. I do not subscribe to using the Qur'an in any way." Good also responded by calling for a curb on Muslim migration to the USA. Blatant xenophobia is no friend to quality public education, which is at the core of healing and DEUCE.

Prager and Good viewed Ellison's decision to be linked to Islam's "civilizational *jihad*" against the West (Southern Poverty Law Center n.d.). Frank Gaffney, the director of the Center for Security Policy,[7] defined "civilizational *jihad*" as "a stealthy, not so much nonviolent as pre-violent form of *jihad*," something that will eventually be used to accomplish strategic goals advocated by ISIS, Al-Qaeda, and Boko Haram. According to Gaffney, the strategy of "civilizational *jihad*" was outlined in a 1991 memo written by Mohamed Akram, a senior Hamas leader and board of directors member for the Muslim Brotherhood in North America. An English translation of Akram's memo became public when the American government used it as evidence in the 2008 trial of the Holy Land Foundation for Relief and Development (HLF). The lengthy trial ended in 2009 with five of the HLF leaders being convicted on charges of providing material support to Hamas, a designated terrorist organization in the USA, under humanitarian aid. Akram wrote in the memo:

> The Ikhwan [Arabic for Muslim Brotherhood] must understand that their work in America is a kind of grand jihad in eliminating and destroying the Western civilization from within and "sabotaging" its miserable house by their hands and the hands of the believers so that it is eliminated, and God's religion [of Islam] is made victorious over all others (see Roach 2016).

The memo, however, is said to have been exaggerated and mischaracterized by Gaffney (Bridge Initiative 2016). It was not a formal plan accepted by the Muslim Brotherhood and it did not have influence in other Muslim circles. Gaffney's claims about civilizational *jihad* may or may not be baseless, but it nevertheless appeals to Americans who are already suspicious of Islam and Muslims.

Akram's assertions – as well as the previous commentary on "civilizational *jihad*" – raise the question of how Jefferson might have theorized and responded to the claim that the West and Islam are locked into a Clash of Civilizations. As a scholar and statesman, Jefferson was inspired by John Locke (d. 1704), the English political theorist whose writings shaped the Declaration of Independence, which Jefferson co-authored alongside John Adams and Benjamin Franklin (Monticello n.d.a.). In addition to co-authoring the Declaration of Independence, he played the lead role in authoring the Virginia Statute for Religious Freedom (1786), a bill that asserted, "Neither pagan nor Muslim nor Jew ought to be excluded from the civil rights of the Commonwealth [of Virginia] because of his religion."

The explicit use of the term Muslim in the Virginia Statute for Religious Freedom might come as a surprise to some readers. As you read about earlier with Bilali Muhammad and Sambo Anderson, there is a hidden history of Islam in the USA. All these examples are reminders that Islam is not a new or recent religion to the country, as worsening Islamophobic polemics seem to suggest.

Jefferson was as much a philosopher and theologian as he was a politician and statesman. It is fair to say that he had a "complicated" relationship with Christianity (Monticello n.d.b.). While he was buried by ministers in the Anglican Church and regularly attended Protestant church services of diverse Christian denominations, he once famously declared, "I am a sect by myself" (Monticello n.d.b.). He often used terms like "our Creator," "our God," and the "Infinite Power" to talk about God, all of which portends a kind of "neutral" language that was common among the leading theist philosophers of the eighteenth century (Monticello n.d.b.). Others claim that he was really a Unitarian, or a theist who rejects the Trinity.

Jefferson's views on Jesus provide further insight into the civilizational interplay between the West and Islam. He is said to have believed more in Jesus's "humanity" than in his "divinity" (Monticello n.d.b.). To Jefferson, Jesus is the "first of human sages" and someone who preached "universal philanthropy, not only to kindred and friends, to neighbors and countrymen, but to all mankind." These kinds of Christological views are similar to the Qur'an's position on Jesus, who is considered a "prophet" – but not the "Son of God" – in the Qur'an. Jefferson and the Qur'an, however, would disagree on whether Jesus performed miracles. The Qur'an states that he did, but Jefferson did not believe so.

As an unorthodox Christian, Jefferson had many "enemies," many of whom were Christian. He was accused of being a "secret Muslim,"[8] an accusation that was considered the "ultimate slur" among Protestants in the eighteenth century (Spellberg 2014). In the American presidential election of 1800, allies of John Adams (d. 1826) – who ran against Jefferson – referred to Jefferson's deist or unitarian beliefs as "un-American." The *Connecticut Courant* wrote in that year that no one seemed to know "whether Mr. Jefferson believes in the heathen mythology or in the [Qur'an]; whether he is a Jew or is a Christian; whether he believes in one God, or in many; or in none at all." Jefferson was clearly a thought leader for his time and for any time, for that matter.

Politically, Jefferson believed that all Americans required complete freedom of religion. Many historians note that the broad diversity of ethnicities and religions in the 13 colonies meant that religious freedom was necessary if the union was to be successful (Monticello n.d.d.). This argument is still valid today given that the American population is significantly more diverse than it was in the eighteenth and early nineteenth centuries. His pluralist vision is more important than ever today as the

USA is increasingly more diversified than it was before, during, and after the American Revolution.

Learning about the interplay between America and Islam is a part of the nation's healing process. When Americans learn more about the pluralist vision of the Founding Fathers, they can begin to heal. And to keep healing, Americans must keep learning about their past and preparing for an even more challenging future.

PART THREE – THE SYNTHESIS OF CIVILIZATIONS

Allyship is central to achieving any kind of synthesis between the West and the Ummah. By standing in solidarity with those who face challenges and conflicts, allies foster unity and promote equality between groups and nations. It is essential in times of strife and in times of peace. If demonstrated effectively, it can nurture more DEUCE and contribute to the synthesis between Christians and Muslims in the USA and beyond.

America's "Magnanimous Friend" in its Darkest Hour

As you know by this point in the book, I was born and raised in a town near Boston, Massachusetts, a city that played a key role in the American Revolution. My father used to take me to Warren's Tavern, a historic building just blocks away from the Bunker Hill monument in Charlestown, Massachusetts, a part of Greater Boston and the site of the Battle of Bunker Hill, the first battle of the Revolutionary War. George Washington is said to have visited Warren's Tavern around the year 1775. As the Commander-in-Chief of the Continental Army, he successfully defended Boston, but following his victory there, King George III (d. 1820) sent the British Royal Navy to sack New York City, the biggest and arguably most important city in the American colonies, at which point Washington was forced to attempt to defend the city.

Unlike Boston, Washington was unsuccessful in defending New York City. Over the next few years, the British seized control of New Jersey and the patriot capital of Philadelphia, Pennsylvania. When Philadelphia fell, Washington was forced to encamp at Valley Forge, a naturally defensible plateau located about 20 miles from Philadelphia. He encamped there on 19 December 1777. Valley Forge is recognized by scholars as one of the lowest points for the American revolutionary cause. I, however, consider it an early microcosm of the Synthesis of Civilizations. American history is replete with these kinds of discrete circumstances that demonstrate a national desire to engage in healing and DEUCE.

The day after Washington encamped at Valley Forge, a Muslim leader – Sultan Muhammad Ibn Abdullah (d. 1790) – supported the American cause by declaring that American vessels sailing with American flags were allowed to enter his ports in Morocco. Sultan Abdullah's declaration provided the struggling American colonies access to a new market to acquire necessary goods to recover from their losses (United States Embassy and Consulates in Morocco n.d.). In granting Americans access to his ports, Sultan Abdullah granted the same privileges to Americans as other nations that had agreements with Morocco.

Interestingly – or should I say "symbolically" – the first representative of the US government to respond to Sultan Abdullah's overture was named Samuel Huntington, the same name as the scholar of the Clash of Civilizations theory. As the President of Congress in 1780, Huntington wrote that it had received a letter dated 28 November 1780 from Étienne d'Audibert Caille, which asked Benjamin Franklin (d. 1790) – the American Founding Father then working in Paris, France – to reply. "Assure him," wrote Huntington, "in the name of Congress and in terms most respectful to the Emperor [Abdullah] that we entertain a sincere disposition to cultivate the most perfect friendship with him" (United States Embassy and Consulates in Morocco n.d.).

Relations between the USA and Morocco entered a different phase when Sultan Abdullah received another letter from Congress in December 1780. It stated:

We the Congress of the 13 United States of North America, have been informed of your Majesty's favorable regard to the interests of the people we represent, which has been communicated by Monsieur Etienne d'Audibert Caille of Sale, Consul of Foreign nations unrepresented in your Majesty's states. We assure you of our earnest desire to cultivate a sincere and firm peace and friendship with your Majesty and to make it lasting to all posterity. Should any of the subjects of our states come within the ports of your Majesty's territories, we flatter ourselves they will receive the benefit of your protection and benevolence. You may assure yourself of every protection and assistance to your subjects from the people of these states whenever and wherever they may have it in their power. We pray your Majesty may enjoy long life and uninterrupted prosperity (United States Embassy and Consulates in Morocco n.d.).

Relations between the USA and Morocco grew even stronger in 1783 and 1784. American diplomats in Paris – among them John Adams, Benjamin Franklin, and John Jay (d. 1829) – urged Congress in September 1783 to initiate a treaty with Morocco. In June 1784, Congress sent Thomas Barclay (d. 1793), an American consul and diplomat, to negotiate a treaty between the parties. In collaboration with Franklin, Barclay traveled to Europe seeking aid and supplies for the Continental Army. Two years later, in June 1786, upon the recommendation of Jefferson, Barclay arrived in Marrakech and subsequently had two meetings with Sultan Abdullah. Barclay himself portrayed the sultan as "a just man, according to this idea of justice, of great personal courage, liberal to a degree, a lover of his people, stern [and] rigid in distributing justice" (United States Embassy and Consulates in Morocco n.d.).

Out of the negotiations came the Treaty of Peace and Friendship, also known as the Treaty of Tripoli – or simply the Treaty of Friendship. It was signed by Jefferson in Paris on 1 January 1787 and by John Adams in London on 25 January 1787. Congress ratified it on 18 July 1787. The treaty extended the previous agreements laid out by the USA and Morocco. It granted permission to American commercial and maritime entities to trade off the coast of North Africa (Considine 2019: 55). Shipping lanes off the coast of North Africa were therefore safe for American vessels, which no longer had to sail in fear of being seized by Moroccan corsairs. The sultan, in other words, committed himself to the defense of his ally.

The Treaty of Friendship marks the official beginning of diplomatic relations between the USA and Morocco. The treaty was the first between any Arab, Muslim, or African state and the USA (United States Embassy and Consulates in Morocco n.d.). Its text is critically important in understanding how the Founding Fathers positioned their nation in relation to the Ummah. Article Eleven of the treaty reads:

The United States of America is not in any sense founded on the Christian religion, as it has in itself no character or enmity against the laws, religion, or tranquility of [Muslims], and as the said States never have entered into any war or act of hostility

against any Muslim nation, it is declared by the parties that no pretext arising
from religious opinions shall ever produce an interruption of the harmony existing
between two countries (Avalon Project n.d.).

While the USA certainly resembled a "nation of Christians" in 1787, we would be misguided to define it as a "Christian nation." Neither the Declaration of Independence nor the Constitution of the USA declares an "official" state religion. Many of the signers of the Declaration of Independence emanated from a range of religious backgrounds, including Anglican, Congregationalist, Deist, Episcopalian, Presbyterian, Quaker, Roman Catholic, and Unitarian.

Article Eleven also reminds Americans and Muslims around the world that the Founding Fathers sought cordial relations – and even political alliances – with Islamic nations. Christianity and Islam, in short, were perceived not as sources of conflict or difference, but as potential areas of civility and common ground. Their example is relevant given the strained relations between the West and the Ummah in the twenty-first century.

Washington, who ushered in the Treaty of Friendship with the help of Adams, Jefferson, and Barclay, remained in contact with Sultan Abdullah in the first year of his presidency, which began in 1789. In a letter dated 1 December of that year, he sent a letter to the sultan that started with a salutation – "Great and Magnanimous Friend" (Mount Vernon n.d.b.). It continued:

It gives me pleasure to have this opportunity of assuring your majesty that I shall
not cease to promote every measure that may conduce to the friendship and har-
mony which so happily subsist between your empire and these. Within our terri-
tories, there are no mines of either gold or of silver, and this young nation, just
recovering from the waste and desolation of a long war, has not, as yet, had time to
acquire the riches [through] agriculture and commerce. But our soil is beautiful,
and our people industrious, and we have reason to flatter ourselves that we shall
gradually become useful to our friends . . . may the Almighty bless your Majesty
with his constant guidance and protection (United States Embassy and Consulates
in Morocco n.d.).

Washington's words show a desire to maintain friendships and har-mony with the Muslims of Morocco, no matter the cost or measure.

Unfortunately, Sultan Abdullah never received his second letter. Sultan Abdullah passed away two months before it arrived at his palace in Morocco. Thankfully, Sultan Abdullah's successor – Sultan Moulay Soliman (d. 1822) – continued the allyship by allowing the USA to establish a consulate in Morocco in the year 1797. In 1821, he gave the Americans a beautiful building in Tangier for its consular representative. This building served as the seat of the principal American diplomat to Morocco until 1956. The building is the oldest piece of non-American-based property owned by the USA anywhere in the world.

Like his father, Sultan Soliman wrote a letter to Washington in which he conveyed his commitment to the Treaty of Friendship, saying "we are at peace, tranquility, and friendship with you in the same manner as you were with our father." He even honored the American people, and said so publicly, by calling them the nation "my father most esteemed" (United States Embassy and Consulates in Morocco n.d.). It is interesting that a progressive treaty like the Treaty of Friendship is an early example of DEUCE that has been lost through the ravages of time. Now is the time to educate Americans on the merits of this example in relation to healing and DEUCE in the USA and beyond.

For the sake of historical accuracy, let me add that the Treaty of Friendship broke down in the early years of the nineteenth century. Maritime disputes and business conflicts sprang up between American vessels and Moroccan vessels off the coast of North Africa. Jefferson, the president at the time, became outraged by Morocco's demands of ransom for civilians captured from American vessels (Wilson 2003). The conflict reached a boiling point when the USS Constitution captured Tunisian vessels that were attempting to blockade American ships from entering the port of Tripoli (Wilson 2003). Jefferson responded by paying the tribute instead of maintaining an American naval presence in the area to protect its shipping from piracy. American merchant vessels had previously become prey for Barbary corsairs.

Frank Lambert, a scholar of the Barbary Wars – as the conflict became known – claimed that the breakdown in relations had less to do with differences between Christianity and Islam and more to do with the effects of piracy and the "natural right" of Americans to freely roam the seas to trade (Lambert 2005: 8). In his review of Lambert's noteworthy book on the topic, Gene A. Smith stated that:

Lambert's study does not perpetuate the idea that religion stimulated the conflict between the US and the North African Barbary States. He does not insist that the pirates represented holy warriors fighting a jihad *against the Stars and Stripes. Nor does he compare the Barbary pirates to modern terrorists. Instead, Lambert maintains that the pirates waged a commercial war where they were motivated by the lure of money rather than religious persuasion (Smith 2006).*

Despite the outbreak of the Barbary Wars, the spirit of the Treaty of Friendship revealed itself again in the winter of 1805, when President Jefferson welcomed Ambassador Sidi Soliman Mellimelli, a Tunisian diplomat, with full military honors at the Navy Yard. He later hosted Mellimelli at the White House during Ramadan.[9] For Muslims, the *iftar* – or the breaking of the daily fast – only occurs at sunset during the Islamic holy month. In a gesture of hospitality to Ambassador Mellimelli, President Jefferson changed the time of the *iftar* so that it would be at sunset (Wilson 2003). While changing the time might seem like a "small" act, it nevertheless sent the message that the president of the USA was willing to make accommodations and adjustments for his Muslim guests to make them feel more at home. Kindness has been shown to decrease stress, improve moods, and contribute to healthier relationships, all of which are crucial if two or more parties wish to heal old and new wounds (Siegle 2023).

It was not for another 109 years that the White House hosted another *iftar*. Former First Lady Hillary Rodham Clinton welcomed 150 Muslims for a meal and reception at the White House to mark *Eid al-Fitr*, the Islamic holy day which marks the end of Ramadan (Wang 2017). Clinton's initiative was continued by the next president, George W. Bush, who said in a White House *iftar*, "All the world continues to benefit from [Islam] and its achievements." He added that Ramadan is a "good time for people of different faiths to learn more about each other. And the more we learn, the more we find that many commitments are broadly shared." President Bush held a White House *iftar* every year he was in office between 2001 and 2009, which might surprise Muslims given his actions following the events of 9/11.

The annual *iftar* tradition at the White House is a reminder of the key role that hospitality plays in healing. Hospitality is a form of engagement that invites human beings to enter the practice of healing by bringing people together despite differences, so that all people can be "nourished" (see Moro 2019). My own firsthand experiences in engaging in DEUCE have taught me that there is something visceral about knowing that I am appreciated and welcomed by my hosts. Hospitality helps to build bonds and foster a sentiment of brotherhood.

Few American cities know more about brotherhood than Philadelphia, a Greek term meaning the "City of Brotherly Love." It is famous for being the residence of Benjamin Franklin, who was an early advocate of DEUCE.

The "Friend of Mankind" and Islamic Values

Benjamin Franklin – one of the more notable Founding Fathers alongside Washington and Jefferson – grew up in a conservative, if not puritanical, environment in Boston. As a young man in 1723, he left his native home for the more tolerant city of Philadelphia. When he arrived there, it had a diverse range of religious groups including Calvinists, Jews, Lutherans, Moravians, Presbyterians, and Quakers. William Penn (d. 1718), the founder of the state of Pennsylvania (in which Philadelphia is located), is famous for ushering in – with the assistance of Tamanend (d. 1701), a Delaware chief – a peace agreement in 1683 which also is known as the Treaty of Friendship. The Penn Treaty Museum described his initial offering of peace:

> *Unarmed, clad in his somber Quaker garb, [Penn] addressed the assembled Native Americans, uttering the following which will be admired throughout the ages: "We meet on the broad pathway of good faith and good-will; no advantage shall be taken on either side, but all shall be openness and love. We are the same as if one man's body was to be divided into two parts – we are of one flesh and one blood" (Penn Treaty Museum n.d.).*

Tamanend's response is equally noble: "We will live in love with William Penn and his children as long as the creeks and rivers run, and while the sun, moon, and stars endure."

While the City of Brotherly Love was more open and tolerant than Boston, it was not immune to intolerance – or even outright violent conflict.

The Treaty of Friendship was violated on 14 December 1763. On that day, 57 members of the Paxton Boys – a Presbyterian Scots Irish group living on the Pennsylvanian frontier – attacked the Native American village of the Conestoga[10] on horseback. The Paxton Boys set their huts on fire and fired guns at the members of the village. They murdered and scalped six Conestoga. One of the elders – Shehaes, who had peaceful relations with his Christian neighbors – was cut to pieces in his own bed.

The Paxton Boys had migrated to Pennsylvania from Peckstang and Donegal in present-day Northern Ireland. Their ancestors had previously migrated from Scotland to Northern Ireland during Oliver Cromwell's invasion of Ireland starting in 1649. Following the French and Indian War (1754–63) and Pontiac's War (1763), the Paxton Boys morphed into a militia group and started encroaching on the land of the Conestoga, which was ceded to them by William Penn in the 1690s.

Horrified by the Paxton Boys' violence, Governor John Penn (d. 1795) – the grandson of William Penn – opened an investigation into the massacre. He and other Lancaster County magistrates met with the Conestoga that had fled the village. After receiving their testimony, Penn decided to comfort the Conestoga by promising them protection in a workhouse building (Franklin 1764). The Paxton Boys were outraged by his decision. In turn, they reassembled their militia and invaded the Lancaster workhouse on 27 December 1763. The Paxton Boys killed all 14 of the remaining Conestoga – six adults and eight children. An eyewitness account by William Henry, a resident of Lancaster, stated that the Paxton Boys cut off Conestoga limbs and split skulls open with their tomahawks. The deadly attack effectively made the Conestoga an "extinct" people.

A year after the massacre, Franklin authored an essay titled *A Narrative of the Late Massacres*. In the text, Franklin wrote that the only crime of the Conestoga is that "they had a reddish-brown skin, and black hair." He characterized the Paxton Boys as "Christian white savages" and "cowards," because brave and honorable men protect and spare civilians, not murder them. Franklin added that the Paxton Boys abused the "Word of God," specifically one of the Ten Commandments – "Thou shall not murder" – by conducting the massacre. He also criticized Lutherans and Presbyterians, who were upset that the Lancaster County government did little to protect the Scots Irish settlers, for sympathizing with the Paxton Boys. Today, it is not unusual to see current vestiges of the Paxton Boys, to a lesser degree, across the country.

Some readers might be wondering, what does Franklin's pamphlet about the Paxton Boys have to do with Islamic civilization or the Ummah? Interestingly, in the essay, Franklin focused on how Prophet Muhammad – and other leaders in Islamic history – were antidotes to the kind of "extremism" exhibited by the Paxton Boys.

Franklin used four specific examples from Islamic history. The first example is a seventh-century story about Prophet Muhammad and Khaled, his companion. Franklin wrote:

> As for the [Muslims], it is recorded in the life of [Muhammad], the founder of their religion, that Khaled [Ibn Al-Walid[11]], one of his captains, having divided a number of prisoners between himself and those that were with him, he commanded the hands of his own prisoners to be tied behind them, and then, in a most cruel and brutal manner, put them to the sword; [however, Khaled] could not prevail on his men to massacre their captives, because in fight they had laid down their arms, submitted, and demanded protection. [Prophet Muhammad], when the account was brought to him, applauded [Khaled and] the men for their humanity; but [Muhammad] said to Khaled, with great indignation, "O Khaled thou butcher, cease to molest me with thy wickedness. If thou [possessed] a heap of gold as large as Mount Obo, and should expend it all in God's case, thy merit would not efface the guilt incurred by the murder of the meanest of those poor captives . . . [Ever] since [Muhammad's] reproof to Khaled, even the cruel [Muslims] never kill prisoners in cold blood (Franklin 1856: 73–4).

By choosing Muhammad and Khaled, Franklin sent the message that the first community of Muslims placed a high degree of emphasis on both humanity and mercy, two concepts that oppose modern-day descriptions of Islam as a violent and extremist religion. The kind of mercy exhibited by Muhammad and Khaled provides promising flickers of light in a darkened world. Mercy can affect a cure, a healing.

Franklin's second example centered on the Third Crusade (1189–92), which you read about in chapter 2. The Third Crusade was an attempt by Frederick I of the Holy Roman Empire, Philip II of France, and Richard I of England, to reconquer Jerusalem from Saladin, who captured the city in the year 1187. Franklin wrote about an encounter between Saladin and some of the notable Crusaders:

> *[W]e read the history of the Wars of the Holy Land, that when the [Crusaders] had suffered a great defeat from Saladin, and among the prisoners were the King of Jerusalem, and Arnold,[12] a famous Christian captain, who had been very cruel to the [Muslims]; these two being brought before the Sultan, then placed the King on his right hand, and Arnold on his left; and then presented the King [Guy of Lusignan[13]] with a cup of water who immediately drank to Arnold; but when Arnold was about to receive the cup, [Saladin] interrupted, saying, "I will not suffer this wicked man to drink, as that, according to the laudable and generous customs of the Arabs, would secure him his life" (Franklin 1764).*

Franklin's writing shows that he valued history and believed that it could be used to enlighten the emerging diverse identities present in Pennsylvania. His utilization of Islamic history helped further educate his peers as they collectively ventured on the path to democracy.

Franklin's third example involved John Bell, a diplomat from Antermony, Scotland. Franklin learned about Bell by reading *Travels from St. Petersburg in Russia to Various Parts of Asia* (1763), Bell's only book. Bell studied medicine in Glasgow and set out for Saint Petersburg when he was 23 years old. There, he joined Artemy Volynsky (d. 1740), a Russian diplomat and statesman who served as the Ambassador of Russia to the Safavid Empire of Iran. Bell and Volynsky traveled together for four years. They journeyed to China, Siberia, and the deserts of Tatar, the historical lands belonging to the Tatars, who you also read about in chapter 2. Soon after completing his journey with Volynsky, Bell was summoned to join Peter the Great (d. 1725) on his expedition to Derbent – a city located in the Republic of Dagestan[14] in Russia – and the Caspian Gates, along the present-day Russian border with Azerbaijan and Georgia. Franklin wrote that Bell appreciated Dagestani hospitality. He described it by claiming that even "if [Dagestan's] greatest enemy comes under their roof for protection [the Dagestani homeowner] is obliged to keep him safe, from all manner of harm or violence . . . and even to conduct him safely through his territories to a place of security." Dagestani hospitality – as with all forms of hospitality – is an asset for community building. A keen sense of community creates feelings of belongingness, which is important in minimizing the potential harmful effects of new wounds opening between Christians and Muslims.

The fourth Islamic example comes from the Andalusian legacy of La Convivencia, which I described in chapter 2. Franklin wrote that the "Moors of [North] Africa" brought a "*punto* of honor" with them to Spain, "the effects of which, remain, in a great degree, [in Spain] to this day" (Franklin 1764). With these words, he suggested that honoring people is a principal element in coming to a collective understanding. Honoring other human beings means that we see each other as having a vital role in each other's lives.

Toward the end of his life, Franklin contributed financially and morally to the building of places of worship of different religious communities in Philadelphia. One place of worship – the Congregation Mikveh Israel – was a Sephardic Jewish community that traced its beginnings in America to around 1740. In that year, Nathan Levy – a Jewish American – received permission from authorities to bury his child in a plot on Spruce Street in Philadelphia (Green 2015). Three years later, Congregation Mikveh Israel started renting a space to serve as a prayer hall. In 1761, its members decided they wanted to create a synagogue, but with the outbreak of the Revolutionary War, the community faced financial difficulties. When the war ended, many of its community members had returned to New York City, where they were originally from. By April 1788, the community was debt-ridden and needed money. Facing default, they reached out to prominent Philadelphians for help. Franklin answered the call by rescuing the debt (Green 2015).

Franklin also contributed a sum of five pounds to a secular hall in Philadelphia in which all people of faith could openly engage in DEUCE. He wanted the hall to be "expressly [used for] any preacher of any religious persuasion who might desire to say something." He added about the new hall – "Even if the *Mufti* of Constantinople [the capital of the Ottoman Empire] were to send a missionary to preach Mohammedanism [Islam], he would find a pulpit at his service" (Franklin 1739). His invitation to the *Mufti* of Constantinople says as much about his views on freedom of speech as it does his views on freedom of religion. He saw freedom of speech and freedom of religion as inextricably linked, as seen in an article he wrote for *The New England Courant* on 9 July 1722:

Without freedom of thought, there can be no such thing as wisdom; and no such thing as public liberty, without freedom of speech; which is the right of every man, as far as by it, he does not hurt or control the right of another (Franklin 1722).

Walter Isaacson, a biographer of Franklin, said that Franklin wanted to build "a new type of nation that could draw from its religious pluralism" (Isaacson 2005: 38). His vision for the new nation was "an aversion to tyranny, a fealty to free expression, a willingness to compromise, the morality of respecting other individuals, and even a bit of humor and humility" (Isaacson 2005: 38). Franklin, Isaacson wrote, "believed in having the humility to be open to different opinions. That for him was not just a practical virtue, but a moral one as well" (Isaacson 2005: 37).

Franklin died in 1790. The *Federal Gazette* in Philadelphia summed up public opinions about him in its brief obituary:

The world has been so long in possession of such extraordinary proofs of the singular abilities and virtues of this FRIEND OF MANKIND that it is impossible for a newspaper to increase his fame, or to convey his name to a part of the civilized globe where it is not already known and admired (National Constitution Center 2023).

On 21 April 1790, the day of his funeral, approximately 20,000 people – or half the population of Philadelphia – paid their respects to Franklin by lining the route of his funeral procession from the State House to the Christ Church burial ground. His casket was carried to his grave by a diverse group of clergymen from around the city in a testament to Franklin's love of humanity and friendships with diverse groups of people.

Appreciating diversity was important to Franklin. He was always willing to talk, listen, and learn. He understood that by increasing our understanding of our own and other's worldview, people can enhance their well-being, strengthen their relationships, and promote a positive outlook on community relations. Following Franklin can help Americans lead happier and more productive lives. More importantly, he can help America treat its wound caused by Islamophobia.

Healing and E Pluribus Unum

Few Americans have ever known more about healing the nation's wounds than Abraham Lincoln (d. 1865), the 16th president of the USA. Lincoln entered the White House as president in 1861, the first year of the Civil War. Two years later, after the Union Victory over the Confederate Army at Gettysburg, Pennsylvania, he delivered his famous "Gettysburg Address" on 19 November 1863 (National Constitution Center n.d.). The brief, two-minute speech pointed to a struggle for the soul of the nation. He said, in part:

> *that from these honored dead [Union and Confederate soldiers] we take increased devotion to that cause for which they gave the last full measure of devotion – that we here highly resolve that these dead shall not have died in vain – that this nation, under God, shall have a new birth of freedom – and that government of the people, by the people, for the people, shall not perish from the earth.*

Lincoln's inspirational words at Gettysburg mirrored the Declaration of Independence's phrase "all men are created equal" (National Constitution Center n.d.). He reinvigorated the American ideals of freedom, liberty, and justice for all. His speech and its myriad themes of reconciliation and sacrifice can be fruitful and important in building bonds between Christians and Muslims, who have had their fair share of conflicts around the West and the Ummah.

President Lincoln's next major speech – his Second Inaugural Address – was given under the newly-completed dome of the Capitol building in Washington, DC, on 4 March 1865. He emphasized the importance of peacebuilding and reconciliation between the Union and the Confederacy in stating:

> *With malice toward none, with charity for all, with firmness in the right, as God gives us to see the right, let us strive on to finish the work we are in, to bind up the nation's wounds, to care for him who shall have borne the battle – and for his widow and his orphan – to do all which may achieve and cherish a just and lasting peace among ourselves, and with all nations (National Park Service 2020).*

With these words, Lincoln showed that the Civil War is best understood as a kind of "divine punishment" for the sin of slavery, a sin for which all

Americans were involved. It is noteworthy that his speech also reframed from words like "me" or "I." He used more inclusive words like "all" or "both" to draw attention to his broader intent (National Park Service n.d.). Just weeks later, he was assassinated in Ford's Theatre by John Wilkes Booth (d. 1865), a stage actor and opponent of the Emancipation Proclamation (1863), which freed the American slaves.

I had the chance to read Lincoln's Second Inaugural Address while visiting Washington, DC, in December 2021. His words are engraved on the north interior wall of the Lincoln Memorial, which stands behind the Washington Monument and adjacent to the Jefferson Memorial at the National Mall. After reading Lincoln's words in quiet reflection, I decided to share my thoughts in a video that I posted to my social media accounts. I turned to three people – Lincoln, Dr. Martin Luther King Jr. (d. 1968), and Prophet Muhammad – as an example of the Synthesis of Civilizations.

The video was filmed on the exact spot where Dr. King Jr. delivered his famous "I Have a Dream" speech in 1963. In it, he stated: "I have a dream that my four little children will one day live in a nation where they will not be judged by the color of their skin but by the content of their character" (King Jr. 1963). With these words, he called on Americans to create an environment where every American can realize his or her dreams, regardless of their identity. They reflect his idea of the "beloved community," where everyone is able to bring their cultural experiences, gifts, and talents to the table for the betterment of the wider community.

King Jr.'s words also mirror the popular transcription of the Farewell Sermon (632), which was delivered by Prophet Muhammad to the Ummah in the last year of his life. In it, he stated:

All mankind is from Adam and Eve. An Arab has no superiority over a non-Arab, nor does a non-Arab have any superiority over an Arab; white has no superiority over black, nor does a black have any superiority over white; [none have any superiority over another] except by piety and good action (Considine 2021: 136).

When I reflect on "I Have a Dream" and the "Farewell Sermon," I am struck by the similarity in their respective languages. I am also reminded of the unofficial motto of America – *E Pluribus Unum* – the Latin term meaning "Out of Many, One." It reveals that inherent in America's very foundation is the ideal that diversity – of opinion and people – is a strength, not a weakness. It is America's most unifying characteristic. It is also the medicine advocated by DEUCE to heal the country's many untreated wounds.

CHAPTER 7

Holiness

The Holy Land

My concluding chapter focuses on the Holy Land, the region of the Middle East that encompasses cities like Bethlehem, Gaza City, Hebron, and Jerusalem, among others. These cities and their surrounding areas are critically important to Jews, Christians, and Muslims. Each population considers these lands to be "holy."

Holiness – the theme of this chapter – is often associated with terms like moral purity, righteousness, and sacredness (New International Version n.d.). At its core, holiness means to separate oneself from moral impurities – or what one might consider harmful or unethical behavior. The term translates the Hebrew word *qadowsh*, which means "to cut off" from the ordinary or the profane.

In the Abrahamic tradition, holiness is linked to the biblical story about God's relationship with Moses and Israel. When God was forging a relationship with the Israelites, he spoke to Moses and said, "Give the following instructions to the entire community of Israel. You must be holy because I – the LORD your God, am holy" (Leviticus 19:2). The verse suggests that following and honoring God – who is forgiving, graceful, just, and merciful – entails being God-like. That means human beings must activate and possess these qualities as they engage with all of God's creation.

Holiness, unfortunately, is out of fashion in today's world, especially in the Holy Land. How has something so central to the Abrahamic tradition become so neglected? How did relations amongst the followers of Abraham become unholy?

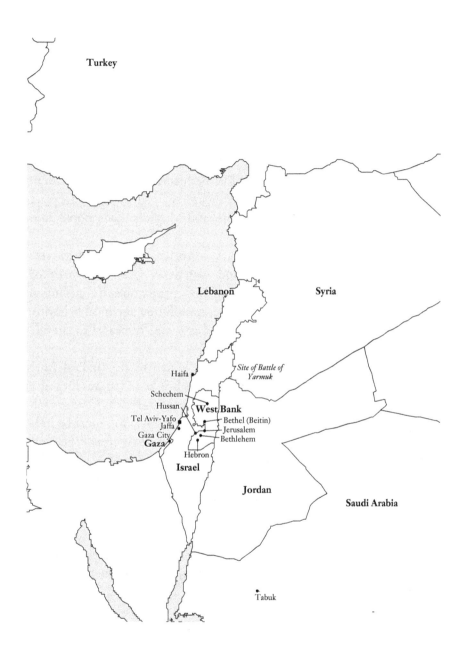

PART ONE – THE CLASH OF CIVILIZATIONS

As has become apparent across this book, the encounters between Christians and Muslims are shaped by a long, shared, and complex history. Throughout this chapter, I will explore the historical backdrop of the Holy Land and the experiences of Jews, Christians, and Muslims within it, dating back to the time of Abraham. Another recurring theme of this book is that relations between Christians and Muslims are historically linked to empire building and the conflicts that come with it. Many problems dividing Christians and Muslims, and indeed Jews in the Holy Land today, are rooted in nineteenth- and twentieth-century wars pitting European nation states against the Ottoman Empire.

The Balfour Declaration and the Partition of the Holy Land

The area of Boston, Massachusetts that I grew up in has a sizeable Jewish population. My hometown – Needham – has approximately 1,000 Jewish people. Newton, its neighboring city, has an even larger community of 30,000 Jews, making it one of the most Jewish cities in the country. The public school systems in the area teach students about the horrors of the Holocaust. I remember my friends telling me survival stories of their grandparents and shared with me the anti-Jewish treatment their relatives received upon arriving on American soil. In my teenage years, I learned about Jewish rituals and traditions by attending about two dozen *bar mitzvah* and *bat mitzvah*. From my peers, I also learned about Israel through their trips on *Aliyah*, the Hebrew term meaning "ascent" and referring to the journeys that Jewish people make to Israel.

Years later, when I moved to Dublin for my PhD program at Trinity College Dublin, I learned about a much more unique perspective of Israel. My education largely came from Dr. Ronit Lentin, an Israeli Irish academic who was then a faculty member of the Department of Sociology at Trinity. A native of Haifa, Israel, Dr. Lentin had written extensively on both Anti-Semitism and Palestinian liberation.[1] I was inspired by her advocacy for a "one-state solution," in which Jews, Christians, Muslims, Israelis, Palestinians, immigrants, and migrants lived in full equality with one another. She also taught me about the

Boycott Divestment and Sanctions (BDS) movement – a controversial movement against Israeli-made goods – and the "right of return," a movement to allow Palestinian families to return to their ancestral lands which they fled during the *Nakba*, the Arabic term meaning "catastrophe" and referring to the Palestinian exodus during and after the Arab–Israeli War in 1948. Studying alongside Dr. Lentin raised my awareness of the Jewish settlements around the Holy Land, which she referred to as "Israeli settler colonialism." While my understanding on these issues have become more nuanced over the years, that part of my education was important in my academic growth.

My experiences while studying in Ireland taught me that it is not a "modern conflict," as many people believe today. History shows us that the Ottoman Empire seized the Holy Land, including Jerusalem, from the Mamluk Empire in 1517. The Ottomans controlled the present-day countries of Israel, Jordan, and the Palestinian territories up until its defeat against France, Italy, Russia, the USA, and the UK during World War I. Prior to its defeat, the empire governed a diverse population of Jews, Christians, Druze, and Muslims, which formed the majority population in the area.

The pre-World War I decades are crucially important in understanding why the Holy Land is a divisive issue between the West and the Ummah today. In 1839 – and again in 1865 – the Ottoman Empire initiated land reforms that allowed the migration of European Jews to cities like Hebron and Jerusalem, two cities that already had sizeable Jewish populations. These European Jews proceeded to shape the Holy Land's educational systems, spoken languages, and general worldviews (Davis 2002: 13). In the Holy Land, the community also maintained links to their former European homes. In 1898, for example, a Jewish community of Jerusalem honored Wilhelm II (d. 1941), the German emperor, when he visited the city, by building a pavilion for him that they decorated with tapestries and Torah scrolls (Ben-David 2023).

The Ottoman Empire's welcoming of Jews to the Holy Land planted the seeds for the movement to establish a nation in the historic land of Israel. The movement's founder – Theodor Herzl (d. 1904), an Austro-Hungarian journalist and politician – called for a Jewish homeland in his influential book, *The Jewish State* (1896), and again at the First Zionist Congress (1897) in Basel, Switzerland. Herzl claimed that creating a Jewish state was a solution to Europe's longstanding mistreatment and persecution of Jews. His proclamation was later recognized in the Balfour Declaration, the single most consequential document and source of controversy in the current state of relations between the West and the Ummah.

On 2 November 1917, Lord Arthur James Balfour (d. 1930) – the British foreign secretary – sent a letter to Lord Walter Rothschild (d. 1937) – a prominent British Jewish banker and politician, promising Rothschild a national homeland for the Jewish people in the Holy Land once the UK gained control of the Ottoman Empire's territories. At the San Remo Conference (1920), European nation states agreed to partition the former Ottoman territories amongst themselves. Two years later – on 24 July 1922 – the agreements of the conference were ratified by the League of Nations, which entrusted the UK with governing Mandatory Palestine and France with governing Mandatory Lebanon. Carving up this part of the Middle East was controversial in its time and it remains so today. Many Muslims saw it, and still see it, as an unholy move that led to future holy wars between Palestine and Israel.

Mandatory Palestine granted permission to European Jews to settle in British territories in the Holy Land. For many Arab Muslims, the UK's decision was perceived as giving special favor to Christians and Jews and amounted to British imperialism in the Ummah. Britain's control of the former Ottoman territories lasted until 29 November 1947, when the United Nations – the follow-up to the League of Nations – enacted the Partition Plan for Palestine. This policy laid the groundwork for the creation of two separate states – a secular Jewish state called Israel, and an Arab Muslim state called Palestine. The former was considered by many Muslims as a "Western colony" designed to further "Westernize" the Ummah. This established some initial barriers to discovering any benefits that could have been undertaken by implementing DEUCE.

When Israel declared its independence on 15 May 1948, it stood as a civic nation based on freedom, justice, and peace as envisaged by the prophets of Israel. Its Declaration of Independence guaranteed freedom of conscience, freedom of expression, and freedom of religion, and added that the Israeli government will "ensure complete equality of social and political rights to all its inhabitants irrespective of religion, race, or sex." It is these civic values and Israel's status as a democracy that are often cited as key considerations of the West's support for Israel, for the Israeli–Palestinian conflict is more than a struggle between Jews, Muslims, Israelis, and Palestinians.

For centuries, the Holy Land has been the battleground of empires. In the twenty-first century, the USA is the dominant foreign influence in the region. Some critics say that the West's alliance with Israel is harmful to peace in the region, while other critics claim that it is vital for the health of democracy in the Holy Land.

After the 7 October 2023 attacks by Hamas on southern Israel and the subsequent launch of an Israeli offensive in Gaza, the response of Western nations such as the USA has been a key flashpoint of international debate. Wherever one might land in the Israeli–Palestinian conflict, it is clear that the Western–Israel partnership is under scrutiny and that its every move is subject to criticism by the Ummah.

The Controversy over the American Embassy in Jerusalem

One of the most contentious and emotional issues in the Israeli–Palestinian conflict is the status of Jerusalem, a city that Israelis and Palestinians both consider their capital. It is also a city that the UN and the USA have long had a strong influence over. The UN partition plan of 1947 envisioned Jerusalem as an "international city" belonging to humanity, but following the Arab–Israeli War of 1948, the UN created the "green line" to separate Israeli controlled West Jerusalem from Jordanian controlled East Jerusalem. In the Six-Day War of 1967, Israel captured East Jerusalem and reunified the city under its control. To this day, the UN considers East Jerusalem to be "occupied territory," meaning that it does not recognize Israel's sovereignty over it.

For Jews, Jerusalem is the holiest city in Judaism. It has served as the center of Jewish life for over 3,000 years, since the time of King David (d. 970 BC). It is the site of the Holy of Holies, the innermost sacred sanctuary of the Tabernacle and later the Temple of Jerusalem. In the Jewish tradition, it hosted the Ark of the Covenant, the chest that protected the tablets of the Ten Commandments as presented by God to Moses. Jerusalem also is home to the Western Wall, the last remnant of the Second Temple where Jews pray today.

In Christianity, Jerusalem also is the site of the Holy of Holies and the metaphorical term representing the sacredness of the innermost sanctuary of the Temple of Jerusalem. For Christians, it is the city where Jesus preached, worshipped, died, and was resurrected.

For Muslims, Jerusalem is known as *Al-Quds* in Arabic. It is the third holiest city in Islam behind Mecca – the site of the Kaaba – and Medina. Muslims refer to the Temple of Jerusalem as the *Al-Haram Al-Sharif*, the Arabic term for "Noble Sanctuary." In the Islamic tradition, it is also the location of the Dome of the Rock, the Al-Aqsa mosque – the third holiest site in Islam – and Prophet Muhammad's ascension to heaven, or the Night Journey.

Given its history and religious importance, it is no wonder that any kind of shift in the status quo of Jerusalem can shake relations between the West and the Ummah and hamper any semblance of DEUCE concepts.

On 6 December 2017, President Donald Trump announced that the American government would recognize Jerusalem as the capital city of Israel, reversing decades of American policies that maintained a neutral position on East Jerusalem's status following Israel's victory in the Six-Day War (1967). Five months later, on 14 May 2018, the USA officially moved its embassy from Tel Aviv – where it had been since the creation of Israel in 1948 – to Jerusalem. Trump claimed that the move was a necessary condition for peace between Israelis and Palestinians (White House 2018). Critics, on the other hand, claimed that the move fanned the flames of the Clash of Civilizations and undermined peace in the region. Experts criticized the US government for "acting like the arsonist" instead of "acting like the fireman" (Underwood 2018). Others were offended by the timing of the embassy's opening – right before what Palestinians call *Nakba* Day (or the Day of Catastrophe) and Ramadan, the Islamic holy month (Underwood 2018). Islamist extremists, on the other hand, used it to craft a narrative that pitted the Ummah against the "crusaders" of the West. ISIS, for instance, responded by uploading social media posts with phrases like "ISIS in Manhattan" and images of an explosive bomb and detonator in Times Square in New York City (Raymond 2017). In the Gaza Strip and the West Bank, dozens of Palestinian protestors were injured in clashes with Israeli forces. Protests also erupted elsewhere in the Ummah, including in Lebanon, Morocco, and Turkey. Needless to say, the challenges to DEUCE are enormous and a lack of DEUCE-oriented opportunities means that holiness is further out of reach in the Holy Land.

Moving the American embassy to Jerusalem has done little to further holiness in the Holy Land. Current perceptions position the USA as pro-Israeli and anti-Palestinian. All parties need to be more attentive to the need to create a DEUCE-like permanent solution that would require immense efforts by both the Israelis and Palestinians, facilitated further by the USA and abetted by the Abraham Accords.

Tensions were heightened again in March 2019, when President Trump shut the American consulate in East Jerusalem, thus downgrading the status of its main diplomatic mission in Palestine. A Palestinian official called Trump's decision "the final nail in the coffin" for the American role as peacemaker in the Holy Land (Harb 2019). One year later, during the Trump administration, the Abraham Accords were signed, which normalized relations between Israel and several Arab nations. Palestinians and their allies typically claim that the Abraham Accords undermine the possibility of a two-state solution, in which the Gaza Strip and the West Bank make up a Palestinian state, neighboring the state of Israel.

For many Palestinian Christians and Muslims in the Holy Land, the American–Israeli alliance is an unholy one. Despite that, for many Israeli Jews, the American–Israeli alliance is a holy one. Herein lies the quandary. Palestine – the hypothetical state of the Palestinian people – is considered by a substantial portion of the West to be the world's epicenter of both Islamism and Anti-Semitism. Israel – the only Jewish state in the world – is considered by a sizeable portion of the Ummah to be a Western-backed, Jewish colonial state that is undertaking a genocide against the Palestinian people. These civilizational dynamics have a significant impact on the experiences of Christians in the Holy Land while rendering considerable challenges to DEUCE.

In the Palestinian territories, Christians are caught between the Israeli–Palestinian conflict and the internal divisions between Hamas – the Islamist organization which governs the Gaza Strip – and Fatah – the Islamist organization which governs the West Bank (Wood 2021). In Israel, conversely, Christians are suspended in-between two groups – Jews and Muslims – and two nationalities – Israelis and Palestinians (Welby and Naoum 2021). While the Israeli Christian population has been growing, the community faces similar circumstances to their peers in the former locations, to which we now turn. In this part of our world, conflict is the norm.

Squeezed Between Israel and Palestine – Christians in the Holy Land

Christians in the Palestinian territories and Israel are often overlooked – and sometimes even forgotten – amidst the Clash of Civilizations in the Holy Land. In the Gaza Strip and the West Bank, their situation is dire, if not grave, as the Christian populations in both locations are dwindling.

Despite having a presence in the Gaza Strip since Philip the Apostle (d. 80) traveled there from Jerusalem in the first century, some experts claim that Christianity in Gaza is on the brink of extinction. Today, Christians are faced with many challenges living under the rule of Hamas, which gained control of the territory in 2007. Ever since then, Christians have been fleeing Gaza due either to the wars between Hamas and Israel, or religious persecution at the hands of Hamas. In 2005, the year that Israel withdrew from 21 Jewish settlements in the strip, the Christian population of the Gaza Strip was around 5,000. As of 2024, there were only 1,300 Christians remaining, most of whom are Greek Orthodox.

The Christian population of Gaza dwindled even further in the aftermath of 7 October 2023. Israel responded with a military campaign that had deadly repercussions for Gazan Christians. On 19 October of that year, an Israeli missile hit the historic Greek Orthodox Church of Saint Porphyrius,[2] killing 17 people. The Orthodox Patriarchate of Jerusalem described the attack as a "war crime" (Mallinder 2023). After 7 October, two Christian women were also killed by an Israeli sniper while walking around the grounds of the Catholic Holy Family Church. A Christian leader responded by lamenting that Christians are squeezed in the middle of two groups that have been fighting for generations (Jaffe-Hoffman 2024).

Given that Christians are suffering (like Muslims) in Gaza, it is unsurprising that both populations express a spirit of solidarity between them. One example of their solidarity occurred in October 2023 when Gabriel Romanelli, the priest of the Holy Family Church, opened his doors to shelter his Muslim neighbors who were sheltering from Israel's military operations (Mallinder 2023).

It is worthy of mention that Palestinian Christians in the Gaza Strip are able to express their faith in public and operate Christian schools. The Rosary Sisters School – one of the four Christian schools in Gaza – decorates a Christmas tree with lights and ornaments every year. Hamas, however, forbids Palestinian Christians from publicly observing Christmas and forces them to observe privately, either in their churches, homes, or organizations (Balousha 2022).

Christians do not fare much better in the West Bank, where they are governed by the Palestinian Authority (PA), whose laws – like those of Hamas – are derived from the Sharia. While the PA allows for freedom of belief and freedom of worship and calls for respect of "all other divine religions," it does so under the watchful eye of maintaining "public morality" (United States Department of State 2019). The PA's leader at the time of writing – Mahmoud Abbas – is widely recognized as being "anti-American" and "anti-Western." A member of the Fatah Central Committee once referred to the American people as "the enemy" and Israel as its "claw in the region" (Hirsch 2022). As mentioned earlier, for many Palestinian Christians and Palestinian Muslims, Israel is viewed as an outpost of the American Empire and its interests in the Holy Land.

But the PA is not the only source of trouble for Palestinian Christians, who are also impacted by Jewish settlements in the West Bank. These settlements are highly controversial and impede progress toward the Dialogue of Civilizations and the Synthesis of Civilizations. Today, there are at least 600,000 Israeli settlers and 146 settlements in the West Bank, which Israel seized in the Six-Day War (1967) (Hudson and DeYoung 2024). The 300,000 Palestinians in the West Bank are under the control of Israeli security forces, which are widely regarded as substantially backed by the American government. Critics claim that the settlements are in violation of the Fourth Geneva Convention, which prohibits the transfer of civilian populations into occupied territories. A sizeable portion of the Ummah sees the USA as enabling what critics refer to as Jewish settler colonialism in the West Bank.

Since the presidency of Jimmy Carter (1976–80), all but two American presidents – Ronald Reagan and Donald Trump – considered the Jewish settlements in the West Bank to be "inconsistent with international law." In 2019, Trump changed course by declaring that his administration did not view the settlements as "illegal." That position was overturned in

2024 by President Joe Biden, who adopted President Carter's original stance (Hincks 2019).

Beyond the legality of these settlements, there is an ugly everyday reality to the separation between the Palestinian communities and Jewish settlements in the West Bank. Critics have claimed that there is nothing "holy" about the "system" of the dividing walls that snake through the hilly and rocky West Bank landscape, which have been described as "imprisoning" thousands of Palestinians (see Schrag 2010). The demolition of Palestinian homes, and the installation of numerous checkpoints, which restrict the ability of Palestinians to routinely move about, have added further to anti-American and anti-Israel hostilities.

In Israel, the overall condition of Christians presents a much more optimistic picture. While the Christian population in Israel has grown in recent years, they still face an uphill battle against second-class citizenship. Israeli Christian leaders claim that the population is experiencing a "historic tragedy unfolding in real time" (British Broadcasting Corporation 2021). One leader claimed that they are subjected to the same "apartheid discrimination" as Muslims and other non-Jews (Hanania 2022). In terms of specific challenges, cases of vandalism against, and the seizure of, church properties are commonplace. Physical assaults and verbal harassment often go unreported.

Christian leaders often blame Jewish extremists – not Muslim extremists – for these kinds of attacks. They point their grievances to events like those that unfolded in March 2023, when a group of Jewish extremists attacked a church in the Garden of Gethsemane, where the Virgin Mary – the mother of Jesus – is believed by some Christians to have been buried. In that event, Jewish extremists entered the church and attacked a priest with a metal rod. Two years earlier – in March 2021 – a Romanian monastery in Jerusalem was vandalized and its entrance set on fire. It was the fourth such attack on the monastery in that month alone (Daily Sabah and Anadolu Agency 2021). Responding to these and other incidents, the Latin Patriarch of Jerusalem at the Holy Family Church – Pierbattista Pizzaballa – said that Jewish extremists felt protected by Israeli Prime Minister Benjamin Netanyahu. Pizzaballa also questioned whether Jewish extremists undercut Israel's commitment to freedom of worship, which, as we saw, is enshrined in the Israeli Declaration of Independence.

It is apparent that the two-state solution represents the most sensible way out of a complex situation, but it has been proven to be insufficient to all parties. The key for any DEUCE-like resolution can only occur when real dialogue, education, and understanding occurs and relevant parties commit themselves to serving others, as service to those in need is an act of holiness.

There are, nevertheless, glimmers of "holiness" in Israel. Consider Michael Ayoub, a Palestinian Catholic, who is famous for serving as a *mesaharati*, the Arabic term for a person who beats a drum to wake Muslims up for *suhoor*, the pre-dawn meal before fasting begins during Ramadan. Ayoub, who hails from Acre, Israel, is by no means a traditional *mesaharati* given his Christian background, but he sees no contradiction in his role. "We are the same family," he told *The Times of Israel*, "There is only one God and there is no difference between Christians and Muslims" (El-Batsh 2016). The Ayoub family has served as *mesaharatis* in Acre for generations. His father, a fervent Catholic, used to listen to readings of the Qur'an every Friday during the main weekly Muslim prayers (El-Batsh 2016). Partly for that reason, Ayoub says he grew up with the idea of coexistence, knowledge, and respect for other religions, all of which signify that he and his family members are committed to living a holy life.

Abraham's Sanctuary in Hebron

A "sanctuary" – the focus of this section – is a sacred place set apart from the profane and ordinary world. Sanctuaries are meant to make human beings feel closer to the divine. They are synonymous with compassion, mercy, and sacredness. I have visited many sanctuaries in my travels over the years. A few experiences are worth noting.

In 2007, I visited Palmyra, New York, where local Mormon leaders gave Dr. Ahmed and me a tour of the sacred grove where Joseph Smith (d. 1844) – the Mormon prophet – received his first revelations. Months later, when we were researching in Salt Lake City, Utah – the primary home of Mormon Americans – we visited the Mormon Church, the iconic building in Temple Square. Our visit, while filled with hospitality and generosity from the Mormon community, did not include a visit to the Celestial Room within the temple. That space, while open to the public for certain events, is typically reserved for Mormons that are in good standing with the Mormon Church. Dr. Ahmed respected their decision, as it was their right to govern and manage their sanctuary according to their desires and needs. To avoid any confusion, he wrote that being in Salt Lake City was like "arriving in familiar territory," adding, "Although I had never been there before, I found nothing but friendliness" (Ahmed 2010: 411).

Other sanctuaries in the world – like the Tomb of the Patriarchs in Hebron, a city in the West Bank – do not conjure up these kinds of feelings of respect and tolerance. As one of the oldest inhabited cities in the world, Hebron has always been a battleground of various civilizations, and it remains one to this day.

In ancient times (around 1010–970 BC), King David was made king of Israel in Hebron, located a little under 20 miles south of Jerusalem, which he made his capital for seven years until seizing Jerusalem. In modern times, the city was administered by the British in Mandatory Palestine (1920–48), by Jordan after the Arab–Israeli War (1948–9), and by Israel following the Six-Day War (1967). In the wake of an agreement in January 1997, it came under the administration of the Palestinian Authority (PA), while parts of it were still under Israeli control.

For the Jewish people, the Sanctuary of Abraham is the second holiest place in Judaism after the Temple Mount in Jerusalem. In Hebron, Abraham is reported to have purchased the Cave of Machpelah as a burial site for Sarah, his wife. The location later became a family sepulcher. According to tradition, Abraham, Isaac, and Jacob – along with Sarah, Rebekah, and Leah, their wives – are buried there.

Also known as the Tomb of the Patriarch or the Ibrahimi Mosque, the Sanctuary of Abraham has been a site of both holiness and unholiness, of prayer and worship, and of bloodshed and division. Around the year 570, Justinian I – the Emperor of Byzantium – built a church on the site. His structure was destroyed in 614 by the Sassanian Empire, which left the site in ruins. Around the year 620, Prophet Muhammad is reported to have visited the Sanctuary of Abraham on his Night Journey to Jerusalem, a journey that made Hebron the fourth holiest city in Islam behind Mecca, Medina, and Jerusalem. In 637, after the Ummah seized Hebron, Muslims built the Ibrahimi Masjid – or Abraham Mosque – on the site of the former Byzantine church. During the First Crusade, the

Crusaders seized control and turned the site back into a church. In doing so, they banned Muslims from entering the holy sanctuary, a policy that was not reversed until Saladin's victory in 1187 during the Third Crusade. Saladin turned the site back into a mosque, but he also allowed Christians to worship there.

Three other empires – the Mamluk, Ottoman, and British – had control of the Sanctuary of Abraham prior to the creation of Israel in 1947. Under the Mamluks, Jews and Christians were forbidden from entering the sanctuary. Under the Ottomans, which governed Hebron from Constantinople as part of the Sanjak of Jerusalem – the site was strictly reserved for use by Muslims. Under the British, which seized Hebron on 8 December 1917 during World War I, the tomb remained closed to non-Muslims, but the area maintained a general peace.

Relations between the Abrahamic populations in Hebron reached a boiling point after World War I. The city was populated by Arab Muslims and had a small Jewish community. In 1929, Haj Amin Al-Husseini (d. 1974) – the Mufti of Jerusalem and a Palestinian Arab nationalist – encouraged riots against the Jews. Sixty-seven Hebron Jews were massacred on 23 August of that year. Seven years later, in 1936, the Hebronite Jewish community moved out of Hebron as a precautionary measure to secure their safety. Only one Hebronite – Ya'akov Ben Shalom Ezra – was allowed to remain in the city. Jordan took control of the West Bank following the partition of Palestine in 1948. The Jordanians banned Jews from entering the building. In 1967, when the IDF seized control of Hebron, the Chief Rabbi of the IDF – Shlomo Goren (d. 1994) – entered the Cave of Machpelah. Since then, Jews have sought to regain their right to pray at the site, which is currently run by the Muslim Waqf (Religious Trust). After Israel's victory over Egypt, Jordan, and Syria in the Six-Day War (1967), Israeli settlers renewed the Jewish presence in the city. Their growth in Hebron was interpreted by many Muslims as unholy because it led to the infringement upon their livelihood and property rights.

The Sanctuary of Abraham became the center of international headlines on 25 February 1994. On that day, Baruch Goldstein (d. 1994) – a Jewish extremist and Israeli American physician – killed 29 Palestinian Muslims while they were praying at the site. Following Goldstein's attack, the Israeli Defense Forces (IDF) shut down the Ibrahimi Mosque for several months. When they reopened it, the mosque had installed a military checkpoint for tourists and visitors. The building also was divided into a Jewish side and a Muslim side, separated by bulletproof glass. As of 2024, only Jews are allowed to enter the southwestern side of the building. Muslims, on the other hand, are only allowed to enter on the northeastern side of the building.

As in the case with the American Embassy moving to Jerusalem, the US government has been accused by local Palestinian leaders of siding with Israel over the status of the Sanctuary of Abraham. The Mufti of Jerusalem – Sheikh Mohammad Hussein – condemned the visit by Mike Pence, the former vice president of the USA, in 2022, and claimed that he had "stormed" the site (Abu Toameh 2022). The term "stormed" is sometimes used in the Ummah to describe visits by Jewish worshippers to the Temple Mount in Jerusalem. The sanctuary also recently attracted attention when Hussein and other Palestinian leaders criticized the Israeli government's plan to "Judaize" the area by excavating its courtyards.

It is also worth mentioning that the building's two sides – one for Jews and one for Muslims – is a sign of potential coexistence. The key to fostering a peaceful environment is to keep at bay the surrounding volatility in Hebron. Although Abraham's sanctuary is a holy site to multiple faiths, it has not yet managed to find a peaceful balance. Treating it as a holy site means that followers of the Abrahamic faiths must be inspired to live in holiness while there or elsewhere.

PART TWO – THE DIALOGUE OF CIVILIZATIONS

For all its history of conflict, the Holy Land is undoubtedly a fertile location for tolerance and understanding between Christians and Muslims. Even amidst invasions and seizure of lands by empires, there have been moments in history when holiness outshone unholiness.

The Pact of Umar and the Jerusalemite Christians

Christian and Muslim relations in the Holy Land date back to the years between 610 – when Prophet Muhammad started receiving revelations on Mount Hira – and 632 – when he died. The first conflict between these two populations was the Expedition of Tabuk (630), during which Prophet Muhammad led his army from Medina north to Tabuk, near the Gulf of Aqaba, in present-day northwestern Saudi Arabia. The battle pitted Prophet Muhammad's army against soldiers of the Byzantine Empire. While no Byzantine army met Muhammad and his army on the battlefield, the moment marked the beginning of the Arab–Byzantine Wars, which would last up until the eleventh century.

During the rule of Prophet Muhammad and Abu Bakr (d. 634) – the first caliph – the Ummah did not expand outside of present-day Saudi Arabia. However, under the rule of Umar Ibn Al-Khattab (d. 644) – the second caliph of Islam – Muslim armies marched north to face the Byzantines in the Holy Land. In 636, Umar sent Khalid Ibn Al-Walid (d. 642) and Amr Ibn Al-'As (d. 664) – his top two generals – to engage the Byzantine army. The two sides met that year at the Battle of Yarmuk, along what are now the borders of Jordan–Syria and Israel–Syria. At Yarmuk, the Byzantines were dealt a decisive blow. One year later, after a long besiegement, Umar conquered Jerusalem.

The Islamic conquest was unlike the bloody Christian conquests during the Crusades, which you read about in chapter 2. The Ummah's seizure of Jerusalem in 637 was a relatively peaceful conquest. According to Islamic tradition, Patriarch Sophronius (d. 638) – a representative of the Byzantine government in Jerusalem – invited Umar to his city so he could surrender it to him. Upon his arrival, Umar was given a tour of the city by Sophronius, who took him directly to the Church of the Holy Sepulcher. Sophronius and the Muslims assumed Umar would pray in the church and convert the site into a mosque, but – in a symbolic gesture of tolerance – he declined the offer, fearing that Muslims would interpret it as a sign of the church's conversion into a mosque.

Instead of seizing the Church of the Holy Sepulcher, the Muslims built a mosque – the Mosque of Umar – on a neighboring site where he instead chose to pray. His decision is vastly different from the seizure of later churches by Muslims, like – most famously – the Hagia Sophia's conversion to a mosque in 1453 after the Ottomans conquered Constantinople, the capital of the Byzantine Empire.

The face-to-face encounter between Umar and Sophronius resulted in the Pact of Umar. This DEUCE-like agreement outlined the obligations and restrictions of Christians and other non-Muslim populations under the Sharia. Christians were considered by the pact to be *dhimmi* – or "protected people" – which meant that they had to pay a special tax – known as the *jizya* in Arabic – to maintain their religious practices in exchange for protection and exemption from military service. Christians were guaranteed protections of their churches, lives, and property. While they were allowed to practice Christianity, they were not allowed to build new churches or publicly display the cross or other Christian symbols. Christians also were required to wear a blue belt to distinguish them from Muslims.

Scholars have long debated whether the Pact of Umar is a symbol of holiness or unholiness. In defense of its holiness, some have claimed that it showed how leaders are able to rise above temporal conflicts, territorial ambitions, and an overall hunger for power. One commentator claimed it was, at the time, "by far one of the most progressive treaties in history" (Alkhateeb 2023). Other critics, however, claimed that it promoted second-class citizenship for the non-Muslims of Jerusalem (Wasserstein 2017). Some critics have even claimed that the pact itself is a fabrication because later Muslim leaders did not apply its generous terms in their agreements with Christians and Jews, which they would have, had the pact actually existed.

The Ummah ruled Jerusalem for the next 462 years, at which point the city returned to the possession of Christians following the First Crusade of 1099. The victorious Crusaders, as noted in chapter 2, slaughtered the city's Jewish and Muslim inhabitants upon seizing control. After changing hands to Saladin in 1187, Jerusalem stayed in the hands of different Islamic empires until after World War I, when Mandatory Palestine came under British control.

The cyclical and deleterious relationship between Christians and Muslims in the Holy Land is still extant to this day, despite relatively positive stories like Umar's. The unstable vestiges of the conflict between the early Arab armies and the Byzantine Empire still hover over Israel and the Palestinian territories.

The Keys to Peace – Muslim Allies at the Holiest Site in Christendom

Living in peace in the Holy Land requires constant effort and compromise from all populations that call it home. It calls for both peacekeepers – people or groups that prevent conflicts from escalating – and peacemakers – people or groups who actively work to establish peace.

Oftentimes, Christians and Muslims need both peacekeepers and peacemakers to settle their divisions and feuds. Sometimes, they are needed within Christian and Muslim communities respectively, to mend their internal divisions and feuds. Only by resolving their inner disputes are communities able to properly mend the divisions across the perceived divides between these two populations.

Such is the case at the Church of the Holy Sepulcher, the holiest site in Christendom. Located in the Christian Quarter of the Old City of Jerusalem, the church is believed to be Calvary (also known as Golgotha) – the site where Jesus was crucified – and the location of the Edicule, the small structure within the church that encloses his tomb, from which Christians believe he resurrected. The original church on the site was ordered by Constantine the Great, the Emperor of Rome, in the fourth century. The current structure reflects a combination of architectural styles, including those from the Romans, the Byzantines, the Crusaders, and the Ottomans.

Given its importance to Christians, it is no surprise that the Church of the Holy Sepulcher is a battleground for the different Christian sects jostling over its control. The current church is split between Armenian Apostolic, Coptic Orthodox, Ethiopian Orthodox, Greek Orthodox, Roman Catholics, and Syriac Orthodox. In other words, none of the six groups that now occupy the church has single authority in managing the building. These denominations have agreed to a status quo whereby each sect controls a different section of the space. The status quo dates back to 1852, when Abdülmecid I – the Ottoman sultan – decreed that the church was to be managed by the Armenian Apostolics, the Greek Orthodox, and the Roman Catholics.

The "Immovable Ladder" is one of the symbols of the tense relationship between Christians at the holiest site in Christendom. The ladder, which stands on a ledge over a church door, was placed there 300 years ago. If any Christian group moves it – or even tries to move it – there would be immediate conflict. Keeping it in its place signaled that the different sects were abiding by the status quo, which was broken in 2002, when a Coptic monk moved a chair on the roof occupied by Ethiopian monks. After the status quo was violated, a fight broke out and 11 monks were hospitalized (Jacobs 2021).

Keeping the relative peace at the Church of the Holy Sepulcher would not be possible if it were not for a 500-year-old cast-iron key that is used to open and lock the church's front doors, known as the Doors of Humility. The key is currently in the possession of the Joudehs, a Palestinian Muslim family that has been keeping the peace at the holiest site in Christendom since the twelfth century. Adeeb Joudeh is the current key holder.

Historians differ on the roots of the arrangement, but historical records suggest that the key may have been first given to the Joudeh family by Saladin, the Muslim hero of the Third Crusade who expelled the Crusaders from Jerusalem. Some historians say that Saladin designated the Joudeh family as the key holders to assert his dominance over Christianity in the city. Others say that he chose a Muslim family to serve as a neutral mediator in conflicts amongst Christians. Either way, few doubt the significant role that a neutral mediator plays at the site.

Being the peacekeepers of the Church of the Holy Sepulcher is more than just a family tradition for the Joudehs. "We coexist and pass peace and love, which is the real Islamic religion," he once told local media (Liebermann 2016). In another interview, he referred to the Church of the Holy Sepulcher as his "second home" (Harash 2017). When Adeeb passes the keys onto the next generation of Joudeh key holders, they are also passing along the holiness that the Church of the Holy Sepulcher represents to Christians.

The Joudeh family are not the only guardians of the Church of the Holy Sepulcher. Another Muslim family – the Nuseibeh family – is responsible for swinging the Doors of Humility open to allow visitors and churchgoers to enter. Wajeeh Nuseibeh, a Palestinian Muslim, is the current "door opener," a service that his family was reportedly authorized to take by Saladin's decree dated to 10 February 1187.

Because of Adeeb and Wajeeh's role as peacekeepers, the various Christian communities at the Church of the Holy Sepulcher are able to coexist in a relative state of harmony. Without them, there would be no peace on the site of Jesus's burial and resurrection. These Palestinian Muslims are both reminders of the vital role that neutral parties play in combatting the Clash *within* Civilizations and fostering the Dialogue of Civilizations in the Holy Land and beyond.

PART THREE – THE SYNTHESIS OF CIVILIZATIONS

While one would be remiss to underestimate the importance of peace-keepers, it is critical to distinguish them from peacemakers. The difference between peacekeepers and peacemakers is similar to the difference between tolerance and pluralism. The former term points to maintaining the status quo, while the latter points to an energetic engagement with diversity. Peacekeeping sets out to maintain peace by avoiding conflict, while peacemaking entails engaging in conflict resolution to bring about stability and unity.

Blessed Are the Peacemakers

Peacemaking was central to the earthly mission of Jesus. In the Beatitudes – the teachings he outlined in the Sermon on the Mount – he described the holiness of peacemakers in stating, "Blessed are the peacemakers, because they will be called sons of God" (Matthew 5:9). These words suggest that peacemaking is holy work. His words also call for action and engagement. Jesus understood that peace never happens by chance, but rather by energy and a commitment to uplifting humanity.

Few leaders in the Holy Land have furthered peace between the Abrahamic faiths more than Rabbi Yakov Nagen. Born in Manhattan, Rabbi Nagen studied at Yeshiva University and settled in Othniel, a small settlement south of Hebron. He was a student of Rabbi Menachem Froman (d. 2013), the former chief rabbi of Tekoa and bridge builder in the Holy Land's religious and political landscape. When Rabbi Froman passed away in 2013, his character was praised by a diverse group of people. Peace Now, a peacemaking group, called him a "brave and very special man who believed with all his heart that Jews and Arabs can live together on this land" (Friedman and Leshem 2013). Ziad Sabatin, a Palestinian Muslim from the town of Husan and an advocate of the Froman-inspired group called Land of Peace, called him "our teacher."

Rabbi Nagen, in taking after Rabbi Froman, is a quintessential example of DEUCE in action. He is the co-chairman of the Abrahamic Reunion, a grassroots organization founded in 2004 to bring together members of the four major Abrahamic religions – Judaism, Christianity, Islam, and Druze – to eat, study, and work together. The Abrahamic Reunion's basic premise is that "religion has been used to divide people in the Holy Land and it can also be used as a force to bring people together while still respecting divergent points of view and cultures" (Abrahamic Reunion n.d.). The organization's founding principles include sharing the belief in one God, understanding other religions, using religion as a force for peace, and relating to all of humanity as though everyone is part of one family. It also uses art and culture as tools in its peacemaking work.

As the director of the Blickle Institute for Interfaith Dialogue, Rabbi Nagen trains individuals to bring about changes to interfaith relations in the Holy Land. Each year, the institute selects a group of 12 people to meet regularly to discuss peacemaking in the West Bank. His vision for the region follows the kind of rapprochement between Jews and Christians that followed the publication of *Nostra Aetate* (1965), the declaration of the Second Vatican Council in Rome. Rabbi Nagen also values the Abraham Accords, which he said are rooted in a shared Abrahamic identity and a common vision on dealing with challenges in the Holy Land. "In the path ahead of us, we cannot do it alone. We need the powerful symbols of Abraham, Isaac, Ishmael, Sarah, and Hagar [the ancestors and distinct heirs of the Abrahamic tradition]," he said, adding, "With these symbols together, perhaps we can change the world." He included that the Abraham Accords could "bring an atmosphere of peace that will benefit both sides." In regard to his Israeli Jewish peers, he encouraged them to adopt "vision mode" rather than the "survival mode" that he claimed they have maintained over the last 2,000 years (Rosenbaum 2023).

The Interfaith Encounter Association (IEA), an Israeli-based and non-profit organization founded and directed by Yehuda Stolov, is another inspiration for peacemaking in the Holy Land. Founded in 2001 shortly after the beginning of the Second Intifada – a major uprising by Palestinians against Israel between 2000 and 2005 – its primary focus is to foster dialogue between the various religious communities in the region. The IEA website lays out a step-by-step process that is similar to

DEUCE (Interfaith Encounter Association n.d.). The first stage entails the IEA inviting people from different faiths from across the Holy Land and beyond to join their groups. Once the groups are formed, its participants engage in meaningful encounters – the second stage – which helps them build bridges. The third stage is tasked with transforming hostility, prejudice, and suspicion into hospitality, friendship, and mutual respect. The fourth stage entails collectively engaging in inter-communal relations and thus serving as a model for peacebuilding.

In an effort to deploy a DEUCE solution, both the Israelis and the Palestinians must follow in Rabbi Nagen and his allies' footsteps. It is also wise to adopt an *E Pluribus Unum* mentality where all entities, including the Christians, are equal. This is a complex and difficult task that could foster a conscientious mindset where all parties are engaged in efforts that promote the Synthesis of Civilizations.

Abraham's Tent and Tikkun Olam in the Twenty-First Century

As we saw in chapter 1 with the Abrahamic Family House, the prophet Abraham – revered by Jews, Christians, and Muslims – is a unifying historical figure in the interplay between the West and the Ummah. He is the name bearer of the Abraham Accords – the peace treaty between Israel and several Arab nations – and an inspiration behind the award-winning film *Amen, Amen, Amen*.

I first learned about *Amen, Amen, Amen* at the inauguration ceremony of the Abrahamic Family House in Abu Dhabi. There, I was fortunate to spend several days with Tom Gallagher, the Executive Director of the film, which explored the journey of a Torah scroll gifted by the Jewish community in Dubai to the president and crown prince of the UAE, in honor of his father, the late Sheikh Zayed, the founding father of the UAE whom you read about in chapter 1. I hosted Gallagher and Livia Link-Raviv, the Consul General of the Israeli Consulate of the Southwest, for a public screening and Q&A discussion at Rice University in September 2023, just weeks before Hamas attacked southern Israel on 7 October. Included in the audience were members of the Ahmadiyya Muslim community, the Gülen movement, students of diverse backgrounds, among dozens of other guests. I was honored to host such a diverse and dynamic group of people, and did my best to show the utmost hospitality, a value emphasized by Abraham himself.

Unbeknownst to many, Abraham lived most of his life as a nomad living out of a tent. According to Genesis (4:20), he pitched a tent in Bethel while traveling through the land of Canaan with his wife Sarah and nephew Lot. Genesis (4:20) adds that Isaac – the son of Abraham, pitched a tent in the valley of Gerard. Isaac's son – Jacob – also is reported in Genesis (33:18) to have pitched a tent in Shechem. The tents of Hebrew patriarchs like Abraham were known for their compassion, generosity, hospitality, and humility, all of which are central to the theme of holiness.

Abraham's tent is the inspiration of an interfaith initiative called the Museum of Tolerance, the brainchild of Teddy Kollek, the former mayor of Jerusalem. Located in Jerusalem, the museum not only connects the Old City of Jerusalem to the New City of Jerusalem, but it is also bridging the gap between people of distinct cultural orientations, ethnicities, and religions (Linde 2022).

The Museum of Tolerance sits on three acres of land that includes an amphitheater, a book and gift shop, and a museum, among other entities. Its plaza – *Tikkun Olam* garden – is named after the Hebrew term *Tikkun Olam*, which refers to "mending and repairing" a world rife with conflict and strife. Its conference center hosts global leaders to promote values like humanity, respect, and tolerance. Its exhibition spaces have included "Social Lab," which allows visitors to build interfaith connections and explore cross-cultural encounters. The museum captures all five layers of DEUCE by promoting dialogue, education, understanding, commitment, and engagement amidst all of humanity.

The Museum of Tolerance, however, is the subject of controversy over land rights in Jerusalem. The museum sits on the corner of Independence Park, which was formerly a large Muslim cemetery (Hecht 2016). In 2006, excavation work on the site was halted after Muslim groups claimed that graves and human remains were uncovered. Despite this controversy, the Museum of Tolerance remains a hopeful symbol of Abraham's spirit in the twenty-first century. Like the Abraham Accords and the Abrahamic Family House, it represents a modern harbinger capable of fostering greater mutual understanding.

Yet, there is still potential for tension. The sheer blending of lands and religions in the Holy Land is what makes peaceful coexistence so difficult. DEUCE and the Synthesis of Civilizations thus become paramount. Building societies around civility and secularism allows people to openly practice their faith. When Jews, Christians, and Muslims uphold civic values – while maintaining the positive values of their own respective religions – they are walking on the path to holiness.

Holy Land, Holy People

The beginning of this chapter mentioned Leviticus (19:2), the biblical verse in which God instructs Moses and the Israelites to be holy because God is holy. This should apply to today as well, and not merely to the Jewish people, but to Christians and Muslims, who are their spiritual cousins.

One commentary on Leviticus 19:2 provided inspiration for how human beings can live in the light of God: "Our words should be holy. Our actions should be holy. Our thoughts should be holy. The way we live should be holy" (Wellspring Christian Ministries 2020). Notice that the commentary did not connect holiness to doctrine or dogma. It focused instead on actions and behavior within and between human beings, who are in much need of DEUCE-oriented solutions. Whatever happens in the Holy Land, it will likely not be perfect, but it will be a vast improvement on the circumstances that prevail today.

Conclusion
DEUCE in Action

I began planning this book in 2021. The world has changed a great deal since then, and so have I. As my country – and the world – seemed to veer toward polarization, extremism, and cancel culture, I yearned for balance, dialogue, and nuance. As Christians and Muslims looked to be more divided than ever, I worked to build bonds between them. As politicians and the media used stories to divide us, I sought positive stories that could unite us. And as the West and the Ummah appeared to be fixated and entrenched in their historical entanglements, I focused on the possibilities for building a better future.

DEUCE and the Synthesis of Civilizations

The two main contributions made by this book – DEUCE and the Synthesis of Civilizations – are key to building bonds between Christians and Muslims, as well as the West and the Ummah. To activate DEUCE, more Grey Zone spaces are needed to foster collaboration between individuals and communities. Critical to the success of DEUCE is the sense of local ownership to ensure that the needs and priorities of all populations are met. Current interfaith initiatives – like the House of One in Berlin, and modern-day bridge builders like Rabbi Nagen – are models for breaking new ground regarding the possibilities for civilizational synthesis. It is also worth remembering that DEUCE also can be nourished amidst areas where inhumanity is present. Ted Hakey Jr.'s transformation after attacking the Ahmadiyya Muslim community mosque in Meriden, Connecticut, and Benjamin Franklin's essay following the massacres of the Conestoga people by the Paxton Boys, are a few of the contemporary and historical examples touched upon in this book.

DEUCE is a vehicle to counter the Clash of Civilizations and further boost the Dialogue of Civilizations and the Synthesis of Civilizations. The latter is the ideal state for Christian and Muslims, as it points to a civic-oriented synthesis that unites diverse people on common democratic principles. The civic synthesis is made possible by pluralism – the energetic engagement with diversity – and not merely by tolerance alone, although I do not question the importance of the latter. It is also furthered when governments and societies uphold and promote secularism – the separation between religion and government – which pushes back against the exclusivism of political philosophies linked to Islamism. Countries that slide towards Islamism – as we saw historically with Maududi and Ul-Haq in Pakistan, and as we see today with Erdoğan in Turkey – are counter to DEUCE and to the Synthesis of Civilizations.

I hope that this book provides useful examples to discuss and elaborate upon the Synthesis of Civilizations in the history of Christian and Muslim relations. There are countless examples to choose from. Arabs, Berbers, Christians, and Jews produced a rich culture in Islamic Spain, with the Cathedral-Mosque of Córdoba serving as its crown jewel. Norman kings like Roger II of Sicily governed in a manner that fused Arab, Byzantine, Islamic, and Norman principles. In British India, Sir Sayyid created Aligarh Muslim University, which united Islamic and Western educational practices and systems. In the American context, George Washington and Sultan Abdullah of Morocco allied themselves based on collective ideas and a similar vision for a freer world. The Abrahamic Family House in Abu Dhabi is an iconic example of DEUCE in action and the civic synthesis that often comes with it. Even in war-torn places like Iraq, cultural programs like Reviving the Spirit of Mosul have successfully brought Christians and Muslims together in creative ways.

The Seven H's – Summary of Chapters

Before closing, let us walk quickly through the seven chapters' locations, focusing on the seven core virtues touched on in each – values which can be shared by Christians, Muslims, and those of other faiths and none, and which, crucially, benefit us *all* as we seek to live fulfilling lives.

The first chapter focused on the fundamental virtue of *humanity* around the Arabian Peninsula. In Saudi Arabia, led by Mohammad bin Salman – its current leader – we see the ushering in of transformational changes to counteract the pitfalls of Wahhabism and recognize the dignity of all human beings. Mohammad bin Salman could tighten the Synthesis of Civilizations even further by bringing Saudi Arabia into the fold of the Abraham Accords. Saudi Arabia's neighbor – the UAE, a signee to the Abraham Accords – has long been a leader in promoting tolerance, a value which respects our common humanity. Traveling to the UAE on multiple occasions has been inspiring for me as a young bridge builder and peacemaker. I am confident that it will continue inspiring future generations of Emiratis, just as it might inspire Americans like me.

Building on humanity, the second chapter turned to *hybridity* on the European continent. Despite the prevalence of Fortress Europe and the baggage of the Crusades, Christians and Muslims in Europe have managed to work together – and even flourish together – in locations like Córdoba, Palermo, and Berlin, where they engaged in projects that synthesize the better qualities of the West and the Ummah. These positive stories of hybridity, however, rarely get the airtime that anti-immigrant and nativist policies on the continent receive.

On Europe's eastern edge, we saw in chapter 3 how Turkey faces an ongoing negotiation of *heterogeneity*, a reality that in our increasingly interconnected and complex world, all parts of the globe need to learn to work and succeed with. How Turkey treats its dwindling Christian population will shape the country's relationship with the West in the generations ahead. Reconverting the Hagia Sophia into a mosque exacerbated the Clash of Civilizations. It is my belief that it serves humanity better by serving as an interfaith monument. The decision was roundly condemned in the West for furthering the dominance of Islamism and neo-Ottomanism in Turkey. These kinds of moves – along with Turkey's colonial presence in Cyprus and its antagonistic relations with neighboring Greece – are at odds with the spirit of the Ottoman Empire's *tanzimat* reforms in the nineteenth century, which gave Christians more dignity and rights in Ottoman society. They are also at odds with Kemalism – with its separation of church and state – and the Gülen movement – with its emphasis on civility, dialogue, and education. But those opposition movements – those alternatives – do exist, and we see hope for heterogeneity which encourages national as well as civilizational flourishing.

Chapter 4 also focused a good deal on Islamism, but through the British Indian and the Pakistani contexts. The theme of that chapter – *honor* – plays a vital role in South Asian societies, and it often ebbs and flows between democracy and theocracy, with the likes of Sir Sayyid and Jinnah promoting the former, and figures like Maududi and Ul-Haq representing the latter. To further the Synthesis of Civilizations, Pakistanis today can look to historical role models like Akbar the Great, who stood for "Peace with All" – and contemporary role models – like Mirza Masroor Ahmad, the current caliph of the Ahmadiyya Muslim community, whose motto is "Love For All, Hatred For None."

The mottos of Akbar the Great and the Ahmadiyya Muslim community align with the notion of *harmony* (*Ubuntu*), explored in the book's journey to various parts of the African continent in chapter 5. At the core of *Ubuntu* is the idea that one person or community's well-being is mutually dependent on the well-being of other individuals or groups. The opposite of *Ubuntu* – conflict, division, violence, and warfare – is occurring in northern Nigeria, a country that I described as the "eye of the storm" for Christian persecution in the world. While the situation facing the Copts of Egypt is not as severe as it is in Nigeria, these Christians still suffer from persecution, too. Egypt's relationship with Christendom and the West has a bright spot in the Wafd Party, the political group whose secular slogan of "Religion is For God, Egypt is For All" is a rallying cry for harmony that could serve as an example across the globe.

The theme of *healing* (chapter 6) centered around American society, and the need for healing will be immediately obvious to all readers, especially in the context of the USA. Americans of previous generations had to deal with slavery, whereas Americans today are dealing with Islamophobia, which has led to a surge in discrimination and persecution toward Muslim Americans, particularly since 9/11. To heal in the years ahead, I encourage readers to uplift the "pluralist vision" of the US Founding Fathers. While they were not perfect, they established the foundation for the flourishment of the civic nation, which is best captured by America's motto, *E Pluribus Unum*, the Latin term meaning "Out of Many, One." This motto, which also captures the essence of the Synthesis of Civilizations, is evident throughout American history, from Pinckney's oath to Jefferson's Qur'an, to Benjamin Franklin's appreciation of Islamic values in his *Narrative of the Late Massacres*.

Finally, *holiness* is a fitting term for the closing chapter of a book concerned with building bonds between Christians and Muslims. The modern-day crisis facing Christians and Muslims in the Holy Land is rooted in rivalries between European nation-states and the Ottoman Empire in the nineteenth and twentieth centuries. Today, Christians are squeezed, to their detriment, in-between many populations in the Holy Land, including between Hamas, the Palestinian Authority (PA), Muslim extremists, Israel, Israeli Defense Forces (IDF), and far-right Jewish extremists. The Pact of Umar, the seventh-century agreement between the Christians of Jerusalem and the leader of the Ummah, provides inspiration for modern changes. Muslims in cities like Jerusalem play a pivotal role in holding the fabric of the Christian community together by serving as peacekeepers in the holiest site in Christendom, the Church of the Holy Sepulcher.

Readers should also not forget about the difference between peacemaking and peacekeeping. Peacemaking requires deliberate action in terms of conflict resolution, while peacekeeping simply maintains the status quo. At the heart of both Christianity and Islam is a call to holiness. While some of the "H" virtues highlighted in this book might appear secular in nature, holiness is certainly the most religious. With eyes simultaneously focused on the other values and the inspiration of DEUCE, however, we can see how holiness demands peaceful coexistence (peacekeeping) and energetic engagement (peacemaking).

Call to Action

The stained-glass window on the cover of this book is a microcosm of the historical interplay between the West and the Ummah. It is located in a room known as the Cenacle, a term derived from the Latin word *ceno*, meaning "I dine." The Cenacle is held by Christians to be the site of the Last Supper, the final meal that Jesus – who is revered by Muslims as a prophet – shared with his Apostles before his crucifixion in Jerusalem.

The sacredness of the Cenacle has led to clashes between Christian and Muslim nations and empires throughout the ages. The Romans, Byzantines, Crusaders, and the British – as well as the Fatimids, Ottomans, and Jordanians – have all controlled the site at various points in history. The present building was built by the Crusaders, the Western European

Christians who conquered parts of the Holy Land from the eleventh to the sixteenth centuries. For Muslims, the Crusaders are a sour reminder of the violent expansion of Christianity and the havoc that Christians committed on Muslim communities throughout times.

In spite of this bleak depiction of Christian and Muslim relations, the window in the Cenacle inspires optimism and offers a worthy challenge for Christians and Muslims. Its Arabic inscription translates to "Judge between the people in truth and do not follow your own desire" (Qur'an 38:26).

These words are a fitting reminder for Christians and Muslims in their dealings with and treatment of the other. Spreading falsehoods or untruths damages trust in human relationships and stalls – or at worse prevents – any progress in fostering constructive interactions between groups of people. Followers of Jesus – both Christians and Muslims – would be wise to heed the Qur'an's advice – always operate in the truth rather than belief or ideology.

Being truthful with each other is essential to growth and maturity and crucial in nurturing peace and unity. Without the truth, there can be no security or even survival. Only the truth will set Christians and Muslims free.

As I conclude this book, let me provide advice on your possible next steps and actions to pursue DEUCE in the future. Firstly, it is crucial to understand the complex history between Christians and Muslims, and between the West and the Ummah. Edmund Burke (d. 1797), the Irish statesman, captured this point best when he said, "Those who do not know history are destined to repeat it." Burke is right. Understanding history provides a necessary context for understanding current events and helps today's human beings avoid the mistakes made by their ancestors. Learning history teaches us about inspiring role models who can serve as guides for the twenty-first century. Knowing history preserves the memories of past events, and thus ensures that Christianity and Islam are preserved for centuries to come.

My second piece of advice is to avoid binaries or thinking that there are only two sides to choose from – in the context of this book, you are either with Christians or Muslims, or with the West or the Ummah. Binary thinking oversimplifies complex situations, promotes assumptions and stereotypes, and leads to conflict and detachment between groups of people. While binaries provide a sense of certainty, they also steer human beings away from clarity and knowledge. To avoid binary thinking, I encourage readers to meet new people, build empathy, be curious about other cultures and nations, and listen to diverse voices with an open mind. Furthermore, I encourage you to move away from the claim that there are two groups and only two groups – the "oppressors" and the "oppressed." If this book proved one thing, it is that Christians oppress Muslims and Muslims oppress Christians. Claiming that one group currently oppresses the other is intellectually lazy, cognitively inert, and detrimental to building bonds between these two populations.

Thirdly, I encourage readers to use more of their energy to build civic nations. While not immune to challenges, civic nations serve as the best hope for the future of humanity and for managing complex diversities. Nations designed around democratic rights and constitutions, rather than race or religion, are better suited for dealing with the challenges of the twenty-first century. Civic nations stand for the essence of terms like *Ubuntu* – which points to mutual dependency – and *E Pluribus Unum*, the American motto meaning "Out of Many, One."

Finally, I would be remiss in not mentioning the current work of former NBA basketball player Enes Kanter Freedom and his founding of the Abrahamic Athletics Academy (AAA). The AAA is intended to offer young people of the Jewish, Christian, and Muslim faiths the opportunity to gain experience about each other's differences and similarities through participating in interfaith learning initiatives through the international game of basketball. The objective of the AAA is to provide a high-quality learning experience with emphasis on diversity and synthesis of knowledge and skills at the global level. I am looking forward to joining the AAA in 2025. Only God knows where it will take me. All I can say with confidence is that DEUCE will be coming along with me.

Notes

Introduction

1 To my knowledge, the term Synthesis of Civilizations has not been deployed by academics who study Christian and Muslim relations or the relationship between the West and the Ummah.

Chapter 1: Humanity

1 Under Ibn Saud and Al-Wahhab's leadership, Diriyah emerged as a center of financing and commercial transactions dealing with caravans and merchants. It also emerged as a pilgrimage spot for faithful Muslims. It is located today in the present-day city of Riyadh, the capital of Saudi Arabia, which Ibn Saud's son – Abdul-Aziz – seized total control of in 1773. Ibn Saud and Al-Wahhab tried to seize all of Diriyah in 1747, but failed to do so.

2 MBS has also been heavily criticized for pursuing a war in neighboring Yemen and for the killing of Jamal Khashoggi, a Saudi journalist, at the Saudi consulate in Istanbul in 2018.

3 The Abraham Accords is the landmark treaty that normalized relations between Israel and its Arab neighbors, Bahrain and the UAE. They were signed by Sheikh Abdullah Bin Zayed Al-Nayhan, the Foreign Minister of the UAE, Benjamin Netanyahu, the Prime Minister of Israel, and Abdullatif Al-Zayani, the Foreign Minister of Bahrain. US President Donald Trump presided over the signing on the South Lawn of the White House.

4 The Oslo Accords were signed on 13 September 1993 by Yitzhak Rabin (d. 1995), the Prime Minister of Israel, and Mahmoud Abbas, the negotiator on behalf of the Palestine Liberation Organization (PLO). As part of the agreement, Israel recognized the PLO as the representative of the Palestinians, while the PLO renounced terrorism and recognized Israel's right to exist in peace. Both sides agreed that a Palestinian Authority (PA) would be established and assume governing responsibilities in the West Bank and Gaza Strip over a five-year period (Office of the Historian n.d.).

5 In the year 2021 alone, the volume of bilateral trade between the UAE and Israel reached approximately $1.154 billion (Maher 2022).

6 The Muslim Brotherhood is the oldest and arguably the most influential contemporary Islamist movement in the world (Vidino 2015: 3). While not shunning violence as a political tool, the Brotherhood advocates a bottom-up, gradual Islamization of society. Its reported goal is to form a purely Islamic society and, as a natural consequence, a new political entity rooted in Islam (Vidino 2015: 3).

7 The seeds of the Dialogue of Civilizations were ironically planted by Mohammad Khatami, the former president of Iran. One year before the attacks on 9/11, he delivered a speech at the United Nations (UN) in New York City, where he claimed that engaging in dialogue promoted cross-cultural and inter-civilizational understanding (Khatami 2000). This followed his 1998 decision to introduce a resolution at the UN proclaiming the year 2001 as the "United Nations Year of Dialogue Among Civilizations" (United Nations 2000).

8 The Comboni order was created by Daniel Comboni (d. 1881), an Italian bishop and missionary. He was born to a poor gardening family near Brescia in northern Italy and grew up under the jurisdiction of the Austro-Hungarian Empire. At the early age of 12, he entered the Religious Institute of Verona, where he completed his studies in medicine and languages. At the institute, he also learned Arabic, English, and French in preparation to enter the priesthood. In 1849, he vowed that he would conduct missionary work in Africa, but two years later – after taking a pilgrimage to Jerusalem in 1855 – he started his missionary activities in Khartoum, Sudan, where he was assigned to the liberation of enslaved children. The group eventually moved eastward and started missions around the Arabian Peninsula.

9 It was inaugurated by Cardinal Jozef Tomko (d. 2022) of Slovakia.

10 About two-thirds of Iraqi Christians are Chaldean Catholics, whose church retains its own liturgy and traditions, but recognizes the authority of the pope in Rome.

11 The Dominicans published the first Bible in Arabic, the first Kurdish grammar book, and many other texts of local interest (United Nations Educational, Scientific, and Cultural Organization 2022: 14).

12 The program also trained 20 local students in cinema production in a joint program with the Theatre of Ghent in Belgium.

Chapter 2: Hybridity

1 When exactly the Crusades began is a matter of debate among scholars. In 1061, the Christian Normans of France arrived to Muslim-controlled Sicily and began their slow takeover of the island. Six years later, the Seljuk Turks took Jerusalem from the Fatimids of North Africa and then invaded territories of the Byzantine Empire in the Holy Land. In 1071, the Seljuk Turks defeated the Byzantines at the Battle of Manzikert, currently a town in eastern Turkey, and founded the Sultanate of Rum, a Muslim state established over the conquered territories of the Byzantine Empire. The Sultanate of Rum then seized Antioch, the last Byzantine fortification in Syria, in 1085. In that same year, Alfonso VI seized Toledo, the capital of the Taifa of Toledo, from Yahya Al-Qadir (d. 1092) of the Dhulnunid dynasty, a Muslim Berber dynasty.

2 Today, the town of Clermont is officially known as Clermont-Ferrand and located in central France.

3 A transcription of Pope Urban II's speech at Clermont first appeared in a chronicle of the First Crusade by Robert of Rheims (d. 1122). My translation was taken from Thatcher and McNeal (n.d.: 1–3).

4 *The Gesta Francorum* is an anonymous Latin chronicle of the First Crusade which details the Crusaders' journey to the Holy Land, particularly their siege of Antioch, the capture of Jerusalem, and the establishment of Crusader city-states like Acre and Tiberias.

5 Saladin ended Fatimid control of Egypt in 1171 and established the Ayyubid dynasty in Cairo. When Al-Din died in 1174, Saladin seized control of Damascus and later Aleppo (1183) and Mosul (1185), thus uniting Egypt and Syria into the larger Ayyubid caliphate.

6 The Fourth Crusade is known as much for its Christian-on-Christian violence as it is for its Christian-on-Muslim violence. In 1203, the Crusaders sacked Constantinople and turned it into a Latin city. They named Alexius I Comnenus (d. 1118) its ruler. He pursued a campaign of Latinizing the Greek-speaking Byzantine Empire. The Fifth Crusade is known for its international scope. It started in Egypt in 1217 when Cardinal Pelagius sought to defeat Sultan Al-Kamil, who based his empire in Damietta, which I return to in chapter 5. In 1228, Frederick II – the Holy Roman Emperor – crusaded in Egypt without papal support. In 1235, the Byzantines retook Asia Minor. Meanwhile, on the Iberian Peninsula, King Ferdinand III (d. 1252) of Castille attacked Córdoba in 1238. Two years later, the House of Aragon seized Valencia, which was then ruled by Muslims. The Sixth Crusade, like the Fifth Crusade, started

in Egypt when Louis IX invaded it in 1248. He seized Damietta, but was later captured at Mansurah and released at ransom. In the same year, the Mamluks seized Egypt from the Ayyubid dynasty. The Byzantines recaptured Constantinople in 1261 from the Crusaders and ended the Latin dynasty of the Byzantine Empire. The Seventh and final Crusade started in 1270 when Louis IX attacked Tunis. A decade later, the Mamluks seized Tripoli and Acre from the Crusaders, who regrouped on Cyprus in 1291.

7 "Tatar" is the name given to the Turkic-speaking semi-nomadic people living on the steppes of the Eurasian continent. The Lipka Tatars emerged during the fourteenth-century dissolution of the Mongol Empire. The Tatars fled from Tamerlane (d. 1405), the Turko-Mongol warrior and joined forces with Duke Vytautas (d. 1430), the Christian grand duke of Lithuania, while seeking asylum in 1397. Duke Vytautas secured the Lipka Tatars their freedom of religion rights and even exempted them from taxation. In return, the Tatars provided the Lithuanians with military assistance.

8 The present-day region of Wallachia in southern Romania and the country of Moldova also fought as Christian vassal states alongside Ottoman forces at the Battle of Vienna.

9 According to the UN, between the period 2010 and 2016, approximately 2.5 million refugees and migrants from predominantly Muslim-majority countries arrived to EU countries.

10 Before his attack on Utøya, Breivik detonated a bomb adjacent to the office of the Prime Minister of Norway.

11 In 1995, the Schengen Agreement was officially implemented, with all but Greece and Italy abolishing its internal border checks. The following years saw Austria (1995), Denmark, (1996), Finland (1996), Iceland (1996), Norway (1996), and Sweden (1996) join the Schengen Zone.

12 The term is believed to be coined by Américo Castro, a Spanish academic, in 1948.

13 Saint Vincent of Lérins was a Visigothic church dating back to the middle of the sixth century.

14 The Visigoths built their church on the ruins of a pagan temple belonging to the Roman Empire.

15 The capital of the Aghlabid Empire was Kairouan or Qariwiyyin, which is located in Fez, Morocco.

16 Michael II (d. 829) was born in 770 into an ethnically Jewish family from Amoria, Turkey. The Amorians, along with Armenians and the Balkan people, made up the majority of the Byzantine army in the eighth and ninth centuries. Under his rule, Crete, a Byzantine territory, was attacked by Muslim exiles from Andalusia. These exiles were likely the rebels of the failed revolt against Al-Hakam I (d. 822) of Córdoba in 818. Michael II lost Crete in 824.

17 The Sicilian civil war was caused by the administrative and political disintegration of the island into petty principalities (Metcalfe 2002: 289).

18 The Greek inscription translates to "Jesus Christ will conquer."

19 The *hijra* refers to the year 622, when Prophet Muhammad migrated from Mecca to Yathrib, which he renamed Medina.

20 The Peace Cathedral is the oldest Baptist church in the Republic of Georgia and a partner of the US-based Alliance of Baptists, a Christian denomination.

21 After World War II, much of Berlin lay in ruins. The defeat of the Nazis led to conflicts of interest between the USA and the USSR, who fought for control of Berlin during the early stages of the Cold War. The USA and the USSR agreed to partition Berlin. The Americans received West Berlin and the Soviets received East Berlin. A wall was built to divide the city in 1961. The Berlin Wall – as it is known – represented the opposite of hospitality.

Chapter 3: Heterogeneity

1 Wisdom, the English translation of Sophia, has been defined in many ways, but the most popular definition came from Cicero (d. 43 BC), the ancient Roman orator, who said, "The function of wisdom is to discriminate between good and evil." In other words, wisdom consists of thinking what is best and doing what is best in any given situation. Similarly, ancient Greek philosophers placed a high degree of emphasis on the importance of seeking and acquiring knowledge, a requisite of wisdom. Socrates, the most important of the ancient Greek philosophers, was known as a lover of knowledge, and thus a wise man. The Islamic tradition, alternatively, has its own word for wisdom, *hikmah*, which is used repeatedly in the Qur'an as a characteristic of the righteous (Qur'an 2:251; 4:54; 5:110) and as a quality of those who truly understand the will of God (Qur'an 31:12). According to the Qur'an, wisdom is one of the greatest, if not the greatest, value a human being can possess.

2 Despite the glories of its architecture, the Hagia Sophia of the sixth century was prone to problems. The dome collapsed in 558, only to be rebuilt to an even greater height in 562. Earthquakes have historically taken their toll on the building. The surviving main structure as of 2022, however, is essentially that which was first built under Justinian I between the years 532 and 537 (Wegner 2004).

3 The supporting arches of the Hagia Sophia's dome were covered with mosaics of six winged angels called hexapterygon. The intricate Byzantine mosaics were made from gold, silver, glass, terracotta, and colorful stones and portrayed well-known scenes and figures from Jesus's life (History 2018).

4 The Commission on Security and Cooperation in Europe, also known as the Helsinki Commission, issued a report in 2016 titled, "Turkey – Human Rights in Retreat" (Commission on Security and Cooperation in Europe 2016). The commission is a US government agency created in 1976 to encourage and monitor human rights around the world.

5 Also called Syrian Orthodox Christians or Syriacs, the Assyrians have seen their population in Turkey dwindle to a mere 25,000 people, a far cry from previous generations in their historical homeland in the Turkish provinces of Hakkari and Mardin (Minority Rights Group International n.d.).

6 In this agreement, Turkey claimed territories stretching from Eastern Thrace (now part of Greece), to Cyprus, and to the eastern Aegean islands (Batuman 2014).

7 The US State Department responded by stating, "President Erdoğan's continued outreach to this terrorist organization only serves to isolate Turkey from the international community, harms the interests of the Palestinian people, and undercuts global efforts to prevent terrorist attacks launched from Gaza" (Arab News 2020).

8 An Apostolic Father refers to the Greek Christians that authored early Christian texts dating to the first and early second centuries.

9 The Huns were a set of Eurasian tribal nations led by a Turkic-speaking aristocracy.

10 In response to the *klephts*, the Ottoman military established the *armatoloi*, or local militias made up of Christians.

11 In 1999, Gülen left Turkey at a time when he was under investigation for undermining the Turkish government, which at that time was still firmly under the control of Turkey's secular elite and backed up by the military (Sanderson 2018). In 2000, he was found guilty, in absentia, of scheming to overthrow the government by embedding civil servants in various governmental offices. Soon after Gülen was found guilty, Erdoğan became prime minister of Turkey. In 2007, under the leadership of Erdoğan, the Turkish state reversed the charges against Gülen, signaling a willingness to cooperate with the cleric and his global movement (Sanderson 2018). By this time Gülen had built up a business empire in self-imposed exile. His networks of media outlets in Turkey and abroad had become increasingly powerful; his schools were educating

the next generation of entrepreneurs and leaders (Sanderson 2018). All the while, Gülen had thousands of followers working in Turkish government positions. His opponents viewed this as a "growing underground army, while his supports stated that they were merely trying to increase democracy and dialogue between various social groups through government channels" (Sanderson 2018).

12 Some of the soldiers captured allegedly confessed to taking orders from Gülen, though it is unknown under what conditions those confessions may have taken place, with allegations of torture amassing since the events.

13 The Gülen movement is referred to by its participants with the term Hizmet, which is translated as "service."

14 A decade earlier Gaspare was appointed to the position of official court architect of Constantinople.

15 Kemal agreed to the Treaty of Lausanne in 1923, which superseded the Treaty of Sèvres.

16 The Treaty of Sèvres also created an independent Armenia, an autonomous Kurdistan, as well as Greek control over the Aegean Sea islands commanding the Dardanelles. The agreement was replaced three years later by the Treaty of Lausanne.

Chapter 4: Honor

1 The Center for Social Justice, a US non-governmental organization, reported that at least 84 people were accused of blasphemy in 2021. At least 16 of those people were charged with blasphemy and sentenced to death (United States Department of State 2021). In 2023, the Pakistani government made concessions to the demands of the Tehreek-e-Labbaik Pakistan (TLP), an Islamist extremist party, which would allow blasphemy cases to be tried under the country's anti-terrorism laws. The government also agreed to establish a "Counter Blasphemy Wing" under the Federal Investigation Agency to act against the dissemination of "blasphemous content" on the internet (Morning Star News 2023).

2 Muhammad agreed to another covenant with the Christians of Najran, whom he had hosted for three days in Masjid Al-Nabawi – The Prophet's Mosque – in Medina around the year 631 or 632. As I explained in a previous book – *People of the Book – Prophet Muhammad's Encounters with Christians* – Muhammad even allowed the Christians of Najran to pray inside his mosque. In doing so, he honored his Christian guests with hospitality, which is an expression of honor and reciprocal relationships.

3 In the aftermath of the bombing, the Pakistani Supreme Court ordered the creation of a national council to curb hate speech, develop a curriculum of peace, implement job quotas, and inculcate religious tolerance (Chaudhry 2022). Observers of the Supreme Court's order, however, have claimed that the Pakistani government never complied with the order.

4 Many Pakistani Christians today have been described as having a multifaceted belief system that emerged out of a synthesis between Hindu and Christian religious ideas and practices (Fuchs and Fuchs 2020).

5 Pakistan's sewage industry requires that its workers go deep into the ground and unclog the sewer system without necessary equipment. As a result, the deadly gasses formed in the sewers often kill Pakistani Christian workers (International Christian Concern 2022b).

6 In November 2021, the All-Party Parliamentary Group (APPG), a collection of British parliamentarians, published a report on abductions, forced conversions, and forced marriages, which revealed that approximately 1,000 girls between the ages of 12 and 25 were forcibly converted to Islam every year (see Bailey 2021).

7 The first coup d'état in Pakistani history occurred on 27 October 1958, when General Ayub Khan (d. 1974) took control of the government after ousting Iskander Mirza (d. 1969), the first President of Pakistan. The second coup d'état happened on 5 July 1977, when General

Muhammad Zia Ul-Haq overthrew Zulfikar Ali Bhutto. The third coup d'état unfolded in 1999 when General Pervez Musharraf overthrew Prime Minister Nawaz Sharif.

8 The hallmark of populism is a dichotomous society that is home to two antagonistic and homogeneous groups – the "pure people" versus the "corrupt elite" (Mudde 2004).

9 The name of the papal bull was *Romanus Pontifex*. It is notable for its role in justifying the exploration and expansion of European powers from the late fifteenth century to the early seventeenth century.

10 Queen Victoria (d. 1901) issued a proclamation in 1858 that ended the East India Company's rule and the beginning of direct British governance in India.

11 The Christian Mission School (CMS) was founded in 1854 by Colonel Henry W. Preedy (d. 1867) of the British Army.

12 The Pakistani Constitution of 1956 was based on the Government of India Act (1935), a piece of British colonial legislation that established the country as a federal republic and a parliamentary democracy.

13 He quickly deposed Bhutto, the previous president, who was controversially tried by the Pakistani Supreme Court and executed in 1979 for allegedly authorizing the murder of Nawab Muhammad Ahmed Khan Khasuri (d. 1974), his political opponent.

14 Here are several codes that have been identified as controversial: 295-B – Defiling, etc., of copy of Holy Qur'an. Whoever willfully defiles, damages or desecrates a copy of the Holy Qur'an or of an extract therefrom or uses it in any derogatory manner or for any unlawful purpose shall be punishable with imprisonment for life; 295-C – Use of derogatory remarks, etc.; in respect of the Holy Prophet [Muhammad]. Whoever by words, either spoken or written or by visible representation, or by any imputation, innuendo, or insinuation, directly or indirectly, defiles the sacred name of the Holy Prophet Muhammad (PBUH) shall be punished with death, or imprisonment for life, and shall also be liable to fine; 298-A – Use of derogatory remarks, etc . . ., in response of holy personages. Whoever by words, either spoken or written, or by visible representation, or by any imputation, innuendo or insinuation, directly or indirectly defiles a sacred name of any wife (Ummul Mumineen), or members of the family (Ahle-bait), of the Holy Prophet (PBUH), or any of the righteous caliphs (Khulafa-e-Rashideen) or companions (Sahaaba) of the Holy Prophet (peace be upon him) shall be punished with imprisonment of either description for a term which may extend to three years, or with fine, or with both.

15 The country's first Foreign Minister – Zafarullah Khan (d. 1985) – was an Ahmadi Muslim who viewed Islamic principles as being compatible with Western interpretations of human rights (Thames 2021).

16 Akbar the Great granted the right to build churches starting in 1597 in Lahore and in 1598 in Agra (Kuczkiewicz-Fraś 2011: 77).

17 The *Biblia Regia* was printed in Antwerp by Christopher Plantin (d. 1589), the French book printer and Renaissance humanist, between the years 1569 and 1572.

Chapter 5: Harmony

1 Under Dan Fodio, the Sokoto caliphate conquered Burkina Faso, Cameroon, Southern Niger, and most of Northern Niger. It was dissolved in 1903 after the British and Germans conquered the area and established the newly constructed Northern Nigeria Protectorate and Kamerun [Cameron] respectively.

2 The name Pentecost is derived from pentēkostē, the Greek word meaning "fiftieth." This Christian festival is celebrated on the fiftieth day after Easter Sunday. According to chapter 2 of the Book of Acts, this is the day when the apostles and other followers of Jesus witnessed the descent of the Holy Spirit.

3 The USCIRF was created by the Religious Freedom Act of 1998.

4 Two political parties dominate Nigeria – the All Progressives Congress (APC) and the People's Democratic Party (PDP). In the 2015 presidential election, the APC's candidate Muhammadu Buhari won the election and was re-elected in the 2019 presidential election.

5 The Protestant churches in Nigeria comprise the Assemblies of God, Baptists, the Evangelical Reformed Church, Methodists, and Presbyterians (Harvard Divinity School n.d.b.).

6 Built by Ptolemy II Philadelphus (d. 246 BC) – the founder of the Ptolemaic dynasty – between 283 BC and 246 BC, this library is said to have housed a copy of every significant piece of scholarship from distinct parts of the ancient world. The reasons for its decline are still debated by scholars today, but they typically agree that it suffered damage during an attack by Julius Caesar (d. 44 BC) – the dictator and military general of the Roman Republic – in 48 BC. Its destruction is often cited as a significant event in the history of education, with the loss of numerous irreplaceable manuscripts and scrolls.

7 The other centers were Antioch (in modern-day Turkey), Constantinople (the city of modern-day Istanbul), Jerusalem (the city of Israel and Palestine), and Rome (in modern-day Italy), which emerged in the following centuries as one of the most powerful cities in Christendom.

8 The New Wafd was banned only months later and then revived after President Sadat's assassination in 1981.

9 One center is the Ahmad Baba Center for Documentation, which began its collection around 1970 through a UNESCO educational grant.

10 The Muslim militias were reportedly armed with weapons they had seized from the armories in Libya following the fall of Muammar Gaddafi (d. 2011), the politician who ruled Libya from 1969 until he was overthrown in the Libyan Civil War between 2014 and 2020 (Worrall 2016).

Chapter 6: Healing

1 See The Gilder Lehrman Institute of American History (n.d.) for a copy of Wood's text.

2 Of those Africans who arrived to the USA, nearly half came from two regions – the area comprising the Senegal and Gambia Rivers and the land between them (present-day countries of Senegal, Gambia, Guinea-Bissau, and Mali) – and the area of west-central Africa, including what is now Angola, Congo, the Democratic Republic of Congo, and Gabon (Pruitt 2023).

3 See Considine (2013) for a deeper analysis on the life of Sambo Anderson.

4 The First Amendment of the US Constitution acknowledges that freedom of religion is a fundamental civil and human right for all people living in the United States (Considine 2019: 61). It states: "Congress shall make no law respecting an establishment of religion, or prohibiting the free exercise thereof; or abridging the freedom of speech."

5 Article Six, Clause Three of the constitution requires that representatives and senators "be bound by Oath or Affirmation to support the US Constitution," and that same clause ends with the declaration that "no religious Test shall ever be required as a Qualification to any Office or public Trust under the United States" (see Herrera 2019).

6 The copy of the Qur'an owned by Jefferson was translated by George Sale (d. 1736) and published in the year 1734. Sale translated the Qur'an from Arabic to English under the sponsorship of the Anglican Christian Missionary Society. In his introduction, he stated that the audience for his translation were Protestants who were seeking to argue against Prophet Muhammad's prophethood. He added, "Protestants alone are able to attack the Qur'an with success, and for them, I trust, Providence has reserved the glory of its overthrow."

7 The Center for Security Policy (CSP) was founded by Gaffney in 1988. It has been criticized for promoting conspiracy theories, but also praised for its work in combatting terrorism.

8 The term "secret Muslim" was also applied to Barack Obama during his campaign for the presidency in 2008. Despite the proliferation of the theory, Obama regularly identified himself as a Christian and attended churches including Trinity United Church of Christ in Chicago.

9 After visiting Washington, DC, Ambassador Mellimelli visited Baltimore, Boston, New York City, and Washington, DC. He is said to have "raised many eyebrows" in Boston (Wilson 2003).

10 The Conestoga, also spelt Conestogoe, and the larger Susquehannock tribe, was part of the Iroquoian (Iroquoa) indigenous people of the Five Nations of the Iroquois Confederacy. They lived along the Susquehannock River in what is now Maryland, New York, and Pennsylvania. In the 1690s, after decades of conflict and disease, they established a settlement on the Conestoga River in present-day Lancaster County, Pennsylvania.

11 Khaled (also spelt Khalid) Ibn Walid [d. 642] was an Arab military commander from Mecca. Originally, he allied himself with the Quraysh, the tribe leading the opposition to the Islamic movement initiated by Prophet Muhammad (he was himself a member of the Quraysh) only then becoming Muslim and joining Muhammad. Ibn Walid served as a commander of Muslim armies under Abu Bakr and Umar during the Ridda Wars (633–4) and the Conquest of Byzantine-Syria (634–8).

12 Raynald (d. 1187), also known as Arnold or Reginald of Chatillon, was a French nobleman, the Prince of Antioch between the years 1153 and 1160, and one of the leading military leaders during the Crusades between 1147 and 1187. His frequent and reportedly misguided raids on Muslim-led trading caravans during periods of truce between Christians and Muslims is sometimes blamed for the gradual loss of influence and territory for the Christians of Jerusalem.

13 Guy of Lusignan's troops were defeated at the Battle of Hattin by Saladin's forces. At the end of the Third Crusade, he ceded the title of King of Jerusalem to Richard the Lionheart, the King of England, in exchange for control over Cyprus. He died in 1194.

14 The word Dagestan is of Persian and Turkish origin and translates to "Land of the Mountains" (dag or "mountain" in Turkish and stan or "land" in Persian). The Dagestani region was conquered by the Arab Muslims in the year 643. In the second half of the eleventh century, the Seljuk Turks conquered the Arab Muslims. The Mongols, Persians, Russians, and Timurids also claimed ownership of Dagestan throughout history.

Chapter 7: Holiness

1 Palestinian liberation refers to the Palestinians' desire to achieve self-determination and sovereignty over their own state, which, they claim, includes – but may not be limited to – the Gaza Strip, East Jerusalem, and the West Bank.

2 The church is named after Saint Porphyrius (d. 420), the bishop of Gaza in the fifth century.

References

9/11 Memorial and Museum. n.d. "Module – Events of the day." https://www.911memorial.org/lea rn/resources/911-primer/module-1-events-day

A Document on Human Fraternity for World Peace and Living Together. 2019. "A document on human fraternity for world peace and living together." Vatican.va, 3–5 February. https://www.va tican.va/content/francesco/en/travels/2019/outside/documents/papa-francesco_20190204_doc umento-fratellanza-umana.html

Abdul-Rahman, Z. 2023. "Why is shirk the greatest sin of all?" Yaqeen Institute, 22 March. https://yaqeeninstitute.org/read/paper/why-is-shirk-the-greatest-sin-of-all

Abrahamic Reunion. n.d. "About the Abrahamic reunion." https://www.abrahamicreunion.org/about-us/

Abu Toameh, K. 2022. "Mufti slams Pence for 'storming' Tomb of the Patriarchs." *Jerusalem Post*, 10 March. https://www.jpost.com/middle-east/article-700905

Adebayo, B. 2019. "Muslim cleric who hid Christians during attacks honored in the US." CNN, 18 July. https://www.cnn.com/2019/07/18/africa/nigeria-cleric-honored-intl/index.html

Agius, D.A. 2007. "Who spoke Siculo Arabic?" University of Exeter. https://ore.exeter.ac.uk/repo sitory/handle/10036/38016

Ahmad, A. 2012. "Dīn-i Ilāhī." Encyclopedia of Islam. https://referenceworks.brillonline.com/en tries/encyclopaedia-of-islam-2/din-i-ilahi-SIM_1863

Ahmad, J. (ed.) 1960. *Speeches and Writings of Mr. Jinnah*, 7th edn. Lahore: Shaikh Muhammad Ashraf.

Ahmed, A.S. 1997. "Understanding Jinnah." *New York Times*. https://archive.nytimes.com/www.ny times.com/books/first/a/ahmed-jinnah.html?_r=1&oref=slogin

Ahmed, A.S. 2003. *Islam Under Siege – Living Dangerously in a Post-Honor World*. Cambridge: Polity.

Ahmed, A.S. 2010. *Journey into America – The Challenge of Islam*. Washington, DC: Brookings Institution.

Ahmed, I. 2021a. "*Asia Bibi v. The State* – The politics and jurisprudence of Pakistan's blasphemy laws." *Third World Quarterly* 42(2): 274–91.

Ahmed, K. 2021b. "Sir Syed – A great man ignored?" *Newsweek Pakistan*, 4 June. https://www.new sweekpakistan.com/sir-syed-a-great-man-ignored/

Alkhateeb, F. 2023. "Capture of Jerusalem – The Treaty of Umar." IslamiCity, 11 October. https://www.islamicity.org/11511/capture-of-jerusalem-the-treaty-of-umar/

Al-Bawaba. 2023. "First-ever church in Turkey to open in Istanbul." Al-Bawaba.com, 6 January. https://www.albawaba.com/editors-choice/first-ever-church-turkey-open-istanbul-1504572

Al-Islam. n.d. "Ahmadiyya Muslim community." https://www.alislam.org/ahmadiyya-muslim-com munity/

Al-Jazeera. 2022. "Turkey condemns US decision to lift Cyprus arms embargo." Al-Jazeera, 17 September. https://www.aljazeera.com/news/2022/9/17/turkey-condemns-us-decision-to-lift-cyprus-arms-embargo

Al-Jazeera. 2023. "Saudi crown prince MBS says Israel normalization getting 'closer.'" Al-Jazeera, 20 September. https://www.aljazeera.com/news/2023/9/20/saudi-crown-prince-mbs-says-israel-normalisation-getting-closer

Al-Sarhan, S. 2020. "Hagia Sophia move shows nothing is off-limits for Erdogan's populist Islamist project." AlArabiya News, 16 July. https://english.alarabiya.net/views/news/middle-east/2020/07/16/Hagia-Sophia-move-shows-nothing-is-off-limits-for-Erdogan-s-populist-Islamist-project

Al-Sherbini, R. 2021. "Al Azhar Sheikh rebuffs calls for 'religion merger.'" GulfNews.com, 9 November. https://gulfnews.com/world/mena/al-azhar-sheikh-rebuffs-calls-for-religion-merger-1.83562666

Alexander, A. 2011. "Egypt's Muslims and Christians join hands in protest." BBC, 10 February. https://www.bbc.com/news/world-middle-east-12407793

Ali, S. 2022. "Dr. Craig Considine – Precious moments with the caliph at the historic mosque opening in Zion." ReviewOfReligions.org, 17 October. https://www.reviewofreligions.org/40302/dr-craig-considine-precious-moments-with-the-caliph-at-the-historic-mosque-opening-in-zion/

Aligarh Muslim University. n.d. "The Founder." https://amu.ac.in/about-us/the-founder

Alimahomed-Wilson, S. 2019. "When the FBI knocks – Racialized state surveillance of Muslims." *Critical Sociology* 45(6): 871–87.

Alketbi, S. 2022. "2 years since Israel, UAE signed Abraham Accords – what's been achieved? – Opinion." *Jerusalem Post*, 7 September. https://www.jpost.com/opinion/article-716469

Anli, I. 2019. "Muslim minorities' dangerous flirt with Erdogan." Ibrahimanli.blogspot.com, 27 February. https://ibrahimanli.blogspot.com/2019/02/muslim-minorities-dangerous-flirt-with.html

Arab News. n.d. "The Coptic miracle – How Egypt's historic Christian church survived and thrived." https://www.arabnews.com/Copts

Arab News. 2020. "Revealed – How a bank in Turkey funded Hamas terror operations." 25 October. https://www.arabnews.com/node/1753671/middle-east

Arab News. 2021. "Most French believe white Christians risk 'extinction' from Muslim migration – poll." 27 October. https://www.arabnews.com/node/1956551/world

Arab News. 2023. "History of Great Mosque of Cordoba being rewritten by church, activists claim." 1 March. https://www.arabnews.com/node/2260411/world

Associated Press. 2020. "Abu Dhabi marks interfaith effort a year after Pope's visit." Voice of America News, 3 February. https://www.voanews.com/a/middle-east_abu-dhabi-marks-interfaith-effort-year-after-popes-visit/6183625.html

Avalon Project. n.d. "The Barbary Treaties (1786–1810) – Treaty of Peace and Friendship, signed at Tripoli (November 4, 1796)." Lillian Goldman Law Library. https://avalon.law.yale.edu/18th_century/bar1796t.asp

Awad, A. 2012. "The true story of sharia in American courts." TheNation.com, 14 June. https://www.thenation.com/article/archive/true-story-sharia-american-courts/

Azeemuddin, M. 2017. "The philosophy of Sir Syed Ahmad Khan of religious tolerance, communal harmony, multiculturalism, and national unity." *International Journal of All Research Education and Scientific Methods* 5(12): 1–9.

Bailey, A. 2021. "APPG for the Pakistani minorities – Abductions, forced conversions, and forced marriages of religious minority women and girls in Pakistan." All-Party Parliamentary Group,

26 November. https://appgfreedomofreligionorbelief.org/appg-for-the-pakistani-minorities-ab
ductions-forced-conversions-and-forced-marriages-of-religious-minority-women-and-girls-in
-pakistan/

Ballard, R. n.d. "The Christians of Pakistan – A historical overview and an assessment of their
current position." Center for Applied South Asian Studies. https://fid4sa-repository.ub.uni-hei
delberg.de/3372/1/christiansinpakistan.pdf

Balousha, H. 2022. "In Gaza, Christian and Muslim Palestinians celebrate Christmas together."
ArabNews.com, 24 December. https://www.arabnews.com/node/2221441/middle-east

Bano, N., Ahmad, H., Hassan, J., and Razaq, R. 2023. "Principles of religious pluralism." *Religions*
14(20): 1–12.

Barkindo, A. and Dyikuk, J.J. 2022. "Nigeria, the church, and religious freedom – Challenges
and opportunities to secure this right." Cornerstone Forum – A Conversation on Religious
Freedom and Its Social Implications 316 (July). Washington, DC: Religious Freedom Institute.

Başaran, E. 2016. "Thinking Gülen is a peaceful scholar is a huge mischaracterization." Hurriyet
Daily News, 28 July. https://www.hurriyetdailynews.com/opinion/ezgi-basaran/thinking-gulen
-is-a-peaceful-scholar-is-a-huge-mischaracterization-102173

Baskan, B. 2019. "Turkey and the UAE – A strange crisis." Middle East Institute, 1 May. https://
www.mei.edu/publications/turkey-and-uae-strange-crisis

Batuman, B. 2014. "The shape of the nation – Visual production of nationalism through maps in
Turkey." *Political Geography* 29(4): 220–34.

Becatoros, E. and Fraser, S. 2022. "Greek foreign minister slams Turkish leader's missile threat."
Associated Press, 12 December. https://apnews.com/article/greece-turkey-athens-recep-tayyip
-erdogan-government-5bee76c2e7b2e1feaea3e2dddf54144c

Ben-David, L. 2023. "The great powers converged on the Holy Land in the 19th century." Jerusalem
Center for Public Affairs, 5 January. https://jcpa.org/the-great-powers-converged-on-the-holy
-land-in-the-19th-century/

Bhabha, H.K. 1994. *The Location of Culture*. New York: Routledge.

Boissoneault, L. 2015. "The Golden Age of Timbuktu." JSTOR Daily, 25 June. https://daily.jstor
.org/golden-age-timbuktu/

Bonesh, F. 2021. "Relations between Copts, government and Islamic groups in Egypt." AlBawaba,
30 November. https://www.albawaba.com/opinion/relations-between-copts-government-and
-islamic-groups-egypt-1457122

Bordoni, L. 2021. "Iraq – Pope's prayer of the sons and daughters of Abraham." VaticanNews
.va., 6 March. https://www.vaticannews.va/en/pope/news/2021-03/pope-francis-prayer-interre
ligious-ur-abraham.html

Bostock, B. 2021. "Inside the evangelical mission to build the first church in Saudi Arabia, the
home of Islam where preaching the Bible can land you in jail." Insider, 8 February. https://
www.insider.com/us-evangelicals-mission-saudi-arabia-first-church-2021-1

Boston Celtics History. n.d. "Ubuntu – I am because we are." https://www.bostoncelticshistory
.com/item/ubuntu-i-am-because-we-are/

Bowie, L. 1977. "The Copts, the Wafd, and religious issues in Egyptian politics." *The Muslim World*,
67(2): 106–26.

Bridge Initiative. 2016. "'Civilization jihad' – Debunking the conspiracy theory." Bridge Initiative,
2 February. https://bridge.georgetown.edu/research/civilization-jihad-debunking-the-conspir
acy-theory/

Bridge Initiative. 2020. "Factsheet – Gates of Vienna." Bridge Initiative, 18 September. https://
bridge.georgetown.edu/research/factsheet-gates-of-vienna/

Britannica. n.d.a. "Dīn-i Ilāhī." https://www.britannica.com/topic/Din-i-Ilahi

Britannica. n.d.b. "Greece under Ottoman rule." https://www.britannica.com/place/Greece/Greece-under-Ottoman-rule

Britannica. n.d.c. "Ibn Saud." https://www.britannica.com/biography/Ibn-Saud

British Broadcasting Corporation. 2020a. "Asia Bibi – Pakistani Christian woman breaks silence in new book." BBC, 30 January. https://www.bbc.com/news/world-us-canada-51317380

British Broadcasting Corporation. 2020b. "Hagia Sophia – Pope 'pained' as Istanbul museum reverts to mosque." BBC, 12 July. https://www.bbc.com/news/world-europe-53371341

British Broadcasting Corporation. 2021. "Israel rejects 'alarm call' by Christian leaders in Jerusalem." BBC, 21 December. https://www.bbc.com/news/world-middle-east-59740356

Broadhurst, R. 1952. *The Travels of Ibn Jubayr*. London: Jonathan Cape.

Brown, P.M. 1924. "From Sèvres to Lausanne 1." *American Journal of International Law* 18(1): 113–16.

Brumley, J. 2022. "In Tbilisi, the Peace Project rises as home for Christians, Jews and Muslims under one roof." Baptist News, 8 June. https://baptistnews.com/article/in-tbilisi-the-peace-project-rises-as-a-home-for-christians-jews-and-muslims-under-one-roof/#.Y495V-zMLeQ

Bulut, M.H. 2022a "Din-I Ilahi – An Indian Shah, Jesuits and a divine religion." Daily Sabah, 13 February. https://www.dailysabah.com/arts/din-i-ilahi-an-indian-shah-jesuits-and-a-divine-religion/news

Bulut, U. 2022b. "Turkey – Jihad against Cyprus." Gatestone Institute, 28 June. https://www.gatestoneinstitute.org/18633/turkey-jihad-cyprus

Burgen, S. 2016. "Córdoba rejects Catholic church's claim to own mosque-cathedral." *The Guardian*, 13 March. https://www.theguardian.com/world/2016/mar/13/cordoba-catholic-churchs-claim-mosque-cathedral

Burke, P. 2018. "A case of cultural hybridity – The European Renaissance." Brewminate, 13 December. https://brewminate.com/a-case-of-cultural-hybridity-the-european-renaissance/

Calderwood, E. 2015. "The Reconquista of the Mosque of Córdoba." *Foreign Policy*, 10 April. https://foreignpolicy.com/2015/04/10/the-reconquista-of-the-mosque-of-cordoba-spain-catholic-church-islam/

Carnevale, A. 2020. "Once upon a time in Palermo, when Islam and Christianity were walking side by side." Conceptual Fine Arts, 25 November. https://www.conceptualfinearts.com/cfa/2015/11/27/the-time-when-in-palermo-islam-and-christianity-were-walking-side-by-side/

Cartwright, M. 2018. "The capture of Jerusalem, 1099 CE." WorldHistory.org, 16 July. https://www.worldhistory.org/article/1254/the-capture-of-jerusalem-1099-ce/

Casper, J. 2022. "Despite drop in deportations, Turkey still troubles Christians." *Christianity Today*, 6 April. https://www.christianitytoday.com/news/2022/april/turkey-christians-deportations-religious-freedom-apc.html

Çevik, S. 2020. "Political implications of the Hagia Sophia reconversion." *Fair Observer*, 17 July. https://www.swp-berlin.org/en/publication/political-implications-of-the-hagia-sophia-reconversion

Chaudhry, K. 2022. "Pakistan still failing to protect religious minorities." Union of Catholic Asian News, 20 June. https://www.ucanews.com/news/pakistan-still-failing-to-protect-religious-minorities/97715

Chimtom, N.K. 2023a. "Christians in Northern Nigeria living 'under bondage,' says archbishop." Cruxnow.com, 13 March. https://cruxnow.com/church-in-africa/2023/03/christians-in-northern-nigeria-living-under-bondage-says-archbishop

Chimtom, N.K. 2023b. "Over 50,000 massacred in Nigeria for being Christian in the last 14 years, report says." NCRonline.com, 12 April. https://www.ncronline.org/news/over-50000-massacred-nigeria-being-christian-last-14-years-report-says

Christianity Today. 2023. "Mali 'at a crossroads' with referendum, says Christian leader."

Christianity Today, 17 June. https://www.christiantoday.com/article/mali.at.a.crossroads.with .referendum.says.christian.leader/140369.htm

Christides, G. and Kuntz, K. 2017. "The refugee scandal on the island of Lesbos." Spiegel.de, 24 November. https://www.spiegel.de/international/europe/conditions-on-lesbos-worsen-for -refugees-and-residents-a-1180209.html

Cimmino, J. 2017. "The Spanish left targets the Catholic Church." *National Review*, 27 July. https:// www.nationalreview.com/2017/07/cathedral-cordoba-belongs-catholic-church/

Cole, J. 2011. "Christians, Muslims 'one hand' in Egypt's youth revolution." Informed Comment, 27 February. https://www.juancole.com/2011/02/christians-muslims-one-hand-in-egypts-youth -revolution.html

Commission on Security and Cooperation in Europe. 2016. "Turkey – Human rights in retreat." Commission on Security and Cooperation in Europe, 9 December. https://www.congress.gov /114/chrg/CHRG-114jhrg23374/CHRG-114jhrg23374.pdf

Connolly, K. 2021. "'House of One' – Berlin lays first stone for multi-faith worship centre." *The Guardian*, 27 May. https://www.theguardian.com/world/2021/may/27/berlin-lays-first-stone -for-multi-faith-house-of-one-worship-centre

Considine, C. 2013. "George Washington was a friend of Muslims." Huff Post, 18 February. https:// www.huffpost.com/entry/george-washington-was-a-f_b_2712606

Considine, C. 2017a. *Islam, Race, and Pluralism in the Pakistani Diaspora*. New York: Routledge.

Considine, C. 2017b. "The racialization of Islam in the United States – Islamophobia, hate crimes, and 'flying while brown.'" *Religions* 8(9): 1–19.

Considine, C. 2019. *Islam in America – Exploring the Issues*. Santa Barbara, CA: ABC-CLIO.

Considine, C. 2020. *The Humanity of Muhammad – A Christian View*. Clifton, NJ: Blue Dome Press.

Considine, C. 2021. *People of the Book – Prophet Muhammad's Encounters with Christians*. London: Hurst.

Cook, S.A. 2018. "Neither friend nor foe." Council on Foreign Relations, November. https://www .cfr.org/report/future-u.s.-turkey

Council of Europe. n.d. "About the Council of Europe – Overview." Council of Europe Office in Yerevan (Armenia). https://www.coe.int/en/web/yerevan/the-coe/about-coe/overview

Crawford, M. 2014. *Ibn 'Abd al-Wahhab*. London: Oneworld.

Daily Sabah and Anadolu Agency. 2021. "Christian church in Jerusalem attacked for 4th time in 1 month." *Daily Sabah*, 2 March. https://www.dailysabah.com/world/mid-east/christian-chur ch-in-jerusalem-attacked-for-4th-time-in-1-month

Damietta Cross-Cultural Center. n.d. "Story of Damietta." Damietta Cross-Cultural Center. https://www.siena.edu/centers-institutes/damietta-cross-cultural-center/story-of-damietta/

Darr, A. 2018. "In the name of God – The Asia Bibi case and its implications for the rule of law and Islam in Pakistan." South Asia at LSE Blog, 6 December. https://blogs.lse.ac.uk/southasia /2018/12/06/long-read-in-the-name-of-god-the-asia-bibi-case-and-its-implications-for-the-rule -of-law-and-islam-in-pakistan/

Davis, R. 2002. "Ottoman Jerusalem – The growth of the city outside the walls." In: Salim Tamari (ed.) *Jerusalem 1948 – The Arab Neighborhoods and their Fate in the War*. The Institute of Jerusalem Studies and Badli Resource Center, pp. 10–29.

Democracy Matrix. 2023. "Ranking of countries by quality of democracy." https://www.democra cymatrix.com/ranking

Director of National Intelligence. n.d. "Boko Haram." https://www.dni.gov/nctc/groups/boko_ haram.html

Du Jarric, P. 2004. *Akbar and the Jesuits: An Account of the Jesuit Missions to the Court of Akbar*, translated with introduction and notes by C.H. Payne. London: George Routledge & Sons, 1926.

Dunne, M. and Hamzawy, A. 2017. "Egypt's secular political parties – A struggle for identity and independence." Carnegie Endowment, 31 March. https://carnegieendowment.org/research/20 17/03/egypts-secular-political-parties-a-struggle-for-identity-and-independence?lang=en

Egypt Today Staff. 2022. "Pope Tawadros says Abrahamic religion 'categorically unacceptable'." *Egypt Today*, 8 January. https://www.egypttoday.com/Article/1/111646/Pope-Tawadros-II-says -Abrahamic-Religion-categorically-unacceptable

El-Batsh, M. 2016. "Tambourine in hand, a Christian wakes up Acre's Muslims for Ramadan." TimesofIsrael, 25 June. https://www.timesofisrael.com/tambourine-in-hand-a-christian-wakes -up-acres-muslims-for-ramadan/

El-Faki, M. 2018. *Copts in Egyptian Politics, 1919–1952*. Alexandria: Bibliotheca Alexandrina.

Ergin, M. and Karakaya, Y. 2017. "Between neo-Ottomanism and Ottomania – navigating state-led and popular cultural representations of the past." *New Perspectives on Turkey* 56, 33–59.

Escarcena, J.P.A. 2022. "Ceuta: The humanitarian and the Fortress EUrope." *Antipode* 54(1): 64–85.

Feder, J.L. 2016. "This is how Steve Bannon sees the entire world." BuzzFeed, 16 November. https:// www.buzzfeednews.com/article/lesterfeder/this-is-how-steve-bannon-sees-the-entire-world

Feierstein, G.M. and Guzansky, Y. 2023. "A mixed report card – The Abraham Accords at three." Middle East Institute, 15 September. https://www.mei.edu/publications/mixed-report-card-abraham-accords-three

Fein, A. n.d. "The visual culture of Norman Sicily." Khan Academy. https://www.khanacademy .org/humanities/medieval-world/byzantine1/x4b0eb531:middle-byzantine/a/the-visual-culture -of-norman-sicily

Filkins, D. 2017. "Turkey's vote makes Erdogan effectively a dictator." *New Yorker*, 17 April. https:// www.newyorker.com/news/news-desk/turkeys-vote-makes-erdogan-effectively-a-dictator

Fiore, M. 2020. "The Abraham Accords and the Palestinian issue." *E-International Relations*, 1 November. https://www.e-ir.info/2020/11/01/the-abraham-accords-and-the-palestinian-issue/

For Human Fraternity. n.d. "Abrahamic family house." https://www.forhumanfraternity.org/ abrahamic-family-house/

France 24. 2021. "US condemns Erdogan 'anti-Semitic' remarks." France 24, 19 May. https:// www.france24.com/en/live-news/20210518-us-condemns-erdogan-anti-semitic-remarks

Franklin, B. 1722. "Freedom of speech – Revisiting a 1722 letter from Benjamin Franklin." North Jersey.com, 16 January 2020. https://www.northjersey.com/story/opinion/2020/01/16/freedom -speech-revisiting-1722-letter-benjamin-franklin/4481802002/

Franklin, B. 1739. "Benjamin Franklin on Rev. George Whitefield (1739)." National Humanities Center. https://nationalhumanitiescenter.org/pds/becomingamer/ideas/text2/franklinwhitefi eld.pdf

Franklin, B. 1764. "A narrative of the late massacres, [30 January? 1764]." Founders Online. https:// founders.archives.gov/documents/Franklin/01-11-02-0012

Franklin, B. 1856. *The Works of Benjamin Franklin; Containing Several Political and Historical Tracts Not Included in Any Former Edition and Many Letters Official and Private, Not Hitherto Published; with Notes and a Life of the Author*. Edited by Jared Sparks. Boston, MA: Whitemore, Niles, and Hall.

Friedman, M. and Leshem, E. 2013. "Thousands mourned beloved, controversial West Bank rabbi." TimesofIsrael.com, 5 March. https://www.timesofisrael.com/thousands-turn-out-to-mourn -beloved-and-controversial-west-bank-rabbi/

Fuchs, M.M. and Fuchs, S.W. 2020. "Religious minorities in Pakistan – Identities, citizenship and social belonging." *South Asia – Journal of South Asian Studies* 43(1), 52–67.

Gates, H.L. n.d. "How many slaves landed in the US?" https://www.pbs.org/wnet/african-americans-many-rivers-to-cross/history/how-many-slaves-landed-in-the-us/

Gehrke, J. 2020. "Turkey used Russian missile system to track NATO fighter jets, US lawmakers suspect." *Washington Examiner*, 9 October. https://www.washingtonexaminer.com/policy/defense-national-security/turkey-used-russian-missile-system-to-track-nato-fighter-jets-us-law makers-suspect

Gehrke, J. 2021. "Behind-the-scenes disputes point to trust gap between Biden and 'troublemaker' France." *Washington Examiner*, 20 June. https://www.washingtonexaminer.com/policy/behind -the-scenes-disputes-point-to-trust-gap-between-biden-troublemaker-france

Giese, F. and Acosta, L.A. 2021. "An endangered heritage – Mudéjar and Neo-Moorish architecture in 20th-century Europe." In: F. Giese (ed.) *Mudejarismo and Moorish Revival in Europe*. Leiden: Brill, pp. 535–50.

Gijs, C. and Fota, A. 2022. "Hungary's Viktor Orbán faces growing backlash over 'race mixing' comments." Politico, 25 July. https://www.politico.eu/article/romania-slams-hungary-viktor-or ban-backlash-race-mixing-comments-unacceptable/

Gilbert, L. 2021. "Turkey's Christians face increasingly dangerous persecution." *Newsweek*, 13 April. https://www.newsweek.com/turkeys-christians-face-increasingly-dangerous-persecution-opini on-1583041

Glick, C.B. 2020. "A tale of 2 White House signing ceremonies." *Israel Hayom*, 16 September. https://www.israelhayom.com/2020/09/16/a-tale-of-2-white-house-signing-ceremonies/

Godwin, M. n.d. "Mythologizing the medieval – Ethnonational symbolism by far-right extremists." Partnership for Conflict, Crime, and Security Research. https://www.paccsresearch.org.uk /blog/mythologizing-the-medieval-ethnonational-symbolism-by-far-right-extremists/

Gomes, R. 2021. "Abrahamic Family House in Abu Dhabi to open in 2022." Vatican News, 15 June. https://www.vaticannews.va/en/vatican-city/news/2021-06/abu-dhabi-abrahamic-family-house -2022-human-fraternity.html

Graham-Harrison, E. 2020. "Asia Bibi – Pakistani woman jailed for blasphemy releases photos in exile." *The Guardian*, 28 January. https://www.theguardian.com/world/2020/jan/28/asia-bibi -pakistani-woman-jailed-for-blasphemy-releases-photos-in-exile

Gramlich, J. and Scheller, A. 2021. "What's happening at the US–Mexico border in 7 charts." Pew Research Center, 9 November. https://www.pewresearch.org/fact-tank/2021/11/09/whats-hap pening-at-the-u-s-mexico-border-in-7-charts/

Grant, K. 2017. "'I owe them' – Convicted mosque shooter embraces Islam." NBC Connecticut, 25 September. https://www.nbcconnecticut.com/news/local/i-owe-them-convicted-mosque-sh ooter-embraces-islam/23036/

Green, D.B. 2015. "This day in Jewish history – 1788: Benjamin Franklin helps floundering Philly synagogue." Haaretz.com, 30 April. https://www.haaretz.com/jewish/2015-04-30/ty-article/ .premium/1788-ben-franklin-helps-save-philly-shul/0000017f-db2c-df9c-a17f-ff3c9f9f0000

Griffith, S. 1997. "Sharing the faith of Abraham – the 'credo' of Louis Massignon." *Islam and Christian-Muslim Relations* 8(2): 193–210.

Häde, W. 2015. "Christians in Turkey as part of a Western conspiracy? A Turkish perspective on Christian missionaries." In: Hans Aage Gravaas, Christof Sauer, Tormod Engelsviken, Maqsood Kamil, and Knud Jørgensen (eds.) *Freedom of Belief and Christian Mission*. 1517 Media, pp. 181–9.

Hall, G.M. 2007. *Slavery and African Ethnicities in the Americas – Restoring the Links*. Chapel Hill, NC: University of North Carolina Press.

Hanania, R. 2022. "Plight of Middle East's Christians deserves more attention." Arab News, 23 September. https://www.arabnews.com/node/2168001

Harash, R. 2017. "Muslim holds ancient key to Jesus tomb site in Jerusalem." Reuters.com, 30 November. https://www.reuters.com/article/idUSKBN1DU17Z/

Harb, A. 2019. "US shuts Jerusalem consulate, downgrades Palestinian mission." Al-Jazeera, 4 March. https://www.aljazeera.com/news/2019/3/4/us-shuts-jerusalem-consulate-downgrades -palestinian-mission

Harvard Divinity School. n.d.a. "Abul A'la Maududi." Harvard Divinity School – Religion and Public Life. https://rpl.hds.harvard.edu/faq/abul-%E2%80%99la-maududi

Harvard Divinity School. n.d.b. "Christianity in Nigeria." Harvard Divinity School – Religion and Public Life. https://rpl.hds.harvard.edu/faq/christianity-nigeria

Harvard Divinity School. n.d.c. "Hassan al-Banna." Harvard Divinity School – Religion and Public Life. https://rpl.hds.harvard.edu/faq/hassan-al-banna

Harvard Divinity School. n.d.d. "Fethullah Gülen." Harvard Divinity School – Religion and Public Life. https://rpl.hds.harvard.edu/faq/fethullah-gülen

Hassan, H. 2022. "The 'conscious uncoupling' of Wahhabism and Saudi Arabia." *New Lines Magazine*, 22 February. https://newlinesmag.com/argument/the-conscious-uncoupling-of-wah habism-and-saudi-arabia/

Hecht, E. 2016. "Museum of Tolerance Jerusalem moves forward." *Architectural Record*, 22 July. https://www.architecturalrecord.com/articles/11815-museum-of-tolerance-jerusalem-moves-for ward

Hedgecoe, G. 2015. "Córdoba controversy – Historic Mosque-Cathedral mired in cultural dispute." Al-Jazeera America, 24 May. http://america.aljazeera.com/articles/2015/5/24/cordoba -mosque-cathedral-controversy.html

Heraclides, A. 2011. "The essence of the Greek–Turkish rivalry – National narrative and identity." Hellenic Observatory Papers on Greece and Southeast Europe, October. https://eprints.lse.ac .uk/45693/1/GreeSE%20No51.pdf

Herbjørnsrud, D. 2018. "The real Battle of Vienna." Aeon, 24 July. https://aeon.co/essays/the-batt le-of-vienna-was-not-a-fight-between-cross-and-crescent

Herrera, J. 2019. "Using a Quran to swear in to Congress – A brief history of oaths and texts." *Pacific Standard*, 4 January. https://psmag.com/news/using-a-quran-to-swear-in-to-congress -a-brief-history-of-oaths-and-texts

Hincks, J. 2019. "The White House says Israeli settlements in the West Bank are no longer illegal. Here's what that means." *Time Magazine*, 19 November. https://time.com/5732752/israeli-settle ments-trump-administration/

Hirsch, M. 2022. "The Palestinian leadership hates the US." Jewish News Syndicate, 23 October. https://www.jns.org/the-palestinian-leadership-hates-the-us/

History. 2018. "Hagia Sophia." 29 September. https://www.history.com/topics/ancient-greece/ hagia-sophia

Holland, S. 2020. "Morocco joins other Arab nations agreeing to normalize Israeli ties." Reuters, 10 December. https://www.reuters.com/article/israel-usa-morocco-int/morocco-joins-other -arab-nations-agreeing-to-normalize-israel-ties-idUSKBN28K2CW

House of One. 2011. "Charter for a partnership of Judaism, Christianity, and Islam." House of One, 12 October. https://house-of-one.org/sites/default/files/house_of_one_berlin_charta_en gl.pdf?t=1ECa4r

Huddleston, A. 2009. "Divine learning – The traditional Islamic scholarship of Timbuktu, Mali." *Fourth Genre – Explorations in Nonfiction* 11(2): 129–35.

Hudson, J. and DeYoung, K. 2024. "White House reverses West Bank policy, calling Israeli settlements illegal." *Washington Post*, 24 February. https://www.washingtonpost.com/national-secur ity/2024/02/23/israel-west-bank-settlements-illegal/

Human Rights Watch. 2012. "Saudi Arabia – Christians arrested at private prayer." Human Rights Watch, 30 January. https://www.hrw.org/news/2012/01/30/saudi-arabia-christians-arrested-pri vate-prayer#

Human Rights Watch. 2024. "Pakistan – Mob attacks Christian settlement." Human Rights Watch, 22 August. https://www.hrw.org/news/2023/08/22/pakistan-mob-attacks-christian-settlement

Hummel, D. 2020. "Legislating Islamophobia – The factors for the existence of anti-sharia laws in the United States." *Public Policy and Administration* 37(3): 317–41.

Huntington, S.P. 1993. "The Clash of Civilizations?" *Foreign Affairs* 72(3): 22–49.

Hussain, T. 2005. "U.S–Pakistan engagement – The War on Terrorism and beyond." https://www.usip.org/sites/default/files/sr145.pdf

Interfaith Encounter Association. n.d. "How it works." https://interfaith-encounter.org/en/

International Christian Concern. 2022a. "Gunmen attack two churches in Northern Nigeria." International Christian Concern, 20 June. https://www.persecution.org/2022/06/20/gunmen-attack-two-churches-northern-nigeria/

International Christian Concern. 2022b. "Christians make up 90% of Islamabad's sanitation workers; but that's not the whole story." International Christian Concern, 23 August. https://www.persecution.org/2022/08/23/christians-make-90-islamabads-sanitation-workers-thats-not-whole-story/

Ioannou, D. 2020. "'Bad news' for Turkey's marginalized Christians." Politico, 5 August. https://www.politico.com/news/2020/08/05/turkey-christians-hagia-sophia-392125

Isaacson, W. 2005. "Benjamin Franklin's gift of tolerance" in Akbar Ahmed and Brian Forst (eds) *After Terror – Promoting Dialogue among Civilizations*. Cambridge: Polity.

Jacobs, F. 2021. "The Christian church so holy that Muslims hold its keys." BigThink.com, 28 April. https://bigthink.com/strange-maps/holy-sepulcher/

Jadaliyya and Ahram Online. 2011. "Al-Wafd Party." Jadaliyya, 18 November. https://www.jadaliyya.com/Details/24643

Jaffe-Hoffman, M. 2024. "Since start of Israel–Hamas war, 3% of Gaza's Christians dead." *Jerusalem Post*, 17 February. https://www.jpost.com/christianworld/article-787453#google_vignette

Jones, D. 2019. "What the far right gets wrong about the Crusades." *Time Magazine*, 10 October. https://time.com/5696546/far-right-history-crusades/

Karlińska, A. 2020. "Treasures from Eastern Europe – Kruszyniany, symbol of tolerance." Resilience-ri.eu, 16 October. https://www.resilience-ri.eu/blog/treasures-from-eastern-europe-kruszyniany-symbol-of-tolerance/

Kassam, A. 2014. "Córdoba's Mosque-Cathedral in name-change row." *The Guardian*, 5 December. https://www.theguardian.com/world/2014/dec/05/cordoba-mosque-cathedral-name-change-row-andalusia

Kennedy, H. 2011. "Muslims return favor, join hands with Christian protesters for Mass in Cairo's Tahrir Square." *NY Daily News*, 7 February. https://www.nydailynews.com/news/world/muslims-return-favor-join-hands-christian-protesters-mass-cairo-tahrir-square-article-1.137961

Khan, S. and Ramachandran, V. 2021. "Post-9/11 surveillance has left a generation of Muslim Americans in a shadow of distrust and fear." PBS.org, 16 September. https://www.pbs.org/newshour/nation/post-9-11-surveillance-has-left-a-generation-of-muslim-americans-in-a-shadow-of-distrust-and-fear

Khatami, M.K. 2000. "Address by H.E. Mr. Mohammed Khatami, President of the Republic of Iran." In: UNESCO (United Nations Educational, Scientific and Cultural Organization), *Round Table: Dialogue among Civilizations*. New York: United Nations.

King Abdullah Abdul-Aziz International Centre for Interreligious and Intercultural Dialogue. n.d. "Who we are." https://www.kaiciid.org/who-we-are

King Jr, M.L. 1963. "Read Martin Luther King Jr.'s 'I Have a Dream' speech in its entirety." National Public Radio, 16 January. https://www.npr.org/2010/01/18/122701268/i-have-a-dream-speech-in-its-entirety

Kingdom of Saudi Arabia. n.d. "Basic Law of Governance." The Embassy of the Kingdom of Saudi Arabia – Washington, DC. https://www.saudiembassy.net/basic-law-governance

Kuczkiewicz-Fraś, A. 2011. "Akbar the Great (1542–1605) and Christianity – Between religion and politics." *Orientalia Christiana Cracoviensia* 3: 75–89.

Kurtzer-Ellenbogen, L., Youssef, H., Barron, R. and Gallagher, A. 2023. "Is a Saudi–Israel normalization agreement on the horizon." United States Institute of Peace, 28 September. https://www.usip.org/publications/2023/09/saudi-israel-normalization-agreement-horizon

Lambert, F. 2005. *The Barbary Wars: American Independence in the Atlantic World*. New York: Farrar, Straus, and Giroux.

Lappin, Y. 2020. "As Turkey's lira tumbles, Erdogan pursues neo-Ottoman visions." The Begin-Sadat Center for Strategic Studies – Bar-Ilan University, 2 November. https://besacenter.org/turkey-erdogan-ottoman-visions/

Library of Congress. n.d.a. "Timbuktu: An Islamic Cultural Center." https://www.loc.gov/collections/islamic-manuscripts-from-mali/articles-and-essays/timbuktu-an-islamic-cultural-center/

Library of Congress. 2007. "Thomas Jefferson's copy of the Koran to be used in Congressional swearing-in ceremony." Library of Congress, 3 January. https://www.loc.gov/item/prn-07-001/

Liebermann, O. 2016. "Two Muslim families entrusted with care of holy Christian site for centuries." CNN, 27 March. https://www.cnn.com/2016/03/26/middleeast/easter-muslim-keyholder/index.html

Linde, S. 2022. "One of a kind – The new 'Abraham's Tent.'" *Jerusalem Post*, 16 January. https://www.jpost.com/israel-news/article-692502

Lowcountry Digital History Initiative. n.d. "Enslaved and freed African Muslims – Spiritual wayfarers in the South and Lowcountry." https://ldhi.library.cofc.edu/exhibits/show/african-muslims-in-the-south/five-african-muslims/salih-bilali-bilali-mohammed

Maher, M. 2022. "Two years on, the Abraham Accords bear fruit." Washington Institute, 26 October. https://www.washingtoninstitute.org/policy-analysis/two-years-abraham-accords-bear-fruit

Mallinder, L. 2023. "Under Israeli attack – Who are the Christians of Gaza?" Al-Jazeera, 1 November. https://www.aljazeera.com/news/2023/11/1/under-israeli-attack-who-are-the-christians-of-gaza

Marie, M. 2022. "Mohammad Ali Pasha Palace, a stunning reflection of Egypt's architectural heritage." *Egypt Today*, 10 March. https://www.egypttoday.com/Article/4/113651/Mohammad-Ali-Pasha-Palace-a-stunning-reflection-of-Egypt-s

Marshall, P. 2021. "Are Egypt's Christians persecuted? Why some Copts say no." Hudson.org, 15 January. https://www.hudson.org/human-rights/are-egypt-s-christians-persecuted-why-some-copts-say-no

Marshall, P. and Shea, N. 2011. "Pakistan." In: *Silenced: How Apostasy and Blasphemy Codes are Choking Freedom Worldwide*. New York: Oxford Academic.

Martany, S. and Al-Khatib, M. 2022. "How Iraq's Christians are rebuilding their ancient churches." Premier Christianity, 1 June. https://www.premierchristianity.com/features/how-iraqs-christians-are-rebuilding-their-ancient-churches/13206.article

Maziad, M. and Sotiriadis, J. n.d. "Turkey's dangerous new exports – Pan-Islamist, neo-Ottoman visions and regional instability." Greek Foreign Affairs Institute. https://fainst.eu/enimerosi/turkeys-dangerous-new-exports-pan-islamist-neo-ottoman-visions-and-regional-instability/

McGarvey, K. 2022. "Christians in Nigeria are under constant attack. Why is so little done about it?" *Irish Times*, 4 July. https://www.irishtimes.com/opinion/2022/07/04/christians-in-nigeria-are-under-constant-attack-why-is-so-little-done-about-it/

219

Metcalfe, A. 2002. "The Muslims of Sicily under Christian Rule." In: Graham A. Loud and Alex Metcalfe (eds.) *The Society of Norman Italy*. Leiden: Brill, pp. 289–321.

Mezquita-Catedral De Córdoba. n.d.a. "The building – Original mosque of Abd al-Rahman I." https://mezquita-catedraldecordoba.es/en/descubre-el-monumento/el-edificio/mezquita-funda cional-de-abderraman-i/

Mezquita-Catedral De Córdoba. n.d.b. "The history – Abd Al-Rahman II." https://mezquita-cated raldecordoba.es/en/descubre-el-monumento/la-historia/

Middle East Monitor. 2017. "21 killed in church bombing in northern Egypt." Middle East Monitor, 9 April. https://www.middleeastmonitor.com/20170409-21-killed-in-church-bomb ing-in-northern-egypt/

Minority Rights Group International n.d. "Türkiye." https://minorityrights.org/country/turkey/

Mirza, A. 2021. "Abrahamia – A new religion on the horizon." *Kashmir Observer*, 22 November. https://kashmirobserver.net/2021/11/22/abrahamia-a-new-religion-on-the-horizon/

Mogul, R. and Saifi, S. 2022. "Imran Khan claims there's a US conspiracy against him. Why do so many Pakistanis believe him?" CNN, 27 May. https://www.cnn.com/2022/05/27/asia/pakistan -imran-khan-us-conspiracy-intl-hnk/index.html

Momeka, D. 2015. "Ancient communities under attack – ISIS's war on religious minorities." Committee on Foreign Affairs (US House of Representatives), 13 May. https://www.govinfo .gov/content/pkg/CHRG-114hhrg94605/html/CHRG-114hhrg94605.htm

Moncelon, J. 1990. "Sous le signe d'Abraham – Louis Massignon, l'ami de Dieu (Khalil Allah)." PhD thesis, Universite de Paris X, Nanterre, Paris.

Monserrate, A. 1922. *The Commentary of Father Monserrate, S.J., on His Journey to the Court of Akbar*, translated from the original Latin by J.S. Hoyland and annotated by S.N. Banerjee, London: Humphrey Milford.

Monticello. n.d.a. "Brief biography of Thomas Jefferson." https://www.monticello.org/thomas-jef ferson/brief-biography-of-jefferson/

Monticello. n.d.b. "Jefferson's religious beliefs." https://www.monticello.org/site/research-and-collec tions/jeffersons-religious-beliefs

Monticello. n.d.c. "Slavery FAQs – Property." https://www.monticello.org/slavery/slavery-faqs/pr operty/

Monticello. n.d.d. "Thomas Jefferson and religious freedom." https://www.monticello.org/research -education/thomas-jefferson-encyclopedia/thomas-jefferson-and-religious-freedom/

Moratinos, M. 2021. "High representative's remarks at the International Day of Human Fraternity." United Nations Alliance of Civilizations (UNAOC), 4 February. https://www.unaoc.org/2021 /02/remarks-international-day-of-human-fraternity/

Morning Star News. 2023. "Pakistan to try blasphemy cases under anti-terror law." *Christian Post*, 30 June. https://www.christianpost.com/news/pakistan-to-try-blasphemy-cases-under-anti-ter ror-law.html

Morning Star News and Casper, J. 2022. "Owo church attack kills dozens of Nigerian Catholics on Pentecost Sunday." *Christianity Today*, 5 June. https://www.christianitytoday.com/news/2022 /june/owo-church-attack-ondo-nigeria-catholic-pentecost-sunday.html

Moro, E. 2019. "Hospitality – The art of healing." Civilgraces.com, 12 February. https://civilgraces .com/2019/02/12/hospitality-the-art-of-healing/

Morris, A. 2021. "Fulani Muslims shout 'allahu akbar' while slaughtering 10 Christians, children, and burning 100 homes." Christian Broadcast Network, 22 November. https://www1.cbn.com /cbnnews/cwn/2021/november/fulani-muslims-shout-allahu-akbar-while-slaughtering-10-christ ians-children-and-burning-100-homes

Mount Vernon. n.d.a. "Biography of George Washington." https://www.mountvernon.org/george -washington/biography/

Mount Vernon. n.d.b. "Morocco." https://www.mountvernon.org/library/digitalhistory/digital-en cyclopedia/article/morocco/#note1

Mozaffari, M. 2007. "What is Islamism? History and definition of a concept." *Totalitarian Movements and Political Religions* 8(1): 17–33.

Mudde, C. 2004. "The populist Zeitgeist." *Government and Opposition* 39(4): 541–63.

Mufila, V. 2023. "Africa, a history to rediscover. 20 – What if Ubuntu saved humanity." Pressenza International Press Agency, 18 January. https://www.pressenza.com/2023/01/africa-a-history-to -rediscover-20-what-if-ubuntu-saved-humanity/

Murphy, K. 2012. "Kansas governor signs bill effectively banning Islamic law." Reuters, 25 March. https://www.reuters.com/article/us-usa-kansas-sharia/kansas-governor-signs-bill-effectively -banning-islamic-law-idUSBRE84O1DJ20120525/

Nabudere, D.W. 2005. "Ubuntu philosophy – Memory and reconciliation." Africa Social Work, September. https://africasocialwork.net/wp-content/uploads/2022/09/PROFESSOR-D-W -NABUDERE-UBUNTU-AND-RECONCILIATION-.pdf

National Constitution Center. n.d. "The Gettysburg Address (1863)." Constitution Center. https:// constitutioncenter.org/the-constitution/historic-document-library/detail/abraham-lincoln-the -gettysburg-address-1863

National Constitution Center. 2023. "On this day, Benjamin Franklin dies in Philadelphia." Constitution Center, 17 April. https://constitutioncenter.org/blog/benjamin-franklins-last-da ys-funeral-and-a-u-s-senate-slight

National Park Service (NPS). n.d. "Valley Forge." https://www.nps.gov/vafo/learn/historyculture /valley-forge-history-and-significance.htm

National Park Service (NPS). 2020. "'With malice toward none . . .' – Lincoln's Second Inaugural Address." 18 April. https://www.nps.gov/linc/learn/historyculture/lincoln-second-inaugural.htm

Neurink, J. 2022. "Iraq – Rebuilding churches as symbols of hope." *Deutsche Welle*, 3 September. https://www.dw.com/en/iraq-rebuilding-churches-as-symbols-of-hope/a-61050614

New International Version. n.d. "What is holiness?" https://www.thenivbible.com/blog/what-is -holiness/

Obiejesi, K. 2018. "As long as I live, I'll keep saving lives, says Muslim cleric who sheltered 300 Christians in Plateau." International Centre for Investigative Reporting, 5 August. https://www .icirnigeria.org/as-long-as-i-live-ill-keep-saving-lives-says-muslim-cleric-who-sheltered-300- christians-in-plateau/

Office of the Historian. n.d. "The Oslo Accords and the Arab–Israeli Peace Process." Department of State – United States of America. https://history.state.gov/milestones/1993-2000/oslo

Ojoye, T. 2018. "I gambled with my life to save over 300 Christians – Imam Abdullahi." Punch ng.com, 5 August. https://punchng.com/i-gambled-with-my-life-to-save-over-300-christians -imam-abdullahi/

Open Doors Australia. 2013. "Stories of Christian persecution – Fatima of Saudi Arabia." Open Doors USA, 25 June. https://www.youtube.com/watch?v=-C23vIlodKw

Open Doors USA. n.d.a. "Saudi Arabia." https://www.opendoorsusa.org/christian-persecution/wo rld-watch-list/saudi-arabia/

Open Doors USA. n.d.b. "Pakistan." https://www.opendoorsusa.org/christian-persecution/world -watch-list/pakistan/

Open Doors USA. n.d.c. "United Arab Emirates." https://www.opendoorsusa.org/christian-perse cution/world-watch-list/united-arab-emirates/

Osama, K. 2016. "Egyptian Christians say there are too few churches." *The Arab Weekly*, 26 February. https://thearabweekly.com/egyptian-christians-say-there-are-too-few-churches

Ottaway, D. 2016. "Saudi Arabia faces the missing 28 pages." Wilson Center, May. https://www. wilsoncenter.org/publication/saudi-arabia-faces-the-missing-28-pages

Ottaway, D. 2021. "Saudi crown prince lambasts his kingdom's Wahhabi establishment." Wilson Center, 6 May. https://www.wilsoncenter.org/article/saudi-crown-prince-lambasts-his-kingdoms-wahhabi-establishment

Ousterhout, R. 2020. "The reconversion of Hagia Sophia in perspective." Oxford University Press blog, 8 September. https://blog.oup.com/2020/09/the-reconversion-of-hagia-sophia-in-perspective/

Pamuk, H. and Lewis, S. 2021. "US hopes Abraham Accords will help Israeli–Palestinian issue – officials." Reuters, 12 October. https://www.reuters.com/world/middle-east/us-israel-uae-launch-working-groups-trilateral-meeting-wednesday-state-dept-2021-10-12/

Paracha, N.F. 2014. "Abul Ala Maududi – An existentialist history." New Age Islam, 1 January. https://www.newageislam.com/islamic-personalities/nadeem-f-paracha/abul-ala-maududi-existentialist-history/d/100793

Penn Treaty Museum. n.d. "William Penn's treaty with the Indians at Shackamaxon." https://penntreatymuseum.org/history-2/peace-treaty/

Pew Research Center. 2005. "The global spread of Wahhabi Islam – How great a threat?' 3 May. https://www.pewresearch.org/religion/2005/05/03/the-global-spread-of-wahhabi-islam-how-great-a-threat/

Pfeffer, A. 2020. "Hamas uses secret cyberwar base in Turkey to target enemies." The Times, 22 October. https://www.thetimes.co.uk/article/hamas-running-secret-cyberwar-hq-in-turkey-29mz50sxs

Phillips, R. 2018. "Tawhid and the Trinity." The Pathway, 5 March. https://mbcpathway.com/2018/03/05/tawhid-and-the-trinity/

Pilkington, E. 2018. "NYPD settles lawsuit after illegally spying on Muslims." The Guardian, 5 April. https://www.theguardian.com/world/2018/apr/05/nypd-muslim-surveillance-settlement

Poljarevic, E. 2015. "Islamism." The Oxford Encyclopedia of Islam and Politics – Oxford Islamic Studies Online. https://www.academia.edu/6916999/Islamism_definition_history_and_the_development_of_the_term_The_Oxford_Encyclopedia_of_Islam_and_Politics

Prager, D. 2006. "America, not Keith Ellison, decides what book a congressman takes his oath on." Townhall, 28 November. https://townhall.com/columnists/dennisprager/2006/11/28/america,-not-keith-ellison,-decides-what-book-a-congressman-takes-his-oath-on-n792991

Prince of Wales. 1993. "A speech by HRH The Prince of Wales titled 'Islam and the West' at the Oxford Centre for Islamic Studies, the Sheldonian Theatre, Oxford." 27 October. https://www.princeofwales.gov.uk/speech/speech-hrh-prince-wales-titled-islam-and-west-oxford-centre-islamic-studies-sheldonian

Proctor, R.A. 2023. "Abrahamic Family House – An architectural symbol of coexistence." Wallpaper.com, 2 March. https://www.wallpaper.com/architecture/abrahamic-family-house-adjaye-associates-abu-dhabi-uae

Pruitt, S. 2023. "What part of Africa did most enslaved people come from?" History.com, 18 July. https://www.history.com/news/what-part-of-africa-did-most-slaves-come-from

Psaropoulos, J. 2022. "New crisis brewing on Cyprus after US lifts arms embargo." Al-Jazeera, 27 October. https://www.aljazeera.com/news/2022/10/27/new-crisis-brewing-on-cyprus-after-us-lifts-arms-embargo

Public Broadcasting Service. n.d. "Interview – Osama Bin Laden." https://www.pbs.org/wgbh/pages/frontline/shows/binladen/who/interview.html

Qazi, A.L. 2017. "How to Islamize an Islamic Republic – Jamaat-e-Islami in its own words." Brookings Institution, 25 April. https://www.brookings.edu/research/how-to-islamize-an-islamic-republic-jamaat-e-islami-in-its-own-words/

Quick, A. 2019. "Timbuktu, Empire of knowledge." Hakimquick.com, 20 November. https://hakimquick.com/timbuktu-empire-of-knowledge/

Radiance Weekly. 2022. "Kansas anti-Muslim Bill 'invites' legal challenge – CAIR." Radiance Weekly, 30 August. https://radianceweekly.net/kansas-anti-muslim-bill-invites-legal-challenge -cair/

Rahman, A.F. 2018. "Getting justice for Asia Bibi." The Hindu, 22 December. https://www.thehin du.com/opinion/op-ed/getting-justice-for-asia-bibi/article25559318.ece

Rahman, A.F. 2021. "The flawed Islamic democracy of Pakistan." The Hindu, 13 December. https:// www.thehindu.com/opinion/op-ed/the-flawed-islamic-democracy-of-pakistan/article379406 09.ece?homepage=true

Raymond, A.K. 2017. "ISIS threatens attacks on US soil after Trump's Jerusalem decision." New Yorker Magazine, 14 December. https://nymag.com/intelligencer/2017/12/isis-threatens-attacks -on-u-s-soil-after-jerusalem-decision.html

Reuters. 2022. "Turkey to re-inforce military presence in northern Cyprus – Erdogan." Reuters, 28 September. https://www.reuters.com/world/turkey-re-inforce-military-presence-northern -cyprus-erdogan-2022-09-28/

Richards, B. 2014. "What drove Anders Breivik?" Contexts 13(4): 42–7.

Roach, D. 2016. "Resist 'civilization jihad,' NRB speakers urge." Baptist Press, 26 February. https:// www.baptistpress.com/resource-library/news/resist-civilization-jihad-nrb-speakers-urge/

Roberts, D.B. 2019. "Reflecting on Qatar's 'Islamist' soft power." Brookings Institution, April. https://www.brookings.edu/wp-content/uploads/2019/04/FP_20190408_qatar_roberts.pdf

Robinson, K. 2022. "Turkey's growing foreign policy ambitions." Council on Foreign Relations, 24 August. https://www.cfr.org/backgrounder/turkeys-growing-foreign-policy- ambitions

Rochford, T. n.d. "Rodolfo Aquaviva." Jesuits Global. https://www.jesuits.global/saint-blessed/ blessed-rodolfo-acquaviva/

Rohan, B. 2017. "Who are Egypt's Coptic Christians and why do extremists target them?" America Magazine, 11 April. https://www.americamagazine.org/politics-society/2017/04/11/who-are-egy pts-coptic-christians-and-why-do-extremists-target-them

Rohmaniyah, I. and Woodward, M. 2012. "Wahhabi perspectives on pluralism and gender: A Saudi-Indonesian contrast." Center for Strategic Communication (Arizona State University), Report no. 1201: 1–10.

Rosenbaum, A. 2023. "Interfaith dialogue – Making religion part of Israel's Middle East peace." Jerusalem Post, 4 February. https://www.jpost.com/middle-east/article-730397

Sadowski, D. 2019. "13th-century encounter points way to greater Christian–Muslim understand- ing." National Catholic Reporter, 8 November. https://www.ncronline.org/spirituality/13th-cen tury-encounter-points-way-greater-christian-muslim-understanding

Saint Mary's Catholic Church Dubai. n.d. "History." https://saintmarysdubai.org/history

Samasumo, P. 2022. "Catholics in Nigeria express shock and horror at the killings in Owo." Vatican News, 6 June. https://www.vaticannews.va/en/africa/news/2022-06/catholics-in-nigeria-ex press-deep-shock-and-horror-at-the-killin.html

Sammons, E. 2023. "The equalization of religions and the troublesome Abu Dhabi declaration." CrisisMagazine, 1 March. https://crisismagazine.com/opinion/the-equalization-of-religions -and-the-troublesome-abu-dhabi-declaration

Sanderson, S. 2018. "From ally to scapegoat – Fethullah Gülen, the man behind the myth." Deutsche Welle, 4 June. https://www.dw.com/en/from-ally-to-scapegoat-fethullah-gulen-the -man-behind-the-myth/a-37055485

Sariyuce, I. and Reynolds, E. 2020. "Turkey's Erdogan orders the conversion of Hagia Sophia back into a mosque." CNN, 26 July. https://www.cnn.com/2020/07/10/europe/hagia-sophia-mos que-turkey-intl/index.html

Scheindlin, D. 2022a. "How to salvage progressive policies from the Abraham Accords." The

Century Foundation, 2 March. https://tcf.org/content/report/salvage-progressive-policies-abra
ham-accords/?session=1

Scheindlin, D. 2022b. "Biden is making a big mistake with the Abraham Accords." Haaretz, 5 July.
https://www.haaretz.com/us-news/2022-07-05/ty-article-opinion/.highlight/biden-is-making
-a-big-mistake-with-the-abraham-accords/00000181-cdbd-df5a-adbf-cfbdc6510000

Schengen Visa Info. n.d. "What is the Schengen Agreement?" https://www.schengenvisainfo.com
/schengen-agreement/

Schleifer, T. 2016. "Donald Trump – 'I think Islam hates us.'" CNN, 10 March. https://www.cnn
.com/2016/03/09/politics/donald-trump-islam-hates-us/index.html

Schmitt, C.B. 1966. "Perennial philosophy – From Agostino Steuco to Leibniz," *Journal of the
History of Ideas* 27: 505–32.

Schrag, M. 2010. "Holy or unholy land?" AnaBaptistWorld.org, 1 September. https://anabaptistw
orld.org/holy-unholy-land/

Shahid, K.K. 2022. "Pakistan's Christians are living in terror." *The Spectator*, 1 February. https://
www.spectator.co.uk/article/pakistan-s-christians-are-living-in-terror

Shanmugasundaram, S. 2018. "Anti-sharia law bills in the United States." Southern Poverty Law
Center, 5 February 2018. https://www.splcenter.org/hatewatch/2018/02/05/anti-sharia-law-bills
-united-states

Sharqawi, Y. 2022. "The new Abrahamic religion – religion in the service of politics." Fanack.com,
3 January. https://fanack.com/society/features-insights/the-new-abrahamic-religion-religion-in
-the-service-of-politics-224806/

Shehata, S. n.d. "Profile of Egypt's new president Mohamed Morsi." Wilson Center. https://www
.wilsoncenter.org/profile-egypts-new-president-mohamed-morsi

Sherwani, L.A. 2005. *Speeches, Writings, and Statements of Iqbal*, 4th edn. Pakistan: Iqbal
Academy.

Siegle, S. 2023. "The art of kindness." Mayo Clinic, 17 August. https://www.mayoclinichealth
system.org/hometown-health/speaking-of-health/the-art-of-kindness

Sikh American Legal Defense and Education Fund. n.d. "The first 9/11 backlash fatality – Balbir
Singh Sodhi." https://saldef.org/balbir-singh-sodhi/

Singleton, B.D. 2004. "African bibliophiles – Books and libraries in medieval Timbuktu." *Libraries
& Culture* 39(1): 1–12.

Smith, G.A. 2006. "The Barbary Wars – American Independence in the Atlantic World (review)."
The Journal of Military History 70(2): 509–10.

Soliman, H. 2022. "Why do Egypt's Christians support Sisi?" Middle East Monitor, 17 January.
https://www.middleeastmonitor.com/20220117-why-do-egypts-christians-support-sisi/

Southern Poverty Law Center. n.d. "Anti-Muslim." http://www.splcenter.org/fighting-hate/ex
tremist-files/ideology/anti-muslim

Spellberg, D. 2014. "Thomas Jefferson's Qur'an." Not Even Past, 7 July. https://notevenpast.org/de
nise-spellberg-thomas-jeffersons-quran/

Stamouli, N. 2021. "Pope Francis denounces Europe's migrant crisis as 'shipwreck of civilization.'"
Politico, 5 December. https://www.politico.eu/article/pope-francis-europe-migrant-crisis-ship
wreck-of-civilization/

Supreme Court of Pakistan. 2018. "Criminal Appeal No. 39-L of 2015. Supreme Court of Pakistan,
8 October. http://www.concernedhistorians.org/content_files/file/le/594.pdf

Thames, K. 2021. "The perils of being Ahmadi in Pakistan." Ink Stick Media, 4 June. https://
inkstickmedia.com/the-perils-of-being-ahmadi-in-pakistan/

Thatcher, O.J. and McNeal, E.H. (eds.). n.d. "Urban II, Speech at the Council of Clermont
(1095)." In: O.J. Thatcher and E.H. McNeal (eds.) *A Source Book for Medieval History: Selected
Documents Illustrating the History of Europe in the Middle Age*. New York: Charles Scribner's

Sons (1905), pp. 518–21. https://media.bloomsbury.com/rep/files/Primary%20Source%20
5.3%20-%20Urban%20II.pdf

The Gilder Lehrman Institute of American History. n.d. "History resources – The horrors of slavery, 1805 (A spotlight on a primary source by Samuel Wood). https://www.gilderlehrman.org/history-resources/spotlight-primary-source/horrors-slavery-1805

The National. 2022. "Iraqi Christians rejoice as restored Mosul church holds first Mass." *The National*, 1 May. https://www.thenationalnews.com/mena/iraq/2022/05/01/iraqi-christians-rejoice-as-restored-mosul-church-holds-first-mass/

The Pluralism Project – Harvard University. n.d. "The first American Muslims." The Pluralism Project. https://hwpi.harvard.edu/files/pluralism/files/the_first_american_muslims_1.pdf

Toksöz, M. 2022. "Why was the Tanzimat an important period in Ottoman history?" Choices Program, 15 March. https://www.youtube.com/watch?v=OH6KIebbN60

Tomlinson, J. 2012. "Cultural imperialism." In G. Ritzer (ed.). *The Wiley-Blackwell Encyclopedia of Globalization*. https://onlinelibrary.wiley.com/doi/abs/10.1002/9780470670590.wbeog129

Toosi, N. 2021. "Christian groups furious at Blinken for removing Nigeria from religious violence list." Politico, 23 November. https://www.politico.com/news/2021/11/23/christian-groups-blinken-nigeria-religious-violence-list-523258

TRT World. 2022a. "With prayers for world peace, Türkiye's Christians celebrate Christmas." TRT World, 26 December. https://www.trtworld.com/turkey/with-prayers-for-world-peace-t%C3%BCrkiye-s-christians-celebrate-christmas-63880

TRT World. 2022b. "Türkiye's President Erdogan extends Christmas greetings." TRT World, 25 December. https://www.trtworld.com/turkey/t%C3%BCrkiye-s-president-erdogan-extends-christmas-greetings-63856

True Islam. 2021. "Is 'Love For All Hatred For None' Islamic?" True Islam, 20 December. https://trueislam.co.uk/articles/what-does-love-for-all-hatred-for-none-mean/

Tugwell, P., Georgiou, G., and Johnson, G. 2022. "Cyprus fears getting sucked into potential Greece–Turkey conflict" Bloomberg, 26 September. https://www.bloomberg.com/news/articles/2022-09-26/cyprus-fears-becoming-weakest-link-in-turkey-greece-tensions?leadSource=uverify%20wall

Tutu, D. 2007. "If I diminish you, I diminish myself." In: *Peace – The Words and Inspiration of Mahatma Gandhi*. Boulder, CO: Blue Mountain Press.

Tzoitis, N. 2021. "Pope's visit to Cyprus and Greece, on the border between Christianity and Islam." Asia News, 29 November. https://www.asianews.it/news-en/Pope%27s-visit-to-Cyprus-and-Greece,-on-the-border-between-Christianity-and-Islam-54606.html

Underwood, A. 2018. "The controversial US Jerusalem embassy opening, explained." Vox.com, 16 May. https://www.vox.com/2018/5/14/17340798/jerusalem-embassy-israel-palestinians-us-trump

United Arab Emirates Government Portal. 2022. "Year of tolerance." United Arab Emirates Government, 18 May. https://u.ae/en/about-the-uae/culture/tolerance/tolerance-initiatives

United Nations. 2000. "United Nations Year of Dialogue among Civilizations, 2001 launched with headquarters round table discussion." United Nations, 5 September. https://www.un.org/press/en/2000/20000905.ga9747.doc.html

United Nations Educational, Scientific, and Cultural Organization. n.d.a. "Historic centre of Cordoba." UNESCO World Heritage Convention. https://whc.unesco.org/en/list/313/

United Nations Educational, Scientific, and Cultural Organization. n.d.b. "Revive the spirit of Mosul." UNESCO. https://www.unesco.org/en/revive-mosul

United Nations Educational, Scientific, and Cultural Organization (UNESCO). 2022. "Revive the spirit of Mosul." UNESCO, July. https://www.unesco.org/sites/default/files/medias/fichiers/2022/07/mosul_20220708_brochure_eng_1_0.pdf

United Nations Security Council. 2006. "Items-in-Cyprus – documents, resolutions, reports by the Secretary General – Security Council documents." United Nations Security Council, 15 June. https://search.archives.un.org/uploads/r/united-nations-archives/2/e/8/2e8ac6f7bf17b964c086 64affd4396cc7407a051c00e6a53816d7c4e70b8b0c1/S-0903-0010-03-00001.PDF

United States Department of State. 2019. "2019 report on international religious freedom – Israel, West Bank, and Gaza." https://www.state.gov/reports/2019-report-on-international-religious-fr eedom/israel-west-bank-and-gaza/west-bank-and-gaza/

United States Department of State. 2021. "Pakistani 2021 International Religious Freedom Report." https://www.state.gov/wp-content/uploads/2022/05/PAKISTAN-2021-INTERNATIONAL -RELIGIOUS-FREEDOM-REPORT.pdf

United States Department of State. 2022. "2021 Report on International Religious Freedom – Turkey." United States Department of State, 2 June. https://www.state.gov/reports/2021-report -on-international-religious-freedom/turkey/

United States Embassy and Consulates in Morocco. n.d. "History of the US and Morocco." https:// ma.usembassy.gov/our-relationship/policy-history/io/

Ünlühisarcıklı, Ö, Tastan, K., and Canbilek, C.A. 2022. "Turkish perceptions of the European Union 2022." German Marshall Fund, 14 April. https://www.gmfus.org/news/turkish-percep tions-european-union-2022

Varadarajan, T. 2022. "'The history of Akbar' review – Enlightening tales of his imperial self." *Wall Street Journal*, 7 January. https://www.aei.org/articles/the-history-of-akbar-review-enlight ening-tales-of-his-imperial-self/

Vidino, L. 2015. "The Muslim Brotherhood in the United Kingdom." Program on Extremism, December. Washington DC: George Washington University.

Virtue, D. 2003. *Archangels and Ascended Masters – A Guide to Working and Healing with Divinities and Deities*. Carlsbad, CA: Hay House.

Waldman, P. 2001. "'Crusade' reference reinforces fears War on Terrorism is against Muslims." *Wall Street Journal*, 21 September. https://www.wsj.com/articles/SB1001020294332922160

Walker, A. 2012. "What is Boko Haram?" United States Institute of Peace – Special Report, June. https://www.usip.org/sites/default/files/resources/SR308.pdf

Wang, A.B. 2017. "Jefferson's White House iftar in 1805 remains a matter of debate today." *Washington Post*, 21 June. https://archive.sltrib.com/article.php?id=5428330&itype=CMSID

Warren, S. 2022. "Dozens of religious freedom groups urge Blinken to designate Nigeria 'Country of Particular Concern.'" Christian Broadcasting Network News, 23 September. https://www1 .cbn.com/cbnnews/world/2022/september/violence-and-murders-continue-dozens-of-relig ious-freedom-groups-urge-blinken-to-designate-nigeria-country-of-particular-concern

Wasserstein, D.J. 2017. "ISIS, Christianity, and the Pact of Umar." Yale Books, 16 August. https:// yalebooks.yale.edu/2017/08/16/isis-christianity-and-the-pact-of-umar/

Watkins, D. 2019. "Pope welcomes new UAE committee to promote human fraternity." Vatican News, 26 August. https://www.vaticannews.va/en/pope/news/2019-08/pope-francis-welcomes -uae-fraternity-committee.html

Wegner, E. 2004. "Hagia Sophia, 532–37." Metropolitan Museum of Art, October. https://www .metmuseum.org/toah/hd/haso/hd_haso.htm

Weinholtz, E. 2021. "A genuine tolerance – The case of the Ottoman Empire." *The Fountain*, 1 November. https://fountainmagazine.com/2021/issue-144-nov-dec-2021/a-genuine-tolerance

Welby, J. and Naoum, H. 2021. "Let us pray for the Christians being driven from the Holy Land." *The Times*, 19 December. https://www.thetimes.co.uk/article/let-us-pray-for-the-christians-be ing-driven-from-the-holy-land-f27wwksdh

Wellspring Christian Ministries. 2020. "Leviticus 19:2 – Be holy." Wellspring Christian Ministries, 14 February. https://wellspringchristianministries.org/leviticus-192-be-holy-2/

White House. 2018. "His promise to open US Embassy in Jerusalem, Israel." TrumpWhite House.Archives.gov, 14 May. https://trumpwhitehouse.archives.gov/briefings-statements/presi dent-donald-j-trump-keeps-promise-open-u-s-embassy-jerusalem-israel/

White House. 2023. "Statement from President Joe Biden on hate crime statistics." White House.gov, 16 October. https://www.whitehouse.gov/briefing-room/statements-releases/2023/ 10/16/statement-from-president-joe-biden-on-hate-crime-statistics/

Wilson, G. 2003. "Dealings with Mellimelli, colorful envoy from Tunis." Monticello Newsletter 14 (Winter). https://www.monticello.org/site/research-and-collections/tunisian-envoy

Wilson, J. and Flanagan, A. 2022. "The racist 'great replacement' conspiracy theory explained." SPL Center, 17 May. https://www.splcenter.org/hatewatch/2022/05/17/racist-great-replacement-con spiracy-theory-explained

Wolf, K.B. 2017. "Convivencia." Center for Intercultural Dialogue, July. https://centerforintercul turaldialogue.files.wordpress.com/2017/07/kc82-convivencia.pdf

Wood, P. 2021. "Is Christianity in the Middle East doomed?" *Prospect Magazine*, 9 December. https://www.prospectmagazine.co.uk/arts-and-books/the-vanishing-twilight-christianity-mid dle-east-janine-di-giovanni-review

Worrall, S. 2016. "'Badass librarians' foil Al Qaeda, save ancient manuscripts." *National Geographic*, 12 June. https://www.nationalgeographic.com/history/article/badass-librarians-joshua-hammer -timbuktu-manuscript-al-qaeda

Yavuz, M.H. 2016. "Social and intellectual origins of neo-Ottomanism – Searching for a post-national vision." *Die Welt des Islams* 56: 438–65.

Yilmaz, I. 2021. *Creating the Desired Citizens: State, Islam, and Ideology in Turkey*. Cambridge: Cambridge University Press.

Yilmaz, I. 2022. "Muslim Brotherhood of Turkey and Pakistan." *Seminar Magazine* 754, June, pp. 43–6.

Yilmaz, I. and Shakil, K. 2021. "Transnational Islamist populism between Pakistan and Turkey – The case of Dirilis – Ertugrul." European Center for Populism Studies, 15 April. https://www .populismstudies.org/transnational-islamist-populism-between-pakistan-and-turkey-the-case -of-dirilis-ertugrul/

Youth Committee of the Italian National Commission for UNESCO. n.d. "Arab-Norman archi-tecture in Palermo." https://artsandculture.google.com/story/arab-norman-architecture-in-palermo-comitato-giovani-della-commissione-nazionale-italiana-per-l-unesco/IAXB_sagsrnt Lw?hl=en

Index

.